Comparative Urban Politics

Comparative Urban Politics

Power and the City in the United States, Canada, Britain and France

---

Michael Keating

Professor of Political Science, University of Western Ontario, Canada

Edward Elgar

Published by
Edward Elgar Publishing Limited
Gower House
Croft Road
Aldershot
Hants GU11 3HR
England

Edward Elgar Publishing Company
Old Post Road
Brookfield
Vermont 05036
USA

British Library Cataloguing in Publication Data
Keating, Michael 1950–
Comparative urban politics : power and the city in the United States, Canada, Britain and France.
1. Local government. Politics
I. Title
320.85

Library of Congress Cataloguing in Publication Data
Keating, Michael, 1950–
Comparative urban politics: power and the city in the United States, Canada, Britain, and France/Michael Keating.
p. cm.
Includes index.
1. Municipal government–United States. 2. Municipal government–Canada. 3. Municipal government–France. 4. Municipal government–Great Britain. I. Title.
JS331.K43 1991
320.8'5–dc20 91–14403
CIP

ISBN 1 85278 155 6

Printed in Great Britain by
Billing & Sons Ltd, Worcester

Contents

Preface

> The municipality is the only association which is by nature so good that, wherever men are brought together they form themselves into a municipality (de Tocqueville, 1986, p. 85).

Local government is an almost universal feature of political systems. It is a mode of administration but at the same time, at least in democratic polities, an expression of right. Liberal democratic theory is infused with the idea that communities should have the right to govern their own affairs autonomously. Yet the nature of this right differs from one society to another, as does the scope of local affairs and the capacity of communities to exercise their rights. In the modern world, the whole idea of local self-government has come into question, given the scale and complexity of modern government, the interdependence of nations and the imperatives of the market. This book addresses aspects of this question through the study of city politics in four countries. The conclusion is that local government still has a role to play, but that the traditional concern with autonomy needs to be replaced by a concern with governing capacity and the economic and political limitations of local action need to be appreciated. On my travels, I found many officials in each country firmly convinced that matters were better elsewhere. Europeans admired what they saw as the strong tradition of self-government in North America and the role of public–private partnership in urban renewal. Americans admired the unity of European systems and the stronger commitment to social welfare. Other observers were equally persuaded of the unique virtues of their own traditions, regarding foreign examples with disdain. I have not sought to judge systems, and am aware of the dangers of transplanting institutions and processes beyond their native soil. Instead, the conclusion draws general lessons and talks in general terms about the conditions for a viable local democracy.

The project was undertaken between 1987 and 1990, supported by a research grant from the Nuffield Foundation to examine local development policies in the USA and a grant from the Social Science and

Humanities Research Council of Canada to look at urban government and policy in Britain, France and the USA. In view of the breadth of the subject, the book is written in general terms but the argument is informed by field work in all four countries, as well as a review of the secondary literature. Elected and appointed officials in some fifteen cities were interviewed and original documents examined. The cities were chosen for their ability to illuminate aspects of the issues examined, but as this is not a series of case-studies I have not given extensive descriptions of them. Further interviews were carried out with officials of higher-level governments. I am grateful to academic colleagues for advice and comments on draft chapters, especially Patrick Le Galès, Andrew Sancton, Clarence Stone and Gerry Stoker. Preliminary findings were presented to a seminar at the Centre d'Etudes sur la Vie Locale at the University of Bordeaux and to the annual meetings of the Urban Affairs Association and the American Political Science Association in 1990, provoking a fruitful exchange of views. My wife Ann tolerated prolonged absences abroad in the interests of scholarship. My son Patrick gained an early introduction to the less gratifying aspects of scholarship, by helping to check the references.

Michael Keating
London, Ontario

1. Introduction

THE COMPARATIVE APPROACH

The subject of this book is urban government in the USA, Canada, Britain and France. Its central themes are the ability of local governments in cities to manage the process of social and economic change; and the openness of these governments to social interests. This involves an examination of the structure and powers of local government, its political and economic environment and the pattern of politics around it. Particular emphasis will be placed on changes in the intergovernmental system and economic environment, the way in which cities respond to these and the consequent effect of local political relationships. The approach is comparative, examining themes rather than looking at individual national systems, on which a substantial literature already exists. As the approach is rather unusual in the study of local government, some explanation is required. This chapter first examines the rationale for and difficulties in studying comparative urban politics, taking each of the words in the title in turn. Then it outlines the theoretical approach adopted in the remainder of the book, based on the idea of urban regimes.

Comparative politics is a device for exploring issues by examining the effects of political processes, policies and institutional mechanisms in different settings. Unlike case-studies or historical analysis, it takes factors out of their temporal and spatial context to compare them across times and places. It provides a yardstick to measure the significance of findings which within a single national context might be exaggerated or trivialized.

In the absence of repeatable experiments, comparison allows some control of variables. If we observe systematic variations in outcomes in two countries with capitalist market systems, we cannot attribute these to market capitalism and must look for physical, social or political explanations. Comparison, by isolating variables in this way, allows the observer to draw conclusions about causes though in the social sciences these must remain tentative, valid only until a better explanation appears. Cross-national comparison also allows the researcher to escape from national paradigms which limit the scope of observation and to discover new questions to ask. Comparison highlights the questions which are not asked in particular countries but which profitably could be. Comparison, finally, has an evaluative role. If properly done, it can aid policy formulation, not by providing blueprints of what 'works' elsewhere but by providing new ways of looking at problems.

The main obstacles are in defining the variables to be examined since these differ among countries, in obtaining a sufficiently large sample of cases and in controlling for the range of influences which can cause variation. Definition of variables is made harder by differing intellectual traditions, the ways in which issues are perceived, the concepts and the language of political and scholarly debate. For example, *aménagement du territoire* encompasses not merely a set of instruments without precise parallel in Britain or Anglophone North America but a whole conception of the policy process as an integrated, goal-oriented activity. The limitation of the term 'official' in British government to appointed career people reflects a distinction between elective and appointive roles which has deep roots in the political culture.

If systematic comparison is to be made, the larger the number of cases the better. Yet, as the number of cases increases, so does the number of variables. Comparison requires common elements as well as variations, allowing the latter to be isolated. With too broad a range of cases, the differences become overwhelming and the common object of inquiry vanishes. Too large a number of cases also leads to an abstraction in which individual national contexts fade away and the reader is left with little idea of how things actually work. This study uses limited comparison, taking a small group of cases with enough in common to allow common issues to be addressed but which differ significantly in relevant respects.

The broad framework for comparison is provided by the dimensions of culture, structure and choice (Warwick, 1990). Cultural approaches emphasize shared national values, organizing principles and beliefs about the sources and nature of authority. A considerable literature exists explaining national political differences in terms of these values. Cultural explanations of national differences in politics and policy are useful but only if used sensitively and with a historical sense. There is a danger of culture becoming a residual category to explain everything which cannot be explained in terms of structures or political choice; or to serve as a *deus ex machina*, to rescue the study from analytical deadlock. As critics of the culturalist approach have noted, it does not itself tell us how cultural specificities came into being and why they are sustained. The historical reductionism which seeks to explain them merely by pointing to their existence in the past is little help. Instead, it is necessary to locate their origins in concrete historical experiences and to appreciate that they do change over time. Values are subject to political manipulation and may be moulded by institutional structures, while cultures, far from being timeless exogenous entities, may be constructed through socialization and the 'invention of tradition' (Weber, 1977; Hobsbawm and Ranger, 1983).

It is necessary also to recognize within-nation differences in political culture, avoiding the temptation to assume national homogeneity simply because data comes in national sets (Keating, 1988a). Some value-sets, such as those of social democracy or liberalism, are cross-national. Others show variation within nations. This study largely chooses national systems as the unit of analysis because there are relevant *national* cultural and structural characteristics, but the analysis is not rigidly limited to cross-national comparisons.

Structural explanations of political outcomes may be economic or institutional. Economic determinism in both marxist and non-marxist forms is rejected in the following chapters, but the profound influence of modes of production, ownership of assets and the division of labour on governments' scope for action is recognized. Institutions also impose structural limits on governments and especially on local governments given their subordinate institutional status and limited ability to change their organizational form. Institutions help to define problems, structure power relationships, form political norms and allocate roles and resources. Yet institutions are human contrivances and in many cases institutional forms are designed by dominant groups to ensure their continued advantage.

Unless culture and structure are seen as determining, there is room for political choice. This, too, can be analysed in two dimensions. The public choice school seeks to reduce all political decisions to the calculations of rational individuals maximizing their own utility. The ideas are not novel, having their roots in classical economics and utilitarian political philosophy but have enjoyed new currency in recent years in the analysis of urban politics. This book criticizes public choice theory in several places, for its unrealistic assumptions and its meagre view of human nature, but it does recognize the element of individual choice in a political system such as local government where, if there is not complete mobility, households do have some choice as to location. More important, however, is collective choice, the willingness and capacity of groups to formulate common interests and of political systems to permit collective decisions to be taken and accepted as legitimate. Public choice theory rests on a type of reductionism, in which all interests are reduced to the self-interested individual, so that collective action can be explained only in terms of individual calculations. Collective choice theories, on the other hand, are given to reification. A given class may be said to have an interest or to pursue a strategy, or a city, a neighbourhood or ethnic group. The analysis here seeks to avoid both pitfalls by recognizing that common interests exist but they are formulated as constructions not reductions, through complex processes of cultural, social, political and economic integration. Common interests may conflict among groups and within individuals, especially in the urban context, given the multiplicity of issues and pressures.

Moving to the second element of the title, the problems of comparison are multiplied in the case of urban politics since the object of study is so imprecise. Cities can be defined spatially, as contiguous built-up areas with a distinct physical form. They can be defined functionally, in terms of the social and economic processes which take place in defined spaces. They can be defined institutionally, by reference to political and administrative units or local government. They can also be seen as 'imagined communities', aggregates of individuals who see themselves as sharing common interests or modes of life. It is difficult to reconcile these definitions to produce an agreed account. Definition of the city and the boundaries are themselves subject to political contention. This book uses two conceptions of the city, focusing on the ability of city *governments* as legally constituted to manage the *city* seen as an urban agglomeration.

Given that cities differ from each other within states, the number of cases and variables threatens to become unmanageable. Certainly, the method of descriptive generalization across the range of cases to be found in four countries would be impossible. Some comparative studies meet this problem by selecting cities within different countries for comparison, supplying details on national factors where necessary (Savitch, 1988; Parkinson, Foley and Judd, 1989; Judd and Parkinson, 1990;

O'Leary, 1987). Others focus on national policies with regard to cities (Barnekov *et al.*, 1989). This book focuses on national systems of local government, generalizing about national styles at the risk of a loss of appreciation of intra-national variation. Existing works on national systems of urban politics compare nations within Europe (Mény and Wright, 1985; Goldsmith and Page, 1987; Ashford, 1982; Mellors and Pijnenburg, 1989; Mabileau *et al.*, 1989); Britain and the USA (Gurr and King, 1987; Barnekov *et al.*, 1989); the USA and Canada (Goldberg and Mercer, 1986); or all three (Pratt *et al.*, 1989). This study bridges this tradition by comparing two North American countries with two in Europe.

If 'comparative' and 'urban' pose conceptual difficulties, so does the third element of this book's title. Politics has two dimensions of relevance here (Stone, 1987, 1989). There is politics considered as problem-solving, the search for technical solutions to agreed problems, for the maximization of generally accepted goals. The emphasis here is on performance, efficiency and management. Secondly, there is politics seen as conflict, the reconciliation of competing interests and the social distribution of scarce resources. While students of national governments traditionally focus on the latter, much of the literature on local government focuses on the former, assuming that the task of local governments is easily defined and that the only problem is finding the most efficient way to discharge it. The argument deployed here is that there are some common interests in cities and, more importantly, that democratic and open city politics can forge common interests. Problem-solving capacity can be improved and consensual solutions forged. Yet urban politics is also about conflict and its management and consensus itself may be the product of manipulation or successful agenda management.

GOVERNING CAPACITY AND URBAN REGIMES

Two central questions are at the centre of this inquiry. The first concerns the governing capacity of local political arrangements, approached through the idea of urban regimes. Specifically, it concerns the ability of elected councils to manage social and economic change. The second is more normative and concerns the openness of local political arrangements to social and political interests.

To a greater extent than in national politics, urban politics is limited by cultural, institutional and economic constraints. These mould the political arena, shape the political agenda and allocate powers and resources unequally. Winning elections is merely the first stage to achieving power. Many traditional analyses discuss this question in terms of local government's autonomy from higher-level governments. Others emphasize the problem of the autonomy of local governments from local social and economic interests (Gurr and King, 1987). Autonomy is certainly important, but governing capacity is more than this. It is the ability to formulate policies and to mobilize powers and resources behind their implementation.

The formal structure and powers of local governments are relevant and these vary considerably among the cases examined. Yet the conditions in which these powers are exercised can change their potential and meaning. Governing capacity depends also on the cultural and ideological assumptions about the scope of government in different societies. This is discussed in Chapter 2. It is also related to the importance of territory in political discourse, the sense of place and the legitimacy of place-based politics in the political culture.

The intergovernmental network is another critical element. This has sometimes been seen simply in terms of centralization versus local autonomy. If higher-level governments increase their power, it is assumed that this must be at the expense of lower-level governments. Yet it is entirely possible for both levels to increase their governing capacity simultaneously. Nor does centralization necessarily entail a reduction in local government capacity. As writers in different systems have noted (Grémion, 1976; Rhodes, 1981, 1988; Wright, 1982; Dente, 1985), intergovernmental power relationships are reciprocal. Both higher-level and local governments enjoy relative degrees of autonomy or dependence on each other, which vary across time and space. Higher governments are thus both a constraint and a source of powers and resources for elected city governments.

Local governments often have substantial service delivery responsibilities. This generates professional bureaucracies which are also both a constraint and a resource for elected officials. The literature on urban managerialism (Pahl, 1964) stresses their role in allocating resources and opportunities. The organizational analysis school (Crozier and Friedburg, 1977; Dupuy and Thoenig, 1985) emphasizes the diversity and pluralism of governments in which competing professional and agency interests seek to guide policy. Public choice theory also gives a large role to bureaucrats assumed to be pursuing their own self-interest (Niskanen, 1973). This implies that a powerful bureaucracy limits the power of elected officials. On the other hand, control over a professional bureaucracy and the instruments of service delivery provides important resources to elected local governments.

The economic environment confronting local governments also affects governing capacity. The local political economy approach provides the dominant paradigm in urban political analysis in the USA, that of the 'limited city'. This emphasizes two key effects of the capitalist economic system. First, most productive resources and a large amount of investment capital needed for successful urban governance are in private hands. Secondly, the city is an open economy in which owners of capital are free to move out and in which production is traded in a competitive market. Some urban political economists see this market constraint as quite determinant, emptying local politics at least in the USA of its meaning (Peterson, 1981). Others treat it as a constraint whose impact varies according to political factors and the market position of the city in question (Stone and Sanders, 1987). A weak market position may force cities to make concessions to investors. A favourable market location and strong links to economic decision-makers could serve to increase the capacity of local government. In other cases, politics might substitute for market advantage. The intergovernmental system could attenuate business pressures by protecting local governments and providing resources to substitute for private capital, so enhancing governing capacity.

Cities are the locus of a variety of distinct social movements. These are mass popular movements around a series of urban policy issues, notably the use of land and the supply and distribution of public services. Both marxist and non-marxist observers have detected a distinct social base for such movements in contemporary urban society (Lowe, 1986; Castells 1978, 1983). Demands are focused on issues of 'collective consumption', of cultural identity and community, and local self-government. The impact of these on urban decision-makers varies. Some systems of local government are open to social demands and new interests. In other cases, varieties of political closure restrict the urban agenda and insulate decision-makers from social demands, especially those involving redistribution. This is discussed further in Chapter 3.

To analyse the complexity of local policy-making, Stone (1987, 1989) has developed the idea of 'urban regimes', consisting of constellations of public and private power within a structurally defined context. Public policy is seen as the outcome of both economic and political power, with the composition of each and the balance between them varying among cities. This gets away both from an exclusive focus on governmental institutions characteristic of much of traditional local government studies and from the economic determinism of some urban political economy approaches. It allows for an urban politics with its own pattern of interests, in which governing coalitions can put together combinations of powers and resources to achieve desired outcomes. It also generates variables to allow a comparison among cities in terms of power balance and policy outcomes.

While the approach has been applied to compare cities within the USA (Stone and Sanders, 1987), it can be extended to international comparison. To do this, further variables need to be added to the analysis filling in the cultural background, the structural constraints – both institutional and economic – and delineating the scope for political choice. Five sources of power can be identified. First, there is political power derived from the possession of local elective office and the legal prerogatives pertaining to it. Second, there is power in the hands of higher-level governments. Third is power derived from the possession of scarce knowledge and skills, which may be in the public or private sectors. Fourth, there is power derived from the private control of resources, notably but not exclusively in the business sector. Fifth, there is power derived from the ability of certain groups to withdraw cooperation or obstruct change. A governing coalition needs to achieve elective office or control those who do but this is not always enough. It must also mobilize resources controlled by the private sector or other levels of government, possess the necessary knowledge and skills to achieve its goals and defuse or circumvent opposition from those with a capacity for obstruction. The cultural context and prevailing ideological assumptions vary more between than among countries and must thus form an element in the comparative analysis. The external economic environment is also critical in defining the limits of city governance. The success of a governing coalition will depend on the incidence of these resources and constraints; equally, it will depend on the degree of difficulty of the task which it faces (Stone, 1989).

Urban regime theory enables us to generate variables sufficiently broad to permit comparison among different national systems and to examine their combination in specific places. The approach here focuses on assessing different national systems of local government in terms of these variables. The cost, freely admitted, is a loss of some of the intra-national differentiation to which the original formulations drew attention. If the object is to test the capacity of local governing arrangements to resolve problems and achieve change, there are many policy areas which could potentially be examined. Local governments do a great many things and deliver a wide variety of services in different places. Some of these are routine and relatively easy to manage. Others are extremely difficult. To test the governing capacity of different regimes, the examples in the chapters on policy capacity (Chapters 6 and 7) are of difficult issues and issues expressed at a sufficiently high level of generality to allow comparison across institutionally differing systems. They are the redistribution of income and opportunities, and the promotion of economic development in cities facing adverse market conditions.

If the question posed is the efficacy of governmental arrangements, we must ask for whom and for what they are efficacious. In studying complex systems, there is a danger otherwise of being reduced to the 'complacent approbation of uncovered interdependencies' (Crozier, 1964, p. 295). Evaluation of effectiveness thus requires that we approach the issue from a particular perspective, that we find the archimedian point. The archimedian point taken here is the elected local leaders and the evaluative issue is their capacity to manage the process of change through urban regimes.

The next stage of analysis involves normative questions. The avoidance of normative questions in much recent writing on local government is in striking contrast to classical writers such as Mill and de Tocqueville, who had an intense concern with the conditions for creating democracy and liberty, or maintaining social cohesion. Behavioural approaches are the most likely to avoid normative issues but they are not alone. The comparative method itself, with its search for functional equivalence across institutionally varied systems, can lead to an assumption that all institutions perform a function, usually related to system maintenance. This helps avoid normative judgements and discourages a search for criteria other than system maintenance with which to evaluate institutions and processes. Partly this is an understandable reaction to early comparative approaches which assumed that the institutions and processes of the USA and Britain represented the ideal standard against which others might be judged, and towards which others should evolve. Some contemporary comparativists still insist that a rejection of normative judgements is an essential part of the comparative approach since norms are essentially ethnocentric (Dogan and Pelassy, 1990). Public choice theory, which is highly prescriptive and value-laden, hides its normative assumptions behind assertions about human nature, refusing to recognize a separate category of normative questions. Even marxist approaches, while suffused with moral indignation, claim to be no more than analyses of reality. Yet, since the very existence of local government implies a set of values about governing, it is impossible to escape making judgements about the object of study.

The normative issue here is the openness of the urban regime, especially to the interests of the disadvantaged. This is not a new question. The American debate on whether cities were dominated by elites or were pluralist touched on it but dissolved in an argument about methodology and competing interpretations of individual cases. What was lacking was a systematic examination of the cultural and structural factors which might encourage or discourage pluralism and access and a comparative approach to put them in perspective. The chapters which follow examine various forms of closure and containment of urban political demands, stemming from economic constraints, institutional structures and political processes. Closure refers to the ability to keep certain issues off the political agenda or to circumscribe debate to a limited range of options. Containment refers to the limitation on the power of groups challenging the prevailing regime through keeping them out of office, preventing them forming coalitions or withdrawing key powers and decisions from elected governments controlled by challenging groups.

The findings highlight a major conflict at the heart of urban politics. The internationalization of the economy, increasing capital mobility and the emphasis on competitiveness have reduced the autonomy of elected urban governments and increased their dependence on the market. Governing regimes have felt obliged increasingly to focus on development within a market order. At the same time, social and economic changes within cities are increasing social demands, breaking through devices of containment and closure. So cities are becoming internally more pluralist while at the same time the policy options of governing regimes are curtailed by the needs of competition. They must be responsive to the needs both of economic competitiveness and of social justice. Both marxist and non-marxist economic determinists tend to claim that this presents a fundamental contradiction, that a distinct urban politics is unworkable. Here it is seen rather as a challenge to systems of urban governance which are called on to manage political conflicts and policy choices more serious than in the recent past. There is scope for an urban politics here but it varies from one place to another. It is a limited politics but not for any deterministic reasons. Rather there is a constant struggle to define the terms of urban politics and an effort to put together governing instruments to resolve urban problems.

Comparative analysis allows these issues to be examined within different cultural and institutional settings. In order to make the project manageable and retain some substantive description of national settings, it is limited to four countries, chosen for their common and contrasting features. All are advanced capitalist societies with liberal democratic political systems. All are urbanized and have systems of local government subordinate to higher levels. Yet there are significant cultural and structural differences. In Europe and Canada, the scope of government is wider than in the USA and the assumptions about the relationship between the economy and the polity differ. France has long been regarded as the archetype of a state-centred, centralized polity, with a limited amount of political pluralism. The USA is usually seen as the opposite – a limited, fragmented, decentralized state with a pluralist political culture. Canada shares not only a continent but to a large extent an economy with the USA, but the culture and political system are different. In Britain, there is a strong tradition of local government but within a unitary, centralized state. It is therefore possible to compare governing capacity within different combinations of public–private and central–local powers.

Comparison highlights structural and cultural differences while allowing them to be examined in terms of common criteria. So we find that formal political pluralism in the USA takes place within a political spectrum which by European standards is extremely narrow. In France, the picture of the dominant state is modified when we take into account both the nature of local power and the existence of an increasingly international private economy. Differences between Canada and the USA which appear large when only the two are compared, fade when European countries are brought into the picture. Britain's tradition of local self-government appears weaker when we take into account the absence of the leverage over higher governments found elsewhere.

The remainder of the book falls into two parts. Chapters 2 to 4 consider the systems of urban government and politics in the four countries, examining differences of culture, structure and the pattern of local politics. In order to achieve comparison and to avoid predetermining the issues, the discussion necessarily ranges quite widely. Chapter 2 considers the cultural beliefs relevant to urban politics and the different structures of local government. Chapter 3 looks at the politics of cities, examining sources of conflict, techniques of closure and containment and the pattern of intergovernmental relations. Chapter 4 examines the relationship between elected local government and economic power and social movements. It then draws some conclusions as to the nature of urban regimes in the four countries. The next three chapters focus on policy. Chapter 5 examines efforts to reorganize local government structures, the reasoning and interests involved and the ability of local elites to control the process. Chapter 6 examines the ability of local elected elites to engage in social redistribution. Chapter 7 looks at their capacity to manage the process of economic change in cities. The effects of these efforts on political alignments themselves are also noted. The final chapter (Chapter 8) reviews the argument and assesses the prospects and preconditions for a democratic and progressive urban politics.

2. Systems of Local Government: Culture and Structure

THE PUBLIC DOMAIN

Liberal democracy recognizes a large domain of private life, in which the public authorities do not, and should not, intervene. Yet the resulting individual freedom produces social and economic inequalities which undermine the civic equality which is the essence of the democratic project. There is a consequent problem of the extent of 'public domain' – the sphere of action in which individuals' self-regarding action is not the dominant mode of behaviour or the sole morally worthy value. French political culture recognizes a large public domain as a distinct sphere of action with its own rationale and procedures. Social solidarity is often invoked as a counterpoint to possessive individualism. Some observers (Birnbaum, 1988; Elkin, 1987; Kemmis, 1990) discern such a notion in the ideals of some of the American Revolutionaries, but lament its displacement in the nineteenth century by a dominant ethos of possessive individualism. In this vision, society and politics are seen as a mere extension of the private market in which rational, selfish individuals seek their own gratification. Social rights and obligations, as well as social justice, are seen largely in procedural rather than substantive terms. The notion of a public domain is more familiar in British culture, but competes with an ethos of individualist utilitarianism. Although some observers (Marquand, 1988) see the latter as the dominant feature of British political culture, it has never been free from challenge. The same can be said for Canada, despite the strong American influence.

The relationship between the market, based on unequal property relations, and the polity, based on universal suffrage, is also moulded by other cultural influences. In the USA, support for private enterprise is a defining characteristic of the nation, part of 'American values'. Large questions about the social control of the economy or criticism of the private system, as opposed to its effects, are off the political agenda.

An ethos of competitive individualism legitimizes inequalities of economic outcome. Acquisitiveness and individualism, liberty and property, are seen as inseparable (Birnbaum, 1988). Together with the fragmentation of the political system on territorial and ethnic lines, this has prevented the emergence of a national welfare state, although steps in this direction were taken in the 1930s and 1960s when precarious progressive national coalitions were formed.

In Europe and Canada, by contrast, collectivist values have been sustained by three separate forces. The first is a form of conservatism seen in traditional British Toryism and continental Christian Democracy, which is suspicious of market liberalism, sees society as an organic whole and, while authoritarian and inegalitarian, is paternalist and supportive of universal social provision. Second is a conception of nationalism which has a substantive social and economic content and emphasizes national solidarity as a condition of survival in a competitive world. This developmental nationalism is a strong element in French culture, from Colbert under the monarchy to Gaullism in the 1960s. In Canada, too, nation-building under adverse conditions including a threat of American takeover, led to a pragmatic but expansive view of government intervention in economic and social matters (Lipset, 1990; McNaught, 1988). Third, there is social democracy, a philosophy rooted in the liberal conception of democracy but criticizing the economic inequalities arising in market capitalism both in themselves and in the way they empty the formal equality of citizenship of real meaning. Social democrats value equality of outcome as much as equality of opportunity, and see liberty for the many as requiring restrictions on the prerogatives of property-owners. Social democracy emerged from the late nineteenth century as a stable alliance of the organized working class with other progressive elements committed to using the state to correct market allocation and achieve greater equality.

Though some American observers conflate these traditions into a single collectivist philosophy (e.g., Lipset, 1990), they are quite distinct in their politics. Social democracy is egalitarian while conservatism and christian democracy are based on social differentiation. Developmental nationalism uses a strong state to achieve modernization, conservatism to preserve an existing order. Yet all have pointed to a stronger sense of the public domain and of collectivism in Europe and Canada than in the USA. Their distinctiveness and the contested position of private capitalism is further emphasized in Europe by a marxist tradition. Associated primarily with Communist parties, this has also had an influence on social democrats. By challenging the moral basis of the capitalist order and threatening revolutionary change, it also spurred the growth of christian democracy in postwar Europe as a means of reconciling traditional order with industrial society while saving the proletariat from godless communism.

The concept of a broad public domain and a tradition of collectivist values makes it easier in Europe – and, to a lesser extent, Canada – to mobilize in pursuit of public goods with diffuse benefits. The existence of alternative traditions means that the prerogatives of capital are not unchallenged: if it is seen as instrumentally useful, its moral worth is contested. Claims to substantive equality are made on grounds of citizenship. Significant areas of activity have been taken out of the market altogether on the ground that market allocation does not produce substantive justice. In the USA, by contrast, justice tends to be seen largely in terms of procedure rather than outcomes, so that the contrast between civic equality and economic inequality is not seen as an affront to the dominant cultural values. These distinctions should not be overdrawn. Market liberalism has gained ground in Europe and Canada, and it was the ideological guiding light of the British Conservative administration after Mrs Thatcher came to power in 1979. Yet the boundary between the public and private sectors remains a subject of debate and not mere assertion, and collectivist traditions remain strong.

Another critical difference pertains to property rights. In Britain and France, the feudal legacy has left ultimate property rights in the hands of the state, a tradition which was inherited in Canada (Cullingworth, 1987). In the USA, the Fifth Amendment of the Constitution provides that private property may not be taken without due process of law and just compensation. Canada's Charter of Rights, by contrast, contains no property provision (Cullingworth, 1987). Although custom and political pressures serve to protect property rights in Europe and Canada, their entrenchment in the USA uniquely defines the limits of urban political action. It would not be possible in the USA to nationalize all rights in development land, as has been attempted several times in Britain, or to control land speculation in the manner of some of the French planning instruments. This both defines the scope of public authority in American cities and moulds the terms of exchange between landowners and city government.

The public domain and the extent of public authority find their articulation in the state, one of the most difficult ideas in social science. Some would confine the notion to continental European societies with an intellectual tradition of speaking of the state, denying that in Britain or the USA the concept has any meaning. Others (Dupuy and Thoenig, 1985) deny the utility of the notion altogether, since the 'state' is not a reified object which can be observed and measured. Yet a state as the embodiment of sovereignty and public authority exists on both sides of the Atlantic. The difference is the form which it assumes. In continental Europe, there is a tradition of the state as an autonomous entity over and above private interest, the embodiment of a national will. The legacy of the French Revolution (secured by the end of the nineteenth century) was the transfer of this authority from the person of the monarch to the people and its democratization. This allows government elites to act in the name of a supposed general will, embodying the 'national interest'. It legitimizes both a wide definition of the domain of public authority and an 'enlightened bureaucracy' consciously pursuing the goal of national development. Americans have no concept of the state in this sense. Instead, they speak of 'government', usually seen as a necessary evil to arbitrate among competing private interests, itself subject to restrictions and divided into countervailing powers.

Both indigenous and foreign observers have often denied that in Britain a state over and above social and economic interests exists (Redlich and Hirst, 1903). There is a state, but with its own distinct form. In the absence of a revolutionary tradition, it is not identified with popular sovereignty or the mobilization of national will. Rather, it has been inherited from the pre-democratic constitution and consists of the doctrine of parliamentary sovereignty. This has left a state endowed with massive legal powers compared with its American federal counterpart but resting on pre-modern foundations. On the left, socialists have sought to use the state for a variety of purposes but without giving much thought to its nature (Jones and Keating, 1985). On the right, conservatives have either seen the state as merely a creation of an ordered moral society and not in itself the source of authority, or have adopted the market liberal view of the state as a machine of no value in itself but necessary for providing essential services. The result was considerable muddle (Dyson, 1980). Compared to its western European counterparts, the British state has widely been seen as ill-adapted to the requirements of national mobilization in the pursuit either of economic development or social justice (Jones and Keating, 1985; Marquand, 1988; Nairn, 1981, 1988). In Canada, there is a similar confusion about the state. The absence of a revolutionary assertion of popular sovereignty and a rooting of legitimacy in traditional authority is compounded by the grafting of federalism onto a parliamentary system and the later addition of a semi-entrenched charter of rights. In both Britain and Canada the populist tradition is weaker than in the USA, social deference greater (Lipset, 1990). While this has weakened democratic and decentralist movements, it has allowed governments scope to define the public interest in broader terms, and permitted parties to 'carry' unpopular items of policy.

What all this means is that in France – and, less clearly, in Britain and Canada – a conceptual distinction can be drawn between private and public interest, and debate joined on the relationship of the two; and that the public power as embodied in the state carries its own legitimacy to define the public good other than as a mere aggregation of competing private interests.

The nature of politics and of authority accordingly varies among countries. Two dimensions to the management of public affairs have been identified earlier. The first concerns problem-solving, the identification of social problems and the design and implementation of solutions. The second concerns conflict and is based on the view that there are no 'objective' or universally recognized problems or solutions, merely differing interests. On either dimension, we can recognize three principles for decision-making and resource allocation. The first is competitive electoral politics. The second is the market, a process of individual exchange among private individuals and corporations. The third is professional competence, the right to take decisions based on the possession of specific skills and training. Each can exist in either type of politics, the conflict mode or the consensual mode. On the other hand, the criterion of professional competence is more likely to be found where politics is seen as a goal-oriented activity, directed to consensual objectives. Electoral competition tends to imply conflict on goals, while consignment of issues to the market reflects a view that there are no common goals. What is interesting for comparative analysis is the differing balances among various systems.

There is a tradition in France of politics as problem-solving, with a large sphere of state autonomy in which national needs are defined other than as aggregations of private interests. This includes matters of long-term planning, of distribution and of social and physical development as well as the classic state functions of security and defence. Decisions are taken in the name of a broad national interest defined through electoral competition, and in the name of technical competence. In the French language, there is no distinction between 'politics' and 'policy', forcing those who do perceive a difference to use the English words (e.g., Gaudin, 1988). *Politique* is seen as a project for social guidance towards an end state, in which divergent interests must be accommodated but which is more than the sum of its parts. In the USA, by contrast, politics is seen in terms of conflict management not so much among competing versions of the public interest as among self-defined private interests, to be mediated by markets or by arrangements in politics which imitate markets. Given the development of American society, these interests in turn have come to be defined and conditioned by the market economy. This is not, to anticipate the argument, to be confused with the ideal-type competitive market of neo-classical economic theory. Like all real markets, it is marked by inequality and bias, traits which are reproduced in the polity.

In Britain and Canada, public affairs are seen in terms both of problem-solving and conflict management. The borderline between state control and the market, collective or individual provision, is a matter constantly fought over, especially in Britain. Many functions (such as health, policing and much of education) are taken out of both market and electoral competition to be managed by technical professionals, but here too the boundary line is subject to challenge, with demands both for more control by elected politicians and for marketization.

COMMUNITY AND PLACE

It is often asserted that a viable system of local government must be based on 'communities', rather than on an arbitrary division of territory. Yet 'community' is one of the most contested terms in the social sciences, both as a descriptive term and as a normative idea.

'Community' has been given as many as 94 meanings (Lyon, 1987); the discussion here will be limited to two. The first refers to a sense of affective solidarity usually, but not necessarily, focused on a place. It is associated with *Gemeinschaft* society, based on solidarity and a cultural attachment to place which over-rides wider or narrower loyalties such as class or individualism. There is local political consensus and an absence of intra-community conflict. This type of community is commonly assumed to be in decline with the advent of modern society based on national and international links and impersonal economic relations. Yet, as a normative ideal, it continues to attract support from both conservatives and radicals, equally opposed to the anonymity of modern society and the reduction of social relationships to the market. Conservatives see community in terms of hierarchy, deference and the traditional order, socialists in terms of egalitarianism and mutual support (Mabileau *et al.*, 1989). A variety of thinkers who might loosely be classified as 'postmodernist' similarly sees in community a means for combating the alienation and powerlessness of the urban masses in modern capitalist society (Cooke, 1990). This type of spatial solidarity can be seen in culturally distinct localities such as rural Wales, the Western Isles of Scotland or parts of rural France and in mining villages, but it is a disappearing phenomenon. In the small towns and suburbs of the USA and parts of Britain, a similar degree of social consensus may be found. In these cases, however, it is less a reflection of interclass community solidarity than of class defensiveness in areas marked by residential segregation. To put the point a little differently, community itself has been remoulded to reflect class interests.

The other meaning of community is as a space for social interaction, within which politics can occur (Mabileau *et al.*, 1989). In this sense, community is the local equivalent of the broader public domain, an arena in which publicly-oriented issues can be debated and decisions reached. This is often valued by liberals who see it as a basis for pluralism, voluntary association and cooperation. Agnew (1987), calling this simply 'place', distinguishes it from community in the earlier sense and complains about the tendency to confuse the two. Place he sees in terms of three elements – *locale*, the settings in which social relations are constituted; *location*, the geographical area encompassing the settings for social interaction as defined by social and economic processes operating on a wider scale; and *sense of place*, the local 'structure of feeling' (Agnew, 1987, p. 28). Place is thus a combination of physical space, the social and economic processes which occur in it and affect it and perceptions of these. Balligand and Maquart (1990) similarly distinguish between *espace*, a purely geographical notion, and *territoire*, which includes the pattern of economic, social and political relations expressed within it and which cannot be reduced to mere market exchange. In this sense, place (or community, as some continue to call it) has not declined in importance. On the contrary, the uneven impact of national and global forces, political trends to decentralization and the differing mixes of forces in different locations have served to enhance the importance of place in politics. It is in specific places that the conflict between a global economic rationality and the requirements of distributive justice, environmental protection and cultural specificity is most keenly felt, providing distinct local forms of politics. For community understood as a space for social interaction does not require social homogeneity or consensus on issues of policy. It is compatible with, and may even require, a rich internal political life, with a multitude of associations and interest groups competing for influence. It can also sustain a sense of spatial solidarity which does not displace, but coexists with, class and other loyalties, based upon shared interests. Places can thus be constituted as civil and political societies and citizens credited with multiple loyalties, based on class, ethnicity, place and other factors.

A sense of place is often a product of history and inherited traditions. It is sustained by patterns of social, political and economic interaction focused on the location. Places with the strongest sense of identity tend to be communities with strong traditions and old-established civic and other institutions. Industrialization typically took place in existing towns and cities which have shown the capacity to adapt to successive changes in markets and technology. Here is found a sense of 'civic community' (Mackay, 1989), an identity with and commitment to a city on the part of social and economic elites. This is the case in many of the cities of France. The sense of place and of civic community are often weakest in communities which were themselves the product of industrialization in one phase of its advance and which have been abandoned by capital as it has restructured. This is the case in much of North America, especially in the west, as well as in the industrial cities of Britain. In these places, without a strong historic sense, the definition of the relevant community is often itself an object of political contention. This is not to fall into the trap of historical determinism. Places can be made and remade through political activity, economic and social interaction, the media and external challenge, but cultural legacies make this easier in some locations than in others.

Community as sense of place in turn supports the notion of a local public domain as an arena for public initiative and action above private property interests. If local citizenship can be separated from property ownership, then citizens can be seen as the stakeholders in the urban form and environment. Place can thus be treated as a public good and not as a mere traded 'commodity' (Logan and Molotch, 1987). It is not necessary for local decisions on the use of space to reflect complete political consensus. They can be the product of political debate and compromise, but there must be a sense in which decisions taken at the community level are seen as legitimate and authoritative. This in turn necessitates both a sense of place and a political culture supporting a public domain distinct from the sphere of private commerce.

The idea of place and of community as social interaction varies in the four countries. The French system provides for the defence of communities as historic 'places' whose common interests can be advanced and in which political interaction can take place. At the same time, traditions of national solidarity and intergovernmental influences ensure that these communities are not left defenceless in the face of market forces. In the USA, fragmentation must be seen as a device for protecting private space and enforcing social homogeneity within it. Social interaction takes the form of competition among places in a market-based system policed by a weak national state. Citizenship has become indissolubly tied to property relations. These tendencies are limited in Canada by a larger sense of the public domain and a more expansive view of government. In Britain, the sense of historic place has been relatively weak though far from non-existent. Partisanship, social heterogeneity and the intrusion of broader political issues into local government have prevented local governments from becoming, as in the USA, mere instruments for the protection of private space. At the same time, the development of the welfare state has involved the cooption of local elites into the administration of national policy. Since 1979, two conceptions of locality have come into conflict. The Conservative government has seen an attempt to devalue the sense of community, to define citizenship as property relationships and to reconstitute places in purely market terms, while centralizing their remaining functions. They have been opposed by revitalized local political movements seeking to reconstitute places and create a more vibrant local politics.

CONCEPTIONS OF SELF-GOVERNMENT

Local self-government is widely praised as a 'good thing' but takes on rather different meanings in differing national contexts. In the USA, self-government stems from individualism and pluralism, rooted in a suspicion of government as a threat to liberty. Local governments are seen as associations of individuals choosing to govern their own affairs, defining their boundaries and negotiating their powers. This gives powerful support to the idea of local autonomy and extends the scope of pluralism within the society. Yet in practice liberty has become tied to the defence of property rights. Local self-government is also limited by the high degree of autonomy which the prevailing ideology accords to private enterprise. The liberal–individualist conception of self-government and the absence of a concept of the state also allow higher levels of government to detach themselves to a degree from the fate of cities, leaving them exposed to the forces of the market. Indeed, local government itself is often seen as a market in which cities compete against each other for the favours of private investors.

On the continent of Europe, Britain is often bracketed with the USA as the home of an 'Anglo–Saxon' notion of self-government. Yet the British tradition is very different. Britain lacks both the concept of popular sovereignty found in regimes with revolutionary origins and the individualist notion of government found in the USA. Nor is there a strong tradition of pluralism or belief in the virtues of divided government. Sovereignty resides in the central Parliament which has been prepared to delegate powers to local collaborators or forces in the periphery which it has been expedient to accommodate. Just as it is Parliament and not the British people who are sovereign nationally, so it is not communities of individuals but municipal corporations who are the beneficiaries of delegated powers. These, like the delineation of local government boundaries, are the prerogative of the central authorities and with the powers come a series of obligations. Like the parliamentary regime itself, this system survived the transition from landed oligarchy to democracy (Bulpitt, 1983), despite occasional attempts from the late nineteenth century to establish local governments as genuine spheres of autonomy. In the cities, the political parties took over the role of territorial management. British central politics came to revolve around the alternation of parties in power at Westminster and, as long as the parties saw this as the main prize, they subordinated territorial politics to it. On the other hand, central political and bureaucratic elites saw great advantage in continuing to devolve responsibility for administration to the localities as a means of relieving the political and administrative burden on themselves. The absence of regime challenges from a reactionary right or revolutionary left (or, outside Ireland, separatists) enabled territorial politics to emerge as a collaborative exercise. For the central political elite and the bureaucracy which developed from the mid-nineteenth century the main concern was the autonomy of central elites from the sort of localist pressures which were so overwhelming in centralized states such as France. The British state system, with its apparent concentration of power at the centre, was embraced by the Labour Party as it saw the possibility of gaining power at Westminster from the 1920s on (Jones and Keating, 1985). By the late twentieth century, however, the national partisan divide began to take on territorial dimensions. The major cities were controlled by the Labour Party committed to defending the postwar welfare settlement, and in some cases to radical policy initiatives, while central government was engaged on a radical agenda of its own which involved attacking the territorial power bases of its opponents. This placed the collaborative pattern of central–local relations under severe strain and forced the parties to face the issue of the proper degree of local autonomy.

Despite structural similarities to the American system, Canadian local government shares these features with Britain. Canada's roots lie in the rejection of the American revolution and the origins of municipal government lay in the attempts by the British authorities to force the dominion to govern its own affairs and provide local services. While provincial independence is jealously guarded and has expanded considerably over the years, municipal autonomy is less highly regarded.

In France, the myth of the unitary and uniform state is an old tradition. Identified under the monarchy with the person of the sovereign, the unitary state was given democratic legitimacy by the Revolution. By destroying intermediate forms of authority and vesting sovereignty in the people, the Revolution both unified and reinforced the state (Birnbaum, 1982), which became identified with the 'general will' of the French people. Decentralization and provincialism came to be associated with counter-revolutionary, reactionary and clerical forces opposed to the spirit of progress. Under the Third Republic, under almost permanent siege from the monarchist, clerical and provincialist right, this 'jacobin' spirit was developed into a doctrine of the strong, autonomous central state, free from competing localist and other pressures. Pluralism was little valued and, in contrast to American thinking, centralization was seen as the prerequisite for democracy and civil equality (Mény, 1974). Alternative traditions did survive. The monarchical right saw decentralization as part of a traditional organic order, hierarchical and undemocratic, but this was finally discredited with the Vichy regime. On the left, an anarchist tradition believed in the dissolution of the state in favour of self-governing communities and, while it was always a minority view, this did influence thinking among the 'new left' from the late 1960s.

In practice, official doctrine was far from reality and the unitary state was gradually captured by local interests (Machin, 1977). Indeed, the central problem with local government for much of the nineteenth and twentieth centuries was not the needs of local autonomy and democracy but the need to secure the autonomy of a strong central state against territorial pressures. Yet the identification of democracy and progress with centralization and reaction with decentralization was to remain a powerful influence in French political life. Local government was not vested with large administrative functions, and was seen as an integral part of the unitary state.

Attitudes to local self-government are intimately tied up with attitudes to other questions. Right and left share both centralist and decentralist traditions which can be justified in terms of their central canons. Broadly speaking, parties of the left and representatives of the working class and the poor have tended in the twentieth century to favour centralization. There are both economic and political reasons for this. The national state has a broader tax base than the locality, and it is more difficult for wealthy individuals and businesses to migrate across national than across local boundaries. The class solidarity found on the European left itself tends to downgrade territorial politics, and it has often proved easier on both sides of the Atlantic to forge progressive coalitions at national than at local level. History has also made the left suspicious of the localities. In France, the jacobin left long associated the provinces and localities with clerical and royalist reaction while in the USA local autonomy, like states' rights, was often seen as a code for business dominance and racial oppression.

Conservatives, for their part, have often favoured decentralized government. For traditionalists, this ties in with the emphasis on community as an arena where class conflicts are muted and a deferential social order maintained as a defence against mass society. For market liberals, the locality is the unit nearer the individual and decentralized local government can serve as a surrogate market. These two visions, while both promoted on the political right, are difficult to reconcile. The organic community of the traditionalists is based on a social conception denying the primacy of individuals and suspicious of the competitive market. For the market liberal, decentralization is a means not an end, and any form of local government at best a necessary evil, at worst a barrier to possessive individualism. The right also has its centralist traditions, emphasizing authority, order and national unity. Market liberals, too, have sometimes favoured centralization to combat locally-based socialism.

In the 1970s and 1980s, the European left modified its stance on centralization. One factor was a need to accommodate new urban and regional social movements mobilizing in a politics of territorial defence. There was a rediscovery of 'community' as an alternative – or supplement – to the waning appeal of class. While a great deal of the new thinking was utopian, based on the idealized imagined consensual community, it did allow the left to engage in the politics of territory and to link together struggles which otherwise might have appeared quite disparate (Keating, 1988b). In Britain, France and the USA, support for local action also stemmed from disillusionment (justified or otherwise) with national programmes in the 1960s and 1970s, and their failure to solve urban problems. In France before 1981 and in Britain and the USA after 1980, there was also a reaction to right-wing national administrations.

STRUCTURES

Local government structures reflect national traditions as well as social and political interests. In France, the most striking feature is fragmentation, with over 36 000 units. There are 36 433 communes, 95 departments and 22 regions. In addition, there are 11 urban communities, which group communes in the major cities for certain purposes, as well as large numbers of single-purpose and multi-purpose syndicates of communes. Yet fragmentation exists within a unitary state of which local governments are part; and the system is uniform throughout mainland France. While there have been many changes in the system over the years, the integration of territorial elites into the state structure has enabled them to avoid radical overhaul, or the suppression of any tier of local government.

Communes are a reflection of historic place. Established at the time of the Revolution, most are based on the ancient parishes. While ceasing to have a close relationship to the facts of contemporary social and economic geography, they have remained the bearers of the sense of place through successive regimes. The population range is considerable, with two communes over half a million, one over a million and 1 053 under 50, but all have identical formal powers and status. The departments were originally a technocratic innovation, a centralizing feature intended to circumvent the traditional territorial power structure. In turn, they took on a life of their own. Directly elected from the mid-nineteenth century, they became important interlocutors of the central power, though lacking their own executive until 1982. Regions were brought into being between 1963 and 1986 as a result of the convergent pressures of central technocrats; modernizers seeking to undermine the old structures which they saw as an obstacle to change; decentralizers who wanted more powerful units; and regional neo-nationalists (Keating, 1988c). Gradually gaining status and power, they became fully-fledged local authorities on their direct election in 1986.

The USA also possesses a fragmented system of local government, but for different reasons and with a different significance. In this case, it reflects the American tradition of pluralism and the lack of a unitary state. Local government developed in individual states according to local needs and pressures. From the late nineteenth century, fragmentation was increased under the impetus of the Reform movement, aiming to curtail the power of political bosses and enhance that of professionals. Boundaries and jurisdictions were further manipulated in the twentieth century by social and economic interests seeking to defend private space. It became common for suburbs to incorporate as separate local government units in order to retain social or ethnic exclusiveness and avoid demands for redistribution. In the absence of political and bureaucratic elites at state level with the interest and power to impose comprehensive schemes for local government, the system tended to develop piecemeal. In 1987, there were 3 042 counties, 19 200 cities and towns and 16 691 townships in the USA, giving 38 933 general-purpose local governments in all. In addition, there are 14 721 school districts and 29 532 special districts grouping local governments for specific purposes. Metropolitan areas tend to be fragmented into multiple jurisdictions.

In Britain, local government structures do have a historic significance. Towns incorporated from the middle ages in order to secure independence from the feudal order of the countryside. Municipal corporations were reorganized with statutory functions in 1835, and gradually democratized, while the historic counties were given their own elected councils in 1888. In the nineteenth century, cities were active in promoting bills concerning their powers and boundaries and in forcing down the threshold for county borough status. In the modern era, however, local government structures have largely reflected the wishes of the central bureaucratic and political elites. By the 1920s, the principle was established that the wishes of the inhabitants should be a subordinate consideration (Onslow, 1927). Convenience, partisan advantage and technical efficiency have been the motives for change which has been imposed from the top rather than emerging from the localities. The structure has been dominated by large units with uniform powers for each category of local government and little fragmentation of major cities. Local interests have been important only at the margin, influencing boundaries to ensure local partisan advantage or the defence of social interests. Britain now has 515 local governments, consisting of 69 metropolitan and London boroughs, 47 English and Welsh counties, nine Scottish regions, 387 English, Welsh and Scottish districts, and three Scottish islands' authorities. In the large cities, where there were upper-tier metropolitan counties between 1974 and 1986, there are special-purpose bodies for common functions including police and fire. Northern Ireland is different since, because of sectarian discrimination, local governments have been stripped of most of their powers.

In Canada, there is considerable variation among provinces. There are 4 836 municipalities or general-purpose local governments in all. Yet city governments are less fragmented than in the USA, with small jurisdictions confined to the rural areas. Provincial governments, like British government, face few obstacles to reorganization and have engaged in considerable structural reform, though they have shared the American tendency to design units for individual cities rather than producing general schemes on European lines.

WHAT DO CITIES DO?

One measure of the power and status of local government is functional responsibilities, though direct comparison is difficult since states use different means of allocating tasks. In France, local governments have traditionally possessed a general competence allowing them to intervene for the general wellbeing of their communities, though subject to the law and the administrative control of high authorities. They were distinguished less by their distinct functions than by their differing constituencies and the stages of the policy process in which they could intervene. So over a wide range of policy areas interventions by several levels of government are possible, usually in the form of joint projects. The building and administration of a school may involve an active role for the commune, the department, the region and central government.

In Britain, local governments have a statutorily defined range of functions which they do not share with each other. They act as agents for the administration of centrally-defined policies in other areas. All other activities are, under the *ultra vires* rule, illegal. They are responsible to their local electors, not for the general wellbeing of the community but for the discharge of their statutory functions, though these may be interpreted in various ways. To do this, they possess substantial administrative resources. This in turn, has required large-scale local governments.

In North America, the *ultra vires* rule applies and local governments are restricted to those activities specified in state and provincial statutes. These vary among jurisdictions and among cities, but the functions available to any local government tend to be restricted. Governmental fragmentation and the legacy of the reform era has dispersed responsibilities among a variety of elected and appointed governmental and quasi-governmental bodies in most cities.

There have been several attempts to build general models of the distribution of functions among tiers of government. Some of these are country-specific but others are comparative. Some are descriptive, assembling the various functions performed by local governments and looking for commonalities (e.g., Goldsmith, 1989), others deductive. Descriptive comparison of responsibilities is difficult because of the differing patterns of shared competence, and because in the federal systems of the USA and Canada there are variations among the states and provinces. Table 2.1 shows where the *predominant* responsibility in a number of key functions lies.

What emerges from Table 2.1 is that local governments everywhere have a concern with land use and its regulation. Land cannot be moved from one place to another, it cannot be reproduced, and there are limits to the extent to which it can be substituted by other factors in production and consumption. Local governments provide certain services requiring geographical proximity, such as refuse collection and leisure and recreation. They also have important responsibilities in social services, though matters here are more complex and variable, stemming from differing definitions of tasks, historical traditions and the relationships among the varying services. In Britain, integrated social

Table 2.1 Allocation of functions to levels of government

	USA	*Canada*	*Britain*	*France*
Land use planning	*L*	*L*	*L*	*L*
Refuse collection	*L*	*L*	*L*	*L*
Culture and recreation	*L*	*L*	*L*	*L*
Local roads	*L*	*L*	*L*	*L*
Urban transport	*L*	*L*	*L*/private	*L*
Water	*L*	*L*	private	*L*
Electricity	*L*/private	*L*	private	*N*
Police	*L*/state	*N*/*L*/province	*L*	*N*
Primary and secondary education	*L*	*L*	*L*	*N*
Vocational education	*L*	province	*L*/*N*	*L*
Health	*L*/private	province	*N*	*N*
Personal social services	*L*/*V*	province/*V*	*L*	*N*/*L*
Cash welfare	*N*/state/ local	*N*/province	*N*	*N*/*L*

Note:
L = Local and regional
N = National
V = voluntary sector

services (or social work) departments have direct responsibility for social care but are separated from the National Health Service. In the USA, local governments share social service responsibility with state governments and private and voluntary agencies. Health care is provided privately, but with a significant role for all three levels of government. Canadian municipalities are almost entirely excluded from social service and health matters in favour of provincial governments and private non-profit agencies (Sancton, 1989). In France, departments since the early 1980s have had the lead responsibility in social intervention, while health care is a central responsibility. In practice, there is a complex mingling of central, municipal and agency roles. Cash payments have tended increasingly to be subject to central control, even where (as in the USA and Canada) they continue to be administered locally, though there has been some decentralization of this in France. Education and policing show large variations, being highly centralized in France, with local governments reduced to a purely supportive role, and decentralized in the USA.

Such a descriptive comparison of functions alone gives a misleading view of the powers and role of local governments. Some countries, like France, have traditionally not sought to divide responsibilities functionally at all, so that the account above is only an approximation to reality. The complexity of modern government is such that functions are highly interdependent and sometimes impossible to disentangle. In all systems, there are ways of getting round restrictions where there is a political motive, and of using powers for different purposes. The more complex the system and the more interdependencies among functions and agencies, the more opportunities of this sort are likely to arise. However functions are allocated, their use and the political, social and economic interests served by them can vary according to quite different considerations. Merely listing functions thus does not tell us about their practical significance, why they are allocated, or the political purposes to which they are put. For this, we need a more sophisticated framework of analysis.

An alternative approach is deductive rather than descriptive, derived from neo-classical economic assumptions. King (1984) distinguishes among allocative, distributive and stabilization functions. The allocation function refers to the provision of services which need to be provided publicly, either because they are 'public goods' – that is, goods from the enjoyment of which nobody can be excluded, like defence or clean air – or because they are 'merit goods' – that is, items whose value might not be appreciated by the consumers, such as health services or education. These can be provided locally where there are no external effects on other areas from decisions taken in a locality. Distribution functions involve transfers from one set of individuals to another, in cash, unequal service provision or progressive taxation. These are usually unsuitable for local control, since there may be a tendency for the wealthy to migrate out of jurisdictions which redistribute in favour of the poor, so undermining the programme, and for the poor to migrate into such areas, overburdening it. The third set of functions, those of stabilization, refer to macro-economic fiscal and monetary policies, the external effects of which make them unsuitable for devolution to sub-national governments.

Peterson (1981), too, divides governmental functions into three categories – in this case, the allocational, the developmental and the redistributive. Allocational functions are those (mainly housekeeping tasks) which neither redistribute income nor affect the economic life of the city. Examples would be street-cleaning and public parks. This is similar to King's (1984) allocative category. Developmental functions are those connected with improving the city's economy and tax base and attracting higher-income residents. Redistributive functions are those which redistribute from one set of residents to another, either through cash transfers or through social programmes funded by progressive taxation. Saunders (1984), examining the British case, divides governmental functions into three similar categories. The first concerns the maintenance of order at home and abroad. The second is aimed at the maintenance of production of goods and services (the production function). The third is aimed at supporting the consumption needs of groups in the population who cannot fulfil all their requirements through the market (the consumption function). In contrast to King and Peterson, it is in this last area that the functional specificity of local government is found to lie, though Saunders (1984, 1986) recognizes that sharp lines between the production and consumption functions are difficult to draw.

These models are ideal types, and are of limited help in explaining the actual allocation of functions in the four countries under consideration. Despite King's (1984, p. 44) claim that 'there is a fair degree of uniformity between countries over the local public goods, or at least the items that are arguably public goods, which are subcentrally provided', a great variety can be observed. The cases of education and police have already been mentioned. Considerations of macroeconomic control have led to some limitations on the power of local governments in borrowing in Britain and France, but there is a large variation in the extent to which local governments are able to entice industry to locate in their areas. There does appear to have been a trend since the Second World War for welfare policies involving explicit redistribution to devolve upwards to national governments, either through direct assumption of responsibility or through intergovernmental transfer payments. Yet the extent of this differs greatly, and redistributive policies cannot be identified exclusively with cash transfers. It is technically possible to bend many other local programmes so as to redistribute resources. Most allocation functions can be used for redistributional purposes, notably merit goods like education and housing. It is therefore necessary to distinguish the allocation of functions from the politics surrounding them, and the purposes to which they are put. In some countries, production interests are stronger at national level, in others at local. Chapter 3 examines the different character of national and local politics in the four countries. This has led to pressures for the allocation of functions to levels differing across countries and times.

Another factor is the technical needs of individual services. There is a large literature on the appropriate unit for the various local functions. It is clear that large-scale spatial planning is appropriate for regional rather than for local units, and that a village commune is unlikely to have the resources or population base to run a higher education system. In the 1970s it was successfully argued in Britain that the needs of the water function dictated authorities based on hydrological boundaries. Thirty years earlier, local government had been found to be an inappropriate level for the modern supply of electricity and gas. Official reports on reorganization in Britain and France are replete with references to the most appropriate tier for the performance of various functions. As a general explanation of functional allocation, however, this will not do. It fails to explain the differing patterns in different countries, why electricity can be supplied municipally in Canada but not in Britain, why school districts in North America are often of a size which would be considered 'non-viable' in Europe. Even where authorities are too small to provide services themselves, they can still retain the functional responsibility while buying in provision. Human intervention can create structures responding to other imperatives and interests, even at the risk of some inefficiency in the technical sense.

Government structures and functions may better be explained in historic terms as the outcome of experiences in problem-solving and conflicts among social forces in specific contexts. The experiences of nation-building and service development are central here. In Third Republic France, education was a vital instrument of socialization, secularization and nation-building, teaching children to be French, to be citizens, to be nationalists. For this purpose, it needed to be centrally controlled and directed. The spirit was recalled by a socialist education minister of the 1980s, Jean-Pierre Chevènement, in his campaign for a return to republican discipline, central control and nationalism. Policing, similarly, was an essential element in maintenance of the state from threats of civil disorder, revolution or counter-revolution. In nineteenth-century Britain, these functions could safely be entrusted to municipal leaders loyal to the constitutional order. There was neither a revolutionary left nor a reactionary–clerical right to undermine the nation-building project (Keating, 1988b). In Canada localities, who often wished to be left alone and spared taxation, were *made* to provide the services under close provincial supervision. In the USA, education and policing were regarded as essentially local matters, of little concern to other jurisdictions. In a country where the state has never even tried to claim a monopoly of the instruments of force, local police forces were never seen as a threat to its sovereignty.

In France, the centralist tradition, running through monarchical, napoleonic and republican regimes alike, was associated with the construction of centralized bureaucracies, subject to a greater or lesser degree of influence by local political elites. In Britain, the absence of regime challenges allowed central government to entrust service delivery to local bodies. This in turn allowed the central bureaucracy to remain relatively small, dominated by generalist administrators and concentrating on policy advice and control. In the USA, the expansion of the frontier in the nineteenth century created a wide variety of conditions and needs and the initiative on service delivery was often left to local leadership. Only in the late nineteenth century did the new school of public administration develop general ideas on the proper shape and scope of bureaucracy. In Canada, service development was encouraged by colonial and provincial governments, seeking to get localities to assume responsibility. Structures of government and functional allocation were based largely on either British or American models.

This historic development in turn spawned bureaucracies and professional interests have developed in their maintenance or change. French professional civil servants and teachers, enjoying a privileged status and possibilities for mobility, have resisted transfer to local control. In the USA and Canada, the turn of the century reform movement saw efforts by service bureaucracies to escape from local political control into structures which would allow them more autonomy. These included separately elected boards and appointed agencies. Agencies have also sprung up in fragmented local government systems where a political and organizational vacuum has appeared. In Canada, the tendency for municipal politics to be dominated by land and development issues has led social service professionals to prefer separate agencies under close provincial and professional control (Sancton, 1983). Local government reform in Britain similarly saw efforts by professions to escape the detailed administrative control which they resented in the local government system. Other professions were able successfully to assert arguments based on technical service needs to justify the creation of regional authorities, a level largely free of either local political control or the centralized control characteristic of ministerial departments. The result was to allow a considerable degree of professional independence (Hogwood and Keating, 1982).

Above all, it is the historical balance of political forces which has moulded the structures and activities of local government, and these have varied from one country to another. Social and economic groups and political formations have sought to take issues to the level at which they possess the advantage and where the resources to address their concerns are available. European social democrats have sought to take both economic issues and matters of social distribution to higher levels, though often retaining administration at local levels. Only since the 1970s has this begun to change. European conservatives, while less concerned with public control of the economy or social equity, have favoured an authoritative central state. Their views on centralization have varied according to the prevailing circumstances. In the USA, conservatives have tended to resist centralization of either economic or social functions, while liberals have favoured a stronger federal role. The federal role has thus expanded more rapidly at times of liberal ascendancy in Washington. In Canada, the marked strengthening of the provinces' role within confederation has overshadowed the issue of municipal autonomy and prevented municipal governments from establishing regular links with Ottawa.

Systems of regulation of local government also follow distinct national traditions, based either on administrative control or law. In France, where local governments have had a general competence, national field administrators have wielded a tutelary power. Until 1982, the prefect had power to veto a wide range of municipal decisions and specialized bureaucracies were able to force local decisions into their own preferred mode. In Britain, administrative regulation has traditionally been less pervasive. Inspectorates exist in various functional areas, but there is no class of general territorial administrators like the prefects working closely with local governments. Instead, the system is regulated by legislation defining local responsibilities and powers, and a series of reserve powers allowing central ministers to over-rule local choices in most policy areas in individual cases. While the very absence of a level of central field administration means that these have been used sparingly, the 1980s saw a large use of over-ride powers in planning. In the absence of a system of administrative law such as exists in France, local councils are subject to the ordinary courts, who have interpreted their scope for policy discretion rather narrowly, often resorting to common law where there is no statutory basis for restraint. In the USA, the bias to law over administrative regulation is even stronger. In a litigious society, local governments are subject not only to state laws governing their status and functions but to interpretations of state and national constitutions. Systems of administrative regulation vary from state to state, but are less comprehensive than in either Britain or France. Canada shares the British tradition of regulation by law, but with over-ride powers available to provincial ministers.

Administrative regulation of the French variety is in some respects more constraining on local governments than a framework of law laying down general rules. In practice, the presence of a field administration of the national government provides opportunities for local elites to penetrate the national administration. Administrative regulation becomes a complex game in which the representatives of the centre seek accommodation and compromise. In the 1980s, the state passed a series of measures lightening administrative regulation and replacing it with *a postiori* legal control. In the USA, local governments with their defined spheres of competence are largely free from arbitrary intervention by state and federal executives. Yet they are unable to bend the rules and seek accommodation with the flexibility found in systems of administrative regulation. Britain and Canada are intermediate cases. There is some scope for bargaining and compromise within functionally defined policy areas, though the scarcity of territorially-based national administrators reduces it.

3. The Politics of Cities

ISSUES AND INTERESTS

Politics in cities, as has already been noted, has two dimensions. The first involves problem-solving – formulating policies, mobilizing resources and implementing programmes aimed at improving conditions. This type of politics puts a premium on cooperation, finding common interests and forging positive-sum strategies. The other dimension concerns conflict, focused on control of scarce resources and opportunities. While analytically distinct, these two types of politics are difficult to distinguish in practice, since many programmes contain elements of both and there are strong incentives to define the agenda and present policy proposals as non-conflictual, justified by a common or general interest, and thereby protect them from attack.

Another distinction is between policies for economic growth and development (the politics of production) and policies for distributing the social product (the politics of distribution). Politics within each sphere has its own characteristics and criteria for decision-making. Issues of production impinge on urban politics because of cities' role in the process of economic growth and change. In economies characterized by the private ownership of productive assets and capital, cities need to maintain their economic base. More specifically economic issues arise because of local governments' responsibility for the regulation of land use. Urban politics is deeply affected by competition for land use, the extent to which it should be determined by markets or political decision-making and the conditions for economic development.

Distributional issues arise because of the way in which the urban form and structure allocates opportunities and resources, and because of the role or urban governments in providing public services. Some observers have sought to give a specifically urban meaning to class by noting the interests which arise in relation to urban service provision and competition for land and resources. Rex and Moore (1967) argued that 'housing classes' could be identified on the basis of people's access to housing. While most urban scholars would distinguish this from social class, reserving the latter term for occupational groups, the phenomenon of differential access to housing and urban services does create patterns of common interests and economic and social stratification. Differences in interests and preferences can then be hypothesized for owner-occupiers and tenants or users of public and private transport (Dunleavy, 1980). This is the basis for the politics of 'collective consumption' and distribution.

The tension between production and distribution is a constant theme in local (as in national) politics. This is partly a matter of policy orientation. Production politics is often characterized by problem-solving approaches and the search for consensus on the premise that growth provides advantages for everyone. Criteria for policy evaluation are market-based and commercial and policy-making roles restricted, with a large role for producer interests. Distribution politics are characterized by pluralist competition, with identifiable winners and losers. Criteria for policy evaluation are contested and highly political. Yet there is also scope for conflict within the production sphere, since in a capitalist system economic development tends to be identified with incentives for the owners of capital. Nor can the politics of growth easily be separated from distribution issues, since the costs and benefits of growth are typically distributed unevenly. The relationship between the two policy spheres and the character of politics and pattern of interests surrounding them is a major theme of the urban politics literature.

Peterson (1981) argues that local politics is limited to matters of production while redistribution is, and must be, a matter for the national level. Given the competition among cities for growth and an enhanced tax base, they have no alternative to concentrating on the politics of development. Redistributive policies will prejudice this by driving away high-income residents and business and attracting welfare claimants. Cities have a unitary interest in promoting development and curbing redistributive demands. Local politics is therefore closed and limited to the conditions for production and growth. National politics is more open and pluralistic, and can encompass issues of redistribution.

Saunders (1984), analysing the British experience, comes to the opposite conclusion. His 'dual state model' presents consumption needs as the essence of local government, with production matters being fought out at central level. This theory allows central–local relations to be tied into wider social conflicts since for both neo-marxists and neo-conservatives there is a permanent tension between the production and consumption functions of the state. 'The first priority of central government is and always has been to maintain private sector profitability, whereas that of local authorities has been to provide for the consumption requirements of various groups in the local population' (Saunders, 1984, p. 28). Conflict is increased by the differing politics of each level. Local politics, focusing on issues of service provision and collective consumption, is relatively open and pluralistic, concerned with citizenship rights. Central politics, focusing on production issues, is closed and characterized by corporatist bargaining among producer interests, concerned with property rights.

Neither Peterson nor Saunders claims to have produced a model applicable equally to all times and places. Peterson explicitly bases his model on the experience of the USA and points out that in other countries, such as Britain, the system of fiscal equalization and guarantee of local debt allows local governments to escape the imperative of growth politics. Saunders (1986) acknowledges national differences. So it is possible to treat the economic and social imperatives as variables, and examine their incidence in various contexts. Both production and distribution politics are found at both levels in all four countries, but the balance varies according to the economic environment, the political structure and the prevailing belief systems. The more cities are exposed to the forces of market competition and the less protected by national equalization schemes, the more they are likely to concentrate on the politics of development as opposed to distribution. Many American scholars would see local politics as structurally dominated by producer and property interests, so that even progressive mayors are pushed into pro-business growth strategies (Judd, 1988; Kantor, 1988). National politics, on the other hand, are at least potentially more open to claims based on citizenship rights, though this is critically dependent on the governing coalition in Washington. In Canada, the cultural climate sustains somewhat more of a challenge to business, but there are structural biases which lead local politics to focus on development politics (Sancton, 1983). On the other hand, issues of distribution, collective consumption and other non-property-based claims do arise in North American cities to pose regular challenges to the development orientation and introduce political pluralism. These in turn have been met by various forms of political containment, to curb redistributive demands within the urban regime.

In Europe, local government has generally been more open to redistributive social demands and less oriented to the politics of economic development. Centralization of private business and its close links with a unitary central state have made this the main focus of production politics. In Britain, the local bias to collective consumption issues is reinforced by the extensive service-delivery functions with which local government has been entrusted. In Europe generally, the division between production and consumption conflicts and that between central and local politics have been bridged by social democratic parties operating at both national and local level, incorporating urban social demands into coalitions based on the traditional working class. In the USA, the absence of social democratic parties produced 'city trenches' (Katznelson, 1981), a disaggregation of the interests of the urban poor. Only in the 1930s (and briefly in the 1960s) could local progressive politics be linked to a larger national programme. Observers on both sides of the Atlantic have noted a decrease in what the Americans call the 'middle class' and the British describe as the skilled or working class, and the emergence of an underclass of the very poor, largely excluded from the job market and occupying sub-standard housing. This 'vanishing middle' has implications for class-based politics in cities by polarizing social relations and weakening the prospects for lower-class-based coalitions such as have from time to time characterized national politics.

Peterson has been criticized (Stone and Saunders, 1987), for defining distributive issues out of American politics altogether. Local government is not just about managing distributive demands, or just about maximizing economic competitiveness. It is about both in varying measures in different societies. There are common factors affecting cities across the western world. The opening of the European and global market, together with the reduction of central protection and support, is subjecting European cities to some of the same competitive pressures felt in the USA. Class politics has been transformed by the emergence of cross-class, place-based development coalitions, committed to the pursuit of 'their' city's interest in a context of inter-urban competition (see Chapter 7). Intra-urban conflict has to some degree been displaced by inter-urban competition. Yet cultural and structural factors continue to influence the balance and the outcomes, and it remains true that in Europe the politics of production is essentially a national matter while in North America it is the essence of local politics. The impact of economic changes and business influence on local government in Europe is mediated to a large degree by central government, while in North America it is more direct.

Another source of cleavage is ethnicity. In the older industrial cities of the USA, politics was long based upon the demands of successive waves of immigrants, defining themselves ethnically, bargaining for resources and then being absorbed into the mainstream of political life. After the Second World War, there was a large-scale migration of southern blacks to the cities; facing obstacles in the form of legal or informal segregation and a pervasive pattern of racial discrimination, blacks were not assimilated into the dominant white culture. Nor, with the decline of the older industrial cities from the 1960s, could they benefit from the upward mobility and opportunities available to earlier generations of ethnic immigrants. On the other hand, with a high degree of political solidarity they were able to gain control of a number of city governments. From the 1970s, Hispanics became an important element in the politics of several cities. In Canada, ethnic rivalries have been most obvious in the French–English conflicts in Montreal (Sancton, 1983) and have played a role in several other cities, but not to the same extent as in the USA. In Britain, ethnic politics before the 1970s was focused on the politics of the Irish community in cities such as Liverpool and Glasgow and parts of London. Since then, there has been a mobilization among the black and Asian communities previously accommodated unobtrusively in the Labour Party. In French cities, there was no ethnic politics before the arrival of immigrants from North Africa in the 1960s. In the 1980s the racist National Front made race an issue in French politics, though the relatively small numbers of immigrants and the fact that most of them lack the vote means that they are the object rather than the subject of racial politics. While the Socialist Party is in principle committed to giving immigrants the vote in local (but not national) elections, it has not hitherto felt strong enough to put this into effect.

There is a tendency for conflicts in cities to focus on neighbourhood issues. This is partly an extension of competition for land; it is also because, outside the workplace, residential neighbourhoods are the most convenient forum for political mobilization. The postwar years have seen an increase in spatial segregation by class and by race, resulting from a combination of economic and political factors. Growing affluence led many members of the middle class, especially in the USA and Britain, to move out of the cities to suburbia. Those who could not afford to do so remained in the cities. This was far from a simple economic matter. It is also a simplification to see suburbia as uniformly middle class and white (Harrigan, 1989). The process was in practice heavily influenced by the exercise of economic and social power to maintain social and racial exclusion around the urban periphery, as well as containing the central city. In the USA, lower-income groups and ethnic minorities were kept out of exclusive suburbs through zoning laws requiring large lot sizes, or banning apartment properties or incorporation as separate jurisdictions (Judd, 1988; Kantor, 1988). In both Britain and the USA, real estate agents and lending institutions 'red-lined' neighbourhoods as undesirable because of their lower-class or minority character, reinforcing the pattern of segregation. Tax subsidies to owner-occupation and nationally-financed highway construction gave an added incentive for the middle classes to disperse. American urban renewal programmes in the postwar period, undertaken by municipal–private partnerships with federal funding, extended and 'improved' central business districts but displaced large numbers of lower-class residents. Racism and the absence of affordable housing forced those who were black into ghettos.

In Britain and France, urban renewal, under more direct public control and subject to comprehensive plans, proved a mixed success. New towns were established to accommodate the urban overspill in balanced communities, with employment and social amenities, but these could cope with only a minority of those seeking housing. Fiscal pressures and land shortages soon led governments to build cheap, high-rise buildings around the urban periphery. The middle classes were simultaneously seeking out individual houses in suburbia, supported by government policy and subsidy – or, in the case of many French cities, remaining in the inner city and pushing up prices. Public housing schemes thus came to be associated with the poorest of the working class. In France, they are occupied increasingly by the immigrant population. In Britain, most immigrants arrived too recently to qualify for public sector housing in the new estates of the 1960s, and have tended to remain in inner city areas vacated by the white middle class. The result has been a large degree of coincidence of economic, ethnic and spatial divisions in the cities of Europe and America. In Canada, the process is less marked, given the absence of tax subsidies to owner-occupiers, nationally-funded urban highways or large-scale urban renewal. Frisken (1986), however, sees signs of Canadian provincial governments favouring suburban development, and suggests that Canada may be moving in the American direction.

Gurr and King (1987) point to another set of interests in cities, that of the central state. Public officials need to establish public order in cities, to secure acceptance of the state's authority among urban populations and to maintain institutions of local government. National governments need cities as sources of revenue and parties need them as sources of votes. Jacobs (1984) sees cities as the generators of the wealth of nations. These interests vary across cities and over time. French governments have feared Paris as the source of revolutions from 1789 to 1968 and the fear of public disorder explains the centralization of the police power. In the USA in the 1960s and Britain in the 1980s, urban rioting posed a challenge to the state's claim to maintain order, though not to the regime itself. The role of cities in national wealth generation is now a matter for dispute, but the major cities are still critical for certain higher-level functions including finance and corporate leadership. Capital cities are important as the seats of government, though there is a marked contrast between the obsessive concern of French presidents with Paris and the indifference of American national administrations to conditions in Washington D.C. There are also contrasts in the electoral stakes which national politicians have in cities. In France and Canada, it is not possible for a party to ignore the big cities and hope to win a national election. In the USA and Britain, on the other hand, residential segregation and the constituency-based system for all national elections has weakened competition for the urban vote. Republicans and Conservatives can win national elections without the major cities, while Democrats and Labour may be able to take them for granted.

THE CONTAINMENT OF URBAN POLITICS

In the urban political arena, it is not simply these interests which are contested. The very form of the arena itself is an object of contest, with social and political groups seeking a form of politics which contains competing demands, defines the agenda to suit their purposes and creates a systemic bias (Stone, 1984) in decision-making. Closure is the process whereby dominant groups have sought to restrict the local political agenda, especially by keeping redistributive questions off it. Containment is the means by which the capacity of popularly elected officials to respond to social demands by mobilizing resources is limited. Such strategies both constitute an element of urban politics and shape the wider context within which conflicts are conducted. Forms of closure and containment include the prevailing cultural norms, the structure of local government itself, the party system, the intergovernmental system and the fiscal system.

PARTIES AND ELECTIONS

There is a longstanding public debate over whether local government ought to be 'political'. Taken literally, non-political local government is an oxymoron (equivalent to non-political politics). What is normally meant is that local government ought to be non-partisan; that local politics should be seen as a matter of problem-solving rather than of conflict; or that the speaker does not like the particular type of politics being criticized. Specifically, attacks on 'politics' or partisanship often mask objections to the use of political power to counteract inequalities in the social or economic spheres. 'Non-partisanship' thus tends to be a conservative rallying cry.

The earliest types of party system were caucus parties comprising members of municipal councils, banding together for mutual support but without programmes or mass organization. In the late nineteenth century, members tended to be people of independent social and economic standing, businessmen or professionals with a stake in the local society. Already, however, a professional political class was emerging whose power basis was municipal government itself, who sustained through patronage their privileged access to administration and an ideology of localism which allowed them to present themselves as defenders of territorial interests.

By the turn of the century, cities were faced with the demands of an increasingly assertive lower class, armed with the franchise. This produced two types of politics – machine politics and socialism. The political machine is best known in its American form as a mechanism for trading votes for individualized favours. It thrived in the era of mass immigration when newcomers to the USA had no resource but their vote, and gravitated to neighbourhoods where members of their own ethnic group were established. Machine bosses professionalized patronage, focusing it on the party rather than on the individual patron, while keeping contacts on a personal basis, and greatly expanding its scope. In return for bribes and kickbacks, contracts could be awarded to business, jobs found on the public and private payrolls. In return for votes, rudimentary social services could be provided to needy families. The machine thrived on corruption and the systematic plunder of public and private funds, but it is common now to point to some of its positive effects. It helped integrate immigrants into American society and provided avenues for upward mobility not available in the business world; and it did provide some social services to the indigent. Yet it systematically prevented the emergence of programmatic politics aimed at changing the social and economic order, while maintaining ethnic divisions within the working class. Barriers were thus formed to socialist politics while trade unions were opposed by the machines, at least until the 1930s (Kantor, 1988).

Socialist movements, more common in European cities and in the Canadian west, aimed to mobilize the newly enfranchised working class for social equality and control over the economy. In Britain – and, to some extent, in Canada – they also linked the worlds of workplace struggle against employers, urban struggles against landlords and city elites, and national politics. They were thus committed to asserting the primacy of politics over economics and, to some degree, denying the specificity of local politics. While there were many experiments in 'municipal socialism' in the late nineteenth and early twentieth centuries, the left generally came to believe that only strong national government could assert control over economic forces and mobilize the resources needed to achieve social equality. Socialist movements introduced a strong class dimension to urban politics, allowing lower-class interests to mobilize on a city-wide basis, while to some extent downgrading neighbourhood and ethnic issues.

It would be a mistake to regard machine politics as a purely American phenomenon, and socialist politics as European. Patronage often continued to flourish in France where the socialists of the Section française de l'internationale ouvrière (SFIO) replaced the old notables of the Radical Party. Municipal Labour parties in British cities such as Liverpool and Glasgow (McLean, 1983; Keating, 1988a) encompassed machines which dispensed jobs, council houses and sometimes business contracts in return for political loyalty. In the USA and Canada, socialist municipalities did emerge in the early part of the century (Kantor, 1988) despite the hostile climate. It is true, though, that class-based political action and the pursuit of broad policy goals rather than individual brokerage is more characteristically European and this, together with the relative absence of ethnic divisions, favoured the stabilization of class politics.

The rise of machines and the advance of socialism were both seen as a problem by sections of the business community and much of the professional middle class. They could be curtailed by limiting the role of the poor and working class in urban politics through institutional reform, and by reasserting the ideology of non-partisanship and 'good government'. The reform movement in North America united business leaders worried both about the costs of corruption and the rise of socialism with professionals scandalized by the dishonesty of the machines. Both found support in the new ideas of 'scientific management' purporting to show that there was only one best way to run any organization, to be discovered by rational inquiry. The reform movement sought to reduce the scope of politics by enhancing the role of qualified career professionals, leaving elected members responsible only for broad policy issues. Non-partisanship was enforced in elections and at-large electoral systems introduced to replace wards. This made it difficult for candidates based in neighbourhoods, those representing ethnic minorities and working-class candidates to mobilize the resources to contest elections – or, given the absence of parties, to make broad class appeals. The number of elected officials was reduced to a minimum and professional city managers introduced. As many administrative functions as possible were hived off to semi-independent agencies operating on the basis of 'good management' principles and free from political patronage in appointments and contracting. In many cities, provisions for citizen initiatives, referendums and recalls of elected officials were introduced to reduce further the role of party. Fragmentation of jurisdictions served further to contain lower-class and minority ethnic demands. Structural reform was accompanied by a sustained assault on socialist movements and organized labour, whose political power had largely been broken by the 1920s.

'Reform' politics in this sense is a distinctly North American phenomenon (arriving in Canada from the USA), though forms of institutional closure and containment did exist elsewhere. In France, municipal councils (except in the three largest cities) are elected at-large on a list system. There are two ballots and, until 1982, the list winning a majority at the first ballot or a plurality at the second took all the seats. While in principle the council chose the mayor from among its members, in practice it was the mayoral candidate who selected the list. Once installed, the mayor retained office for the full six year term. While this was intended partly to contain the left, the effect was to encourage partisanship on both sides while insulating political leaders from social pressures and neighbourhood demands. By the 1970s, it served to exaggerate left-wing success at municipal elections, and the socialists were wary of changing it. In the 1982 reforms, they instituted a modest degree of pluralism. Lists can now be merged between ballots, so allowing for coalition formation and the cooption of smaller political movements, and the opposition is now represented in council. While the winning list still takes a majority of seats, the rest is distributed proportionately among all the lists gaining more than 5 per cent of the votes. The effect of this has been a containment of social demands and insulation of French political elites – though not, as in the USA, to produce a corresponding rise in business influence. Rather it protects the interests of the integrated national–local political elite. Containment in France is further aided by the disenfranchisement of most of the immigrant underclass.

Another device to contain the rise of working-class politics, on both sides of the Atlantic, was the promotion of 'non-partisan' anti-socialist coalitions. In many reformed North American cities, especially in the Canadian west and American south, such coalitions continue to dominate the local political scene with the backing of the business community. In the older cities of the American North East and Mid West, partisan politics continues, though party reform, the assimilation of immigrant groups, legislation on hiring practices and the greater availability of welfare services has greatly reduced the power of the machines.

Anti-socialist coalitions survived in some parts of Britain and France until the 1960s. Gradually, they gave way to the national conservative parties, though in France these often remain loosely organized, reflecting the need for conservative politicians to acquire a party label to survive in a partisan environment (Dion, 1986). The result has been an increasing assimilation of national and local electoral politics (Dupoirier *et al.*, 1985; Miller, 1988). It is common to decry this as taking the meaning out of local elections since these are now decided according to 'national' rather than local issues and personalities. Yet it has also served local democracy by widening the agenda beyond the institutional limits of municipal government, raising larger social and economic issues. The closure of municipal politics in non-partisan systems, limiting it to issues defined by municipal jurisdiction, divides radical politics functionally and territorially and, by presenting issues in a forum where the parameters of action are so tightly defined, helps maintain the status quo. In the USA, urban politics is detached from national politics even in partisan systems, largely devoid of ideological or programmatic content and fragmented by race, preventing the emergence of a class-based system and subject to the limitations of city politics identified by Peterson (1981) and others. In Europe, urban politics forms part of a wider political project.

The individuals elected to municipal office reflect these institutional factors. In turn, they mould the character of municipal institutions. In reformed North American systems, election requires a 'non-partisan' appeal, often across the whole city. This requires considerable resources to establish name-recognition and largely precludes divisive appeals or redistributive politics. So election campaigns focus on issues which can be presented as in the interest of the city as a whole, notably growth and development. Individuals attracted to municipal office tend in turn to be those with an interest, either intellectual or financial, in these fields. Ninety-two per cent of big city mayors in the USA in 1987, owned their own companies or occupied managerial–professional positions. Twenty-six per cent were lawyers, 9 per cent in real estate and development and 6 per cent in retail and wholesale trade (Page *et al.*, 1987). Members in non-partisan councils in Canada show a similar tendency.

In Britain and France, elective office was the prerogative of the local bourgeoisie in the late nineteenth century, but gradually the representatives of large business dropped out, leaving locally-based businessmen and professionals facing the rising socialist movement. In the twentieth century, the social base of municipal councillors expanded considerably through the agency of the British Labour and French Communist parties which brought working-class candidates to office. The French Socialist Party was dominated more by white-collar workers and public sector professionals, notably teachers. The 1950s appears to have been the high point of working-class politics in Britain and France (Hindess, 1971; Keating *et al.*, 1989; Jones, 1969; Garraud, 1988). An urban political elite was thus created owing nothing to business sponsorship and marked by discipline and traditions of class solidarity. Recent years have seen a decline in blue-collar municipal councillors and their replacement on the left by public sector professionals and career politicians. In France, the percentage of manual workers among councillors in a sample of 500 communes fell from 24 per cent in 1945 to 11 per cent in 1983, while the number of teachers and civil servants increased from 20 per cent to 38 per cent (Garraud, 1988). Teachers are particularly prominent in the Socialist Party, accounting for 63 per cent of Socialist mayors. The trend was less stark in Britain, with 21 per cent of British councillors (and 35 per cent of Labour councillors) in 1985 having a manual working-class background (Gyford *et al.*, 1989). Among middle-class Labour councillors, a large number come from working-class families. Thirty-six per cent of all British councillors were employed in the public sector, over half of them as teachers. While this is in line with the proportions in the population as a whole, in the large cities, the figure rose with the opportunities presented by two-tier local government between 1974 and 1986 in England, and since 1975 in Scotland. More than half the metropolitan county councillors in 1985 worked in the public sector, as did 52 per cent of both regional and district councillors in Glasgow (Widdicombe, 1986; Keating *et al.*, 1989). Most of these were in white-collar jobs, about half as teachers.

On the right, the evidence is more patchy. In France, the independent businessman or lawyer appears to have given way to the public or private sector manager. The proportion of Gaullist mayors from public sector occupations increased from 20 per cent in 1947 to 40 per cent in 1983, most of these being managers rather than teachers. Among Radical mayors, the public sector proportion stood at 64 per cent. In Britain, the available data do not allow us to make such fine distinctions. Fifty-three per cent of Conservative councillors were professionals, employers or managers, but it is not clear how many of these owned their own businesses.

While it is impossible to infer councillors' policy positions from their backgrounds, there is likely to be an effect on their role perceptions and relationships, both to the bureaucracy and the private sector. Councillors drawn from occupations related to development and real estate, as is common in North America, will have a concern with – and possibly a material interest in – development issues. They may be expected to share ideological assumptions with business leaders, and to defer to business definitions of urban problems. Councillors from knowledge-based occupations without a direct stake in the local economy are less likely to share this assumptive world, and may be inclined to publicly-oriented solutions. They may also be able to deal on equal terms with the local technical bureaucracy and managerial elites in the private sector. There is some evidence in Britain and France of less willingness to defer to permanent officials, and a greater insistence on political leadership in policy development (Gyford *et al.*, 1989; Dion, 1986; Fayolle, 1989). This trend has also been helped by the rise of full-time councillors, a development also noted in Canada (Sancton and Woolner, 1990). While this may enhance the governing capacity of local elected officials, however, it may be at the cost of their social representativeness (Gaudin, 1989; Walker, 1983).

Recent years have seen pressure for the opening of local politics, with the rise of new social and political movements. In American cities where blacks have attained a majority or near-majority, black politicians have used the Democratic Party as their vehicle to gain office. Elsewhere they have challenged at-large elections which have served to limit their influence. In Britain and France, a new left, less tied to the old politics of class and more open to new issues including environmentalism, feminism, ethnicity and participation, has challenged the traditional party machines. Containment has thus become an increasingly difficult enterprise.

POLITICS AND BUREAUCRACY

Earlier this century, it was common to distinguish between 'policy', made by elected responsible politicians and 'administration', carried out by appointed professionals. The distinction is a hazy one, especially since implementation research shows that the way in which policies are carried out can affect outcomes as much as broadly defined policy. This is particularly important in local government when the basic outlines of policy have been established at higher level but decisions on priorities and modes of implementation have been devolved. Bureaucracy is also important in the urban political arena as an intermediary between local government and other agents, including higher-level governments and the private sector.

Politicians and bureaucrats share common interests and need each other for problem-solving. At the same time, if bureaucrats have their own goals, they may limit the capacity of elected officials or create conflict. Public choice theorists, for whom the analysis of bureaucracy is central, tend to a characteristically reductionist approach. Bureaucrats are seen as self-interested individuals intent on maximizing their own benefits such as salary, perquisites, reputation, power, patronage and ease of management (Niskanen, 1973). In most accounts, this is reduced to maximizing their own budgets, either because this is the prerequisite for other personal goals (Niskanen, 1973), or because that is the easiest thing for researchers to examine (Schneider, 1989). Other public choice theorists have recognized that bureaucrats' goals might include satisfying their clients, but count this too as a form of self-seeking behaviour on the grounds that they must derive individual gratification from it (Parks and Ostrom, 1981). This characteristic piece of reductionism defines away the central issue, the distinction between self-interested bureaucratic behaviour and actions directed at social needs.

Bureaucratic behaviour is in practice more complex and varied. Public servants certainly have individual interests in salaries and working conditions; but cultural and structural factors heavily qualify this. Their training and socialization and their professional organization create other values and interests. There is a belief in the subordination of appointive to elective authority which limits the extent to which public servants in the four democracies examined here cynically exploit their position. At the same time, there are beliefs about the prerogatives of knowledge and specialized skill. Most public servants genuinely believe in the social need for the service they provide, and many are imbued with a professional ideology about the way in which it should be provided. These ideologies are diffused and reinforced through training, while working together consolidates this and creates a sense of solidarity. Differences in state traditions and notions of public service create different role expectations in the public service. In France, civil servants are imbued with the idea of the state as the leading force in social and economic development, above the demands of sectional interests. An enlightened bureaucracy is a central element of that state, and entitled to corresponding prerogatives. This does not prevent rivalries among the various *corps* of administrators, but subordinates them to a common language of discourse. Some of this philosophy penetrates the British public service and at times can be pronounced – for example in Scotland in much of the postwar period (Midwinter *et al.*, 1991). For most of the time, though, it is moderated by public servants' subordination to party control and the power of organized interests. The same is true of Canada. In the USA the weakness of the state and the culture of pluralist bargaining reduces the public service to one interest among others – or, rather, to a set of competing interests defined by agency boundaries. It is significant that most public choice analyses are generalizations from American experience, though even there due weight should be given to professional values.

Sense of mission as well as self-interest leads bureaucrats to seek greater autonomy, but the extent of this varies. Similarly, they may or may not seek to maximize their budgets or to resist change, depending on whether this fits in with their complex goals. Attitudes and styles vary across culture and services. We find in some places a traditional conception of the bureaucratic role in providing stability and assisting elected authority. Elsewhere, bureaucrats have developed a more expansive view of their own authority. In some places, a new brand of radical public servant has emerged, identifying with the needs of clients against his or her own employer and challenging traditional professional norms.

Bureaucratic power is also complex and varied. A key element is control of knowledge and information. In some fields, this is reinforced with the possession of the specialized skills necessary to task performance. In addition to these 'cognitive competences', bureaucrats may have 'normative competences' – the ability to define social needs themselves (Laffin, 1986). Claims to exclusive competence are usually associated with professionalism, the creation of a *corps* of individuals deemed to possess the requisite qualifications. Control and autonomy may be further advanced by professional self-regulation, with restrictions on entry, the creation of scarcity and exclusive claims to posts. Professional boundaries may be entrenched by the creation of agencies insulated from political control or market forces. Professional influence may be enhanced where it operates in both public and private sectors, and at more than one level of government. Where a profession has a substantial private as well as a public sector, the former may be able to set standards and influence public policy (Dunleavy, 1980). For example, in both Europe and North America, the urban planning profession exists in both sectors. While the public sector is dominant in France, in North America private development interests are more easily able to define issues and set the agenda.

Professionalism has been developed in the local public service primarily (but not exclusively) to maximize efficiency. With the increased technical complexity of social problems and services, more specialized skills are needed and more differentiation of tasks has resulted. Professionalism is also a means of depoliticizing services and decisions by subjecting them to technical criteria. Often this had its origins in attacks on political patronage and its replacement by merit systems of appointment and promotion. More contentiously, it has involved moving the boundary between political and professional choice. Higher-level governments may also have an interest in promoting professionalism as a means of defining common norms for the system as a whole, to provide central guidance to urban governments and to reduce the local electoral input to administration.

The role and power of professional bureaucracies vary across the four systems of government examined here. Local government accounts for 58 per cent of public civilian employment in the USA (ACIR, 1989b) and just under half in Canada. In North America, the turn of the century reform movement focused on the separation of politics and administration, and sought to put as much as possible into the latter category. 'Civil service' systems of appointment and promotion on merit were written into state legislation and city charters, and the main professions organized themselves into self-regulating associations. In Canada, merit appointment and promotion systems are universal. Separate boards and commissions have also been established to take functions such as planning, utilities and policing out of direct political control and place them under professional influence. Public service, however, remains relatively low in prestige and the fragmentation and weakness of the public sector in matters of planning and urban development has led to a dependence on private leadership, especially in the USA. While this tends to benefit business, pluralism and competition may sometimes be bent to the needs of deprived groups through techniques such as 'advocacy planning'. This is based on the belief that the system is not 'neutral' but can be used to achieve change. Advocacy planners are committed lawyers and professionals who use their skills to combat systematic bias and maximize the opportunities which the system provides for communities.

In Britain, local bureaucracies are large, comprising 40 per cent of all public servants, some four times as many as central civil servants (CSO, 1990). Heavy administrative responsibilities are combined with a high degree of professionalism and a separation of political and administrative roles which allows permanent officials to serve successive leaders of different political persuasions. Departmental boundaries correspond to professions and are usually headed by a qualified professional. Professional insulation is reinforced by legislation mandating the appointment of specific chief officers and a functionally differentiated central government which gives them direct access to their central sponsoring department. As senior civil servants in central government tend to be generalists, much of the technical skill lies at the local level, though there are policy communities linking the two levels and a great deal of central–local relationships is mediated through professional officials dealing with their Whitehall opposite numbers.

In some fields, such as health and water provision, professional interests have been able to escape local political control altogether through special-purpose regional authorities (Hogwood and Keating, 1982), though in the 1980s these were brought under stricter central government control or privatized. Within local government, professional influence varies depending on the salience of the policy, the organization of the profession, central–local linkages and the policy environment. Laffin (1986), for example, notes the greater influence of highway engineers operating in a specialized field than of housing professionals, less well-organized and operating in an area of high political salience in which elected members also considered themselves competent. The planning profession was very influential in the 1960s when it appeared to offer solutions to the problem of urban renewal but the very comprehensiveness of their visions led to disillusion as planners were blamed for all varieties of urban ill. Social workers had a similar experience from the 1970s. There have been conflicting trends in the professionalization of British local government. On the one hand, professional differentiation has increased as successive groups have staked claims for recognition and unique expertise. The committee system, entrusting the executive function to committees largely corresponding to the departments of government, has created further vested interests. On the other hand, there has been growing criticism of the fragmentation which this produces in the approach to social and economic problems. A movement for 'corporate management' in the 1970s sought to subordinate specialized professionals to overall management strategies, but had limited success due to professional resistance and the statutory definition of services.

In the 1980s, a number of radical councils appointed non-professional policy advisors and administrators in a challenge to professional conservatism. Defended as a means of restoring political control and accountability, this was criticized for obscuring the distinction between political and professional roles, and as a return to patronage. From the 1960s, a breed of radicalized official had emerged, often working at community level and identifying with the needs and goals of the community rather than those of the employing authority. In a similar manner to the American advocacy planners, these officials have sought to maximize the influence of deprived communities, stepping outside their professional role to do so. In some of the larger cities, it became common for appointed officials in one council to serve as elected members on another, further challenging the role distinction. This trend was, however, reversed by the abolition of the metropolitan counties and legislation restricting the political activity of local government employees.

France has a strong tradition of bureaucracy as servant of a purposive state. Public service has high prestige, and through the system of *pantouflage* public servants are able to colonize top positions in the private sector. Senior officials are recruited through a system of specialized public service schools through competitive examination and are organized into *corps*. The *grands corps* represent the most prestigious public servants whose privileges include job tenure and the ability to leave public service to enter politics or business and return with no loss of seniority. They develop the generalist skills which allow them an important role in the policy process (Hayward, 1982) while not surrendering their monopoly of technical skill. Individual *grands corps* dominate specific ministries and agencies and there is a high degree of solidarity and mutual support even where members are in different agencies. Most service provision agencies are run not by local government but by outposts of the central ministries. The prefects are generalist field agents of the central state without parallel in Britain or North America. Until 1982, they acted as the executive arm of the departments as well as exercising a supervisory power, the *tutelle*, over the communes, including the power to veto communal acts. The need for local governments to use specialized field agencies of central government to carry out major works gave rise to a *tutelle technique*, the imposition of detailed conditions on works reflecting the preferences of the technical bureaucracy. A financial *tutelle* was exercised by the *Comptrolleur Payeur Général*, a central official responsible for handling local government finances.

The French public service has consistently striven to retain its national status and organization (Dion, 1986), and to resist local control; it has remained an important element in the definition and execution of major programmes for cities. The power of local elected officials has, however, been increasing in recent years. Despite the rhetoric of the unitary state, prefects and state technical officials need to get on with elected local leaders, especially the *grands notables* holding national as well as local office (see below). While there is conflict in the relationship, territorial officials of the central government and the local political elite share common interests in local development, and may jointly promote local interests at the centre. So complex games of collusion and cooperation develop (Worms, 1966; Machin, 1977; Crozier and

Friedberg, 1977). Divisions among field agencies and *grands corps* which compete for the business of local governments also enhance the power of the elected element. There is a long-running rivalry between the *génie rural* and the *ponts et chaussées* over contracts with local government and control of infrastructure agencies (Ashford, 1982). Attempts to strengthen the coordinating and directive role of the prefect in 1964 and 1982, to provide a single central interlocutor for local governments, were largely ineffective.

The decentralization programme of the 1980s served further to strengthen elected officials against the bureaucracy. The prefectoral *tutelle*, already much reduced, was abolished and limits placed on the various types of *tutelle technique*, a more difficult operation. Departments and regions gained their own elected executives. Functions were transferred from central to local government and with them a number of staff, while others were 'placed at the disposal' of councils. Local government administrators gained their own *corps*, ensuring them national status, with uniform salaries and promotion based on examination and only limited discretion allowed local governments in hiring. There has been a gradual increase over the years in the number of professional officials working directly for local government. The large cities had established their own technical bureaucracies before 1982, while some departments and regions had built up semi-legal services to parallel those of the prefect. Many of the left-wing mayors elected in the 1970s established their own *cabinets* of personal advisors to help formulate policy and control administration (Dion, 1986). In the early 1980s considerable numbers of the prefectoral corps moved into the service of local government, often preferring to work with conservative local councils than with the new socialist government. This served to create a more politicized tier of bureaucracy, while the increase in professional and public service workers among elected members created a political class able to engage in a dialogue of equals with the technical bureaucracy. The decentralization reforms thus largely preserved the integrity of the political–administrative elite while increasing the weight of the political element. They also served further to differentiate local governments, as the smaller towns without the resources to establish their own bureaucracy remained dependent on the prefect and central services.

THE INTERGOVERNMENTAL NETWORK

At one time, attention focused on just two aspects of the relationship between cities and higher levels of government – the scope for autonomous decision-making at the municipal level and the degree of central control over the locality. It is now recognized that even in systems characterized by formal separation of functions there are complex patterns of collaboration and interdependence among governments (Wright, 1988), while in formally centralized systems the influence is not all one way (Grémion, 1976; Rhodes, 1981). In federal systems, the notion of a 'centre' itself is problematic, since there are two higher-level governments each of which may have links to municipalities. This is particularly important in the USA, less so in Canada, where the federal government has little contact with local government. In Britain and France, there is only one centre, but the development of the European Community (EC) and its increasing autonomy from national governments is creating new patterns of relationships. Instead of talking simply of centre and locality, then, it is necessary to speak of an intergovernmental system of greater or lesser complexity. The system may be constraining, limiting the autonomy of local government. It may also serve to protect local elites from market influences, supply resources and allow local politics to escape the forms of containment discussed above. A tidy separation of central and local roles may enhance the functional autonomy of local government. It may equally deprive it of opportunities to intervene and forge alliances in the intergovernmental system. The governing capacity of local elected officials in each regime will depend not simply on the degree of autonomy from other levels, but on the precise relationship to the intergovernmental network. Local influence over higher levels of government depends on the channels of access which local political leaders have to the centre, the permeability of the centre itself and the power resources which local elites can use there. This influence may be used collectively, to protect the interests of the local government system as a whole, or individually to gain advantage for particular municipalities.

In Britain, centralization (especially in economic policy matters) means that city–business interactions are largely mediated through central government, providing a degree of protection to local governments. The presence of national political parties in local politics creates a set of shared interests between national and local politicians, and widens the political agenda. Yet there is a separation between central and local political elites. While it is common for local councillors to be elected to Parliament, they sever their municipal connections, though continuing to serve constituency interests. Adversary politics and party discipline at Westminster have meant that in the twentieth century Parliament has not easily been penetrated by localist pressures. Nor are municipal leaders major political figures in their own right. It is rare for a local government leader to be elected to the Labour Party National Executive Committee and in the Conservative Party municipal leaders have a subordinate role. The re-election prospects of MPs depend almost entirely on the national fortunes of their parties. Central–local party links are rather weak (Gyford and James, 1983) and both Conservative and Labour governments have been prepared to override the demands of their own local supporters. This is not to imply that the national parties have no stake in cities. Each has had its own interpretation of urban problems and the weight of urban interests in the national ruling party does affect the distribution of resources and the willingness to accommodate city pressures. Yet the weak sense of place means that national political initiatives, even those directly affecting local government, tend to be seen in partisan or class terms, dividing centre and locality on the same lines. Historically the separation of central and local politics has left a certain room for local autonomy – this is the basis for the tradition of local self-government admired on the continent. It has also served to ensure central autonomy from local pressures (Bulpitt, 1983). Central government has not lacked the means or political ability to intervene where it chose to do so. It is this combination of detachment with power which has allowed governments to impose drastic and repeated changes on the urban government system since the 1960s. They have taken into account their own local party stakes in this process, but have not been restrained in attacking the power bases of their opponents.

Most central–local interactions in Britain take place through the bureaucracies. These are separate both institutionally and in terms of recruitment, the central senior civil service being dominated by generalists concerned with broad policy issues while the local bureaucracy is led by technical specialists. Yet there is a dense network of linkages within functional areas and through professional policy networks which serve to attenuate the separation of central and local roles (Rhodes, 1988). Central–local relations, except in Scotland and Wales, are conducted through a series of functional departments of central government. The absence of a ministry of the interior with overall responsibility for territorial government can enhance local autonomy by fragmenting central direction. Yet is also means that there is no obvious pressure point for territorial lobbying except in the peripheral nations. The absence of a generalized national field administration has similar ambiguous effects. It means a lower degree of detailed supervision of local governments than in continental prefectoral systems. Yet, outside Scotland and Wales, it deprives local governments of locally-based intermediaries, and leaves them facing central departments from a position of weakness. For its part, central government has (at least until the 1980s) striven to simplify central–local relations to relieve itself of the political and administrative burden of detailed control and the pressures which stem from this. The uniformity of the structure and the relative cohesiveness of central government means that central policies tend to be matters of general application, with relatively few opportunities for individual municipalities to extract extra concessions.

In the USA the decentralist tradition, while enhancing formal autonomy, provides less protection for local governments against market forces. The intergovernmental system can nevertheless be used to enhance governing capacity. American municipalities have the advantage of two centres, the state and federal governments, both of which provide resources to municipalities. Executives and bureaucracies at both levels are further fragmented, allowing multiple points of access. As in other countries, functional alliances can emerge between central and local bureaucracies, but the control of allocation by legislatures means that this does not necessarily produce resources. Certainly, the weakness of party discipline makes state and federal legislatures permeable by local interests. The proliferation of special programmes and the practice of legislative log-rolling provide opportunities for cities to gain special favours. Yet this has been limited by the rural and later suburban biases of many state legislatures, which have led them to support measures of urban containment including ‘reform’ structures and metropolitan fragmentation. Alliances made within the intergovernmental system to extract resources for local purposes depend on a favourable climate. In the 1960s, a liberal pro-urban coalition in Congress secured extensive nationally-funded urban programmes. By the 1980s, however, American cities, like their British counterparts, were no longer a significant part of the electoral base of the administration, though retaining some influence in the House of Representatives.

Intergovernmental linkages through the party system are now weak. Even in partisan cities local leaders are not major figures in national politics. In the past, nominations to Congress were controlled by local machines (ACIR, 1986) and some urban bosses were able to use state-wide party machines to wield influence at a higher level, but this is now comparatively rare. The spread of primary elections and of media campaigning means that state and federal legislators are less dependent on the party, though more on private fund-raising. In contrast to Britain and France, there is a diminishing tendency for individuals to proceed from municipal to national politics (ACIR, 1986). So while 'pork-barrel' politics continues to thrive and members of Congress are increasingly obliged to cater to local interests, city officials no longer play a significant mediating role.

Although Canada has a federal system, municipal leaders have limited opportunities to extract collective and individual advantages. At both federal and provincial levels, a British-style parliamentary system, with strong Cabinet government supported by disciplined legislative parties, serves to reduce the permeability of the centre by local interests. This separation is increased by the absence of involvement in local politics by the national and provincial parties. There is a stronger tradition of 'pork-barrel' than in Britain, but the link with municipal government is rather weak. Nor can Canadian municipalities play the federal and provincial governments off against each other, since the federal level has no direct links with local governments and provides virtually no resources for them. In both Canada and the USA, efforts at 'disentanglement', clarifying and separating the roles of territorial levels, are likely to reduce opportunities for local governments to play the intergovernmental system.

It is in France that the most elaborate pattern of central–local interactions prevails, with local elites exercising considerable influence as territorial intermediaries. On the elective side, much of this is attributable to the *cumul des mandats*, the possibility of holding multiple offices. Many city mayors and presidents of the departments and regions are members of the national or European Parliament, or even ministers in the government while the second chamber, the Senate, is elected from local government. In 1988, 80 per cent of the candidates for the legislative elections had a local mandate, while of those elected, 48 per cent were members of departmental councils, 45 per cent mayors and 27 per cent regional councillors (Criqui, 1990). Cumulation provides for collective influence of local government on national urban policy and explains, for example, why local elites have been able to control the process of local government reform. On the other hand, while 45 per cent of members of parliament are mayors, the existence of 36 000 mayors means that a tiny fraction of them are members of parliament. These *grands notables* can outrank the local representatives of the state and forge direct links with national ministries. So there is great inequality in the access of municipalities to central government. The permeability of the central government has varied from time to time. Under the Third and Fourth Republics, when governments were made and broken in the legislative chamber and the party system fragmented, local interests could hold great influence. Under the Fifth Republic, the downgrading of the Parliament, the elimination of proportional representation and the consequent emergence of disciplined parties have reduced the permeability of the centre by individual territorial interests. On the other hand, the restoration of constituency-based parliamentary elections meant that local power bases became important. Gaullist leaders established such bases in the 1960s, often after 'parachuting' into constituencies while the opposition parties of the left consolidated their position locally in compensation for exclusion from the national coalition. By the 1970s 'parachuting' had become difficult as a local implantation became almost essential for a national career (Fayolle, 1989). The establishment of a national party system has thus not in itself weakened the influence of local government. In the 1980s, limitations were placed on the accumulation of mandates to promote greater local responsibility and relieve pressure on the centre. Politicians are now limited to two significant mandates (mayor or deputy mayor of a large city, president of a regional or departmental council, member of the national or European Parliament) but this has not produced an independent local political class. Territorially-based notables do not exert influence merely within their own parties. Opposition mayors may be equally powerful. The abolition of the Greater London Council (GLC) by the Conservative Government in the 1980s contrasts with the failure of the French Socialist Government, motivated by similar partisan considerations, to cut down the council of Paris. In both cases, the national government got the worst of the public argument. The difference was that in France the issue had a major electoral potential and the mayor of Paris was the leader of the national opposition.

Territorial intermediation in France is also carried out by the central government field administrators. While before the 1982 reforms the role of the prefect was to act as executive to the department and exercise a *tutelle* over the communes, observers (Machin, 1977; Worms, 1966; Grémion, 1976) have long recognized that the relationship involved complex patterns of cooperation and collusion. Officially charged with maintaining the integrity of the unitary state and imposing centralized order, the prefects in practice enjoyed considerable discretion in interpreting their orders in the light of local circumstances. Both they and the field officials of the state services recognized the importance of cooperation with local political leaders to avoid conflict and promote local interests. It is not true, as some observers (such as Ashford, 1989) claim, that this makes the French system more 'decentralized' than the British, if that implies a capacity for autonomous local action. Rather it allows an integrated national–local elite access to powers and resources to enhance their governing capacity in cities. Yet the very complexity of this and the mingling of central and local roles allows them to avoid responsibility. As in the other countries, central government has periodically tried to simplify central–local relations and decentralize administration precisely to reduce the political and administrative burden on itself and increase local accountability. In the 1980s considerable powers were transferred from the field administration of central government to the locally elected councils. This has had a considerable impact on the departments. In the large cities, the consensus is that mayors already possessed the substance of the powers transferred to them but that decentralization served to emphasize the autonomous nature of these powers and thus enhanced accountability.

REVENUE AND SPENDING

A critical element in local government's power is finance. As a subordinate level, local government can levy only those taxes which the higher level permits and this is everywhere tightly restricted, with higher-level governments tending to reserve the most buoyant taxes for themselves (Heidenheimer *et al.*, 1983). Local governments also receive grants from higher-level governments with greater or lesser discretion in how they may be spent. Borrowing is sometimes considered a third source of finance, though this has to be repaid from revenue. In addition, local governments may levy charges for various services.

In Britain, local governments have traditionally levied taxes on residential, industrial and commercial property, though their freedom was progressively restricted in the 1980s. Losing the power to tax non-residential property, they were reduced to taxing private households, through a poll tax, and later a form of property tax (in flux at the time of writing). In France, councils have a wider tax base, including property taxes and the *taxe professionnelle*, a business tax calculated in a complex way according to turnover and payroll size. In the USA, municipalities mostly rely on a property tax but a variety of other taxes are used, notably on income and sales. In Canada, municipalities are largely restricted to a property tax, though some provinces provide for small amounts from other sources.

Borrowing is everywhere restricted. In Britain and Canada, borrowing can be undertaken only for capital spending and is tightly controlled by the higher government, though in Britain the controls apply to spending totals and not to individual projects. British councils are also allowed to increase their capital spending through capital receipts – that is, the proceeds of land and property sales. In France, capital spending and borrowing are effectively regulated through the provision of matching grants for approved projects and through the rule that borrowing is not permitted for current spending. Traditionally, control was also exercised through access to the *Caisse de Depôts et Consignations* as the main source of loan funds. This was able to offer privileged rates of interest because its own payments to small savers were tax exempt. Access to the *Caisse* in turn was conditional on obtaining a state subsidy for the investment in question. In the 1980s, the financial advantages of borrowing have largely disappeared and subsidies have been globalized. The proportion of local borrowing accounted for by the *Caisse* has fallen but largely been replaced by the *Crédit Local de France*, another state agency. Together the two agencies account for some three-quarters of local borrowing, with the rest raised mainly in the European capital market (Guengant and Uhaldeborde, 1989). In the USA, control tends to be by law rather than administrative regulation. Forty-six states place limitations on borrowing in the form of statutory ceilings or referendum requirements (ACIR, 1989a).

The financial autonomy of local governments is a function of the size and buoyancy of their tax base and the legal and political restrictions on raising taxes. These combine severely to circumscribe local governments. Property and poll taxes are non-buoyant since, unless properties are revalued yearly, the tax rate has to be increased in times of inflation merely to maintain revenues. They are also obtrusive, not deducted at source like income tax or levied in small amounts like sales taxes. Consequently, there are political difficulties in raising them, and pressure from households and business to keep them down.

This poses a severe constraint on financial autonomy in American and Canadian municipalities. In Britain, where the gearing effect of the local tax (the percentage by which the tax must be raised to produce 1 per cent extra revenue) is very high (about fivefold on average), raising expenditure is very costly. In France, raising residential taxes is difficult and the *taxe professionnelle* is widely unpopular as a tax on jobs.

There are also statutory and administrative limits on local revenue raising. Forty American states have property tax rate limits and eight impose expenditure ceilings (ACIR, 1982). The anti-tax atmosphere of the late 1970s and 1980s saw a growth in such limits. In Britain, government assumed responsibility for setting business rates centrally in the 1980s and can (and does) intervene in individual cases to limit tax levels. The very complexity of the system of control, though, gives some scope to local governments who have engaged in various forms of 'creative accounting' in order to evade the limitations. Canadian provinces do not generally impose limits on local taxation, though the assessment of property for taxes is usually undertaken by the province. In France, local councils are now free to decide both the level of taxation they wish to levy and its distribution among the various taxes; in practice only the largest authorities have the capacity to do this and smaller communes tend to follow the advice of central officials.

Financial support from higher levels of government is an important source of revenue, accounting for 35 per cent of local government revenue in France (Ministère de l'Intérieur, 1988; Joyeux *et al.*, 1989); 38 per cent in the United States (ACIR, 1989a); 45 per cent in Britain; and 45 per cent in Canada. These overall figures need to be qualified significantly. In the federal countries, they conceal large variations among states and provinces. They also exclude assigned taxes which are centrally set but distributed locally, and charges for services. It is often argued that a high level of central support in itself constitutes a restriction on the freedom of local governments. It is true that the larger the central grant, the lower the discretion of local government is likely to be; this is because the smaller the proportion of local expenditure met from local sources the higher the percentage tax increase needed for a given increase in expenditure. The effect of central grants on the governing capacity of local officials, however, depends on the conditions under which the grants are made and the restrictions on their use. Block or unconditional grants which can be spent freely serve to enhance the independence of local government by reducing its dependence on local individual and business tax payers. Block grants themselves can take various forms. The simplest are equal *per capita* payments to municipalities. More sophisticated versions seek to equalize for needs or resources. Needs equalization takes into account the differing costs and needs of areas and gives out unequal amounts so as to provide the same capacity to meet needs everywhere. So communities with a larger land area might need to spend more on roads, those with a high percentage of children more on schools. Resource equalization recognizes that the amount raised by a given tax depends on the wealth of the community. It therefore distributes more to poor areas in such a way that they will be able to provide the same level of service as other areas for the same 'fiscal effort'. With perfect resource equalization, the higher government would underwrite whatever level of expenditure the locality chose. Equalization thus serves to increase local autonomy and governing capacity.

Since the 1960s, many higher governments have moved to consolidate grants into block form, in the interests of clearer financial control and bureaucratic simplicity. Most British grants were consolidated into a single Rate (now Revenue) Support Grant. Initially, this provided for a high degree of needs and resource equalization. In the 1980s, however, resource equalization was reduced and finally eliminated. Now councils receive a grant based on assessed needs, together with a share of the national business rate distributed on a *per capita* basis. Any additional expenditure must be raised entirely from the local tax . As national revenue support has been cut, statutory services which councils are obliged to provide consume larger proportions of their revenues, leaving less discretionary surplus. Starting in the mid-1970s, central support was cut from 66 per cent to 45 per cent of eligible expenditure (Travers, 1989). Also in the 1980s there was some reversal of consolidation, with block grants falling from 71 per cent to 61 per cent of the total (Treasury, 1990) as central government sought to tighten its control. France started to consolidate grants in the 1970s, a process completed under the socialists' decentralization programme from 1981. There is a provision for both needs and resources equalization (Bélorgey, 1984; Keating, 1988d), though not as sophisticated as the British system. The decentralization reforms of the 1980s were accompanied by a consolidation of grants and the assignment of additional revenue sources to local government. It is difficult to make precise calculations because of the changing functional balance and uncertainties over the way costs would have developed in the absence of the programme. It does appear that central government largely maintained its levels of support

(Hoffmann-Martinot and Nevers, 1989; Mény, 1989; Bernier, 1991) though there has been some limitation since the late 1980s. In 1989 the block revenue grant (the DGF, previously linked to Value Added Tax receipts in a manner providing steady real increases) was tied to the consumer price index (Ministère de l'Economie, 1989). Local leaders have complained that the centre has devolved functions whose expenditure projections are increasing, and certainly the devolution of responsibility for some social assistance was intended as a means of keeping costs under control. In Canada, most grants to local governments are conditional and require a matching contribution from the municipality. This is particularly limiting to local autonomy since it reduces the proportion of councils' own source revenue available for discretionary spending.

American local governments received 33.3 per cent of their revenue from state and 4.8 per cent from the federal level in 1987. Most of this is in the form of categorical grants, 61 per cent of the state total being for education (ACIR, 1989b). The average figures mask considerable variations, with some cities critically dependent on federal support. Grants have proved a major subject of political conflict. American municipalities are highly dependent on local business for their tax base and must retain a pro-business image in order to retain their credit rating. This greatly inhibits the raising of local taxes for redistributive social programmes, even where they have the legal right to do so. Federal and state grants do not threaten the existing base and so can increase local government's capacity. Unconditional grants are subject to the same local political process as own-source revenues and, given the competition among cities for investment, are likely to be used for business development and are often used to keep down local taxes (Ladd and Yinger, 1989). So American liberals have tended to favour conditional grants tied to social programmes as a means of freeing communities from economic pressures. They have also favoured a centralization of welfare expenditure such as happens in other countries, so that in the decade 1967–77 the federal share rose from 58 per cent to 70 per cent (ACIR, 1982). Of the non-federal share, states were responsible for over 80 per cent, leaving localities with the main responsibility in only a few places, such as Denver and New York. State and local governments themselves have been among the most avid supporters of federalization (ACIR, 1980). The 1960s also saw a rapid growth in federal specific grant programmes intended to by-pass the states – and, in some cases, city governments as well. Conservatives for their part have favoured block grants, and both the Nixon and Reagan administrations moved to consolidate grants, the latter cutting them considerably in the process so that federal grants to state and local government fell from 3.4 per cent to 2.4 per cent of GNP between 1980 and 1989 (ACIR, 1989a). Under Nixon, a variety of urban programmes was merged into the Community Development Block Grant (CDBG) and a General Revenue Sharing Scheme instituted. The evidence shows that the creation of CDBG and its later devolution to states led to a shift away from social programmes towards business-related expenditures (GAO, 1983). Later the General Revenue Sharing programme, which has some equalizing effect, was eliminated by the Reagan administration. That some conditional grants have survived is due to the nature of the American legislative process in which committees and individual members of Congress seek to preserve 'their' programmes by attaching conditions to them.

So it is a great oversimplification to assert that dependence on grants necessarily reduces the autonomy of local government. It may free localities from the constraints of market competition for tax revenues. In the American context, even the statutory limits on local taxation and borrowing may have helped local autonomy at times, since they were originally introduced in order to free cities from business demands to subsidize development in railways and canals. The wider political context is critical in determining the terms of the relationship. The central state can be oppressive, or it can be a resource allowing localities to escape other forms of dependence. It can allocate gratifying functions with a large political return and adequate resources, or unpopular and difficult functions together with non-buoyant revenue sources. This, in turn, depends on the weight of local elites in the national political system and their ability to forge coalitions to extract resources on their own terms. In Britain, a move away from grant consolidation in the 1980s represented a ploy by central government to take discretionary resources out of the hands of its urban opponents. In the USA, a move towards grant consolidation was partly motivated by the desire to remove resources from the congressional forum where redistributive demands were better received and urban social advocates had allies and place them in the local political arena where development interests predominated. In France, local governments have been better able to extract resources on their own terms, maintaining their governing capacity even in times of national retrenchment.

CONCLUSION

The scope of local politics depends on the functions which local governments are given, but also on the political structures within which they operate, as well as general assumptions about the scope of government. In North America, this is limited by governing assumptions (in the USA), statutory restrictions and the fragmentation of local political power. This produces a closure of American local politics, despite a culture emphasizing decentralization and democratic equality. Local politics tends to be dominated by production issues, with a strong bias to the politics of development. Intergovernmental politics has served to open up the agenda periodically but cities' weight in American national politics has diminished. In Britain, there is less fragmentation and the parties serve to broaden the political agenda, so that issues of distribution and service development are central to local politics. Yet the weak linkage of central and local politics limits the impact of local interests in national politics and the governing capacity of cities. In France, the integration of national and local politics weakens the formal autonomy of local government but can serve to enhance local governing capacity by providing access of non-local powers and resources. Local elites are able both to enlarge the scope of local politics to encompass both production and distribution and enhance their own influence by their presence in the national state. Chapter 4 extends this analysis to the local political environment.

4. Economic and Social Interests and the City

BUSINESS AND THE CITY

The role of private business interests is a central issue in the politics of capitalist countries. In many accounts of urban politics, the issue is seen as preponderant, given the open nature of urban economies and the restricted powers of city governments in the economic domain.

Early marxism saw power relations determined by the ownership of capital with the state as a mere superstructure. Later marxist theories recognize a separate domain of political activity in which the state is credited with a 'relative autonomy'. They also recognize that governments often do things which the representatives of capitalism oppose, notably in the field of taxation, public expenditure and welfare programmes. This is sometimes reconciled with the belief that all government activity is determined by the interests of capital through the ingenious but circular argument that, since capitalists are often unaware of their own long-term interests, the state needs to intervene to safeguard the long-term future of the system. As O'Connor (1973, p. 69) puts it, the state is not an instrument but a structure through which capitalist class interests emerge 'unintentionally'.

Contemporary neo-marxists are less deterministic, seeing the state as an arena of class struggle. In local government, neo-marxists have increasingly recognized a distinct politics, potentially more accessible to non-capitalist interests (Dearlove, 1979) and dominated by consumption or distribution issues. Class conflict 'has been displaced from the shop floor to city streets and neighbourhoods' (Cummings, 1988, p. 18), with different characteristics from that at national level. Some neo-marxists (Dearlove, 1979; O'Connor, 1973) see institutional reforms and local government consolidation as a ploy to reassert class domination. Others see the urban arena as a focus for an attack on capitalism itself (Castells, 1983) putting their faith in urban social movements as a surrogate for the traditional working class. Together with a new willingness for marxist scholars to supplement the deductive method with empirical research this has encouraged a recognition of the independent role of politics and of the differences among cities and societies in the capitalist world.

Ironically, the most economically-determinist theories of urban politics are now found in the writings of non-marxist scholars. Peterson (1981) sees cities as obliged to pursue economic development policies and avoid redistributive measures; any other strategy risks driving away wealthy taxpayers and undermining itself. Peterson claims that economic development is in the interest of the whole city and further identifies it with the growth of private business; business interests must therefore set the urban political agenda. Only at the national level is a different sort of politics possible. The argument is deductive, purporting to show that cities have no choice but to pursue development and that city politics *is* limited to the growth agenda. In practice, Peterson is forced to recognize that challenges to business dominance do occur, and that city government and business interests need to contain these politically. He also explicitly recognizes that his conclusions rest on features specific to the American federal system.

In capitalist societies, it is true, economic growth, employment and income are largely provided by private business. This control of the means of production allows business to make unique claims to legitimacy as more than a mere sectional interest group (Lindblom, 1977). Its claims can be presented as in the interest of society (or the locality) as a whole. Legal provision for property rights and competitive markets limit the role of government and render it to a greater or lesser degree dependent on resources controlled in the private sector. This is *a fortiori* true of local governments which are unable themselves to change the legal framework in which they operate. In so far as local governments wish to promote employment or tap private resources for wages for their citizens and taxes for themselves, they need to accommodate business interests. Where business is free to move its capital across local boundaries, local governments are more dependent on private decisions.

Yet not all these factors have the same strength in all societies, or in all cities. The ideological hegemony of private enterprise is challenged in European and Canadian culture more than in the USA. Property rights are not entrenched in their constitutions, and there is a greater willingness to use the power of the national state to control business mobility. Britain, Canada and France have all had national regional development programmes devoted to this, though varying greatly in scope and effectiveness. Where private enterprise has proved deficient, the state has undertaken investment in productive industry and steered investments in accordance with wider policy considerations. This is not to suggest that government in the USA is not involved in the productive economy, but its interventions are justified in terms of the logic of private enterprise, and use private instruments. Where this fails, they are usually justified in terms of the other uncontested value, the military effort.

Nor are individual cities equally dependent on private investment. Some are centres of government employment. Others have natural locational advantages which allow them to extract a rent from industry which cannot profitably move, though technological change may alter this. Cities which are booming economically may not want additional investment, or may even oppose it as a threat to their environment. Such cities will be much less subject to investor demands, and may be able to impose their own demands in the form of taxes and regulation. By contrast, declining cities in need of new investment may have to make larger concessions to the demands of capital. This has the ironical result that it is often cities with the neediest populations, whose leaders are most dependent on lower-class support, which are under most pressure to accommodate business interests. This 'reverse welfare state' (Lubove, 1969) is found in all countries, but is most marked in the declining cities of the USA. Again, however, political factors are important, notably the complexion of city government. In prosperous cities controlled by the free market right, there is no inclination to impose social costs upon business. Where more collectivist-minded conservatives are in office, there is a greater willingness to use local wealth for social objectives. On the other hand, in declining cities dominated by ideologically conscious lower-class interests, there may be a distaste for appeasing business demands and a more combative attitude towards the private sector.

The structure of local government also influences the urban agenda. In Britain, general-purpose municipal governments have widely drawn functions and need to balance the pressures and needs of a variety of services and clients. In Canada, local politics is largely defined by issues of land and development (Sancton, 1983), giving business and developers a more prominent role. France, with its wide conception of the scope of local government (despite its restricted service-delivery role) is close to the British model. The USA is closer to Canada, though with variations in the breadth of the urban agenda. In so far as the urban agenda is defined by development and city governments concentrate on economic development policies, business may have a further advantage as acknowledged depository of wisdom on how things should be done. Again, this depends on prevailing values and the structures of public authority. It is particularly marked in the USA because of the identification of development with business expansion and because of the rudimentary state of many city planning departments. These often rely heavily on private sector organizations for data, analysis and the formulation of plans. In France, the broad conception of the state as a definer of values and a purposive policy actor creates a different set of values. A strong, self-conscious bureaucracy sustains a conception of the state as the leading force in development and provides the technical resources to allow the public authorities to dominate the process. Britain does not have such a comprehensive notion of the state but British local authorities are well-endowed with planning and technical skills compared with their American or their Canadian counterparts.

Urban governments in all four countries are dependent to some degree on business for their tax base. This, it is frequently argued, means that city governments must adopt policies to attract business and avoid those which drive business away. The effect, however, varies according to the fiscal system in place. In the USA limited fiscal equalization means that cities depend on business property taxes and the income, sales and domestic property taxes generated by local economic activity. In the Canadian provinces, in Britain and in France, equalization schemes attenuate the effects of business movements. The reform of British local taxes in the late 1980s, intended to make councils more responsive to local interests and encourage pro-business policies, may paradoxically have had the opposite effect. Domestic property taxes were replaced by a flat rate poll tax unrelated to income while business property taxes were to be set nationally and distributed to councils on the basis of population. It therefore made no difference whatever to local budgets whether there was a healthy business sector in the city or not. In fact, were they to behave rationally according to Petersonian or public choice principles, councils might seek to divert business development beyond their boundaries but within commuting distance for their residents, in order to enjoy the benefits of economic development without the costs. At the same time, they would seek to attract low-income residents, since these paid the same poll tax while making lesser demands on public services than the middle class. The fact that they did not behave this way exposes the weakness of the theory. In Canada, property taxes on business are generally higher than on residential property (Bird and Slack, 1983). While there are resource equalization provisions varying from one province to another, councils still have an incentive to attract business taxpayers. In France, councils depend heavily on business for their revenues, through the *tax professionnelle* and industrial and commercial property taxes. There are resource equalization provisions to benefit poorer municipalities, but again they do not eliminate all the variation. The need to expand their tax base is increasingly cited as a justification for local policies, but cities are still able to turn to the centre for relief. In 1989, when concern was expressed about the inequitable effects of the *taxe professionnelle* in favour of areas with large business bases, further equalization was introduced to redistribute the proceeds in favour of the less well endowed.

Local governments' susceptibility to business pressures on taxation also depends on the extent to which they are able to respond to them. In Britain, even before the nationalization of the business rate, local governments were unable selectively to lower rates for business in general, or for selected business. The same is largely true of Canada. In Britain and Canada, local governments have powers to help industry through the provision of land and premises, but this is regulated by higher governments. American cities, by contrast, often possess powers to grant tax abatements to selected firms. Some cities have established tax increment districts, whereby revenues generated from improvement in business districts are earmarked for expenditure within that district. There is little control over the supply of land and buildings, or the terms on which these can be made available. In France, local governments have limited powers to exempt businesses from the *taxe professionnelle*. Although in principle such exemptions must apply to whole classes of business and not individual firms, it is often easy to tailor the rules so as to benefit individuals. As in the USA the existence of these exemptions has led firms to demand them as a matter of routine as rewards for investing in a locality. On the other hand, central regulation has meant that this pressure is a great deal less than in the USA. Councils in France are also able to make grants and loans to firms and to provide land and buildings at privileged rates but this, too, is subject to central control.

Another aspect of dependence on business involves the conditions under which cities borrow for capital expenditures and to cover intervals between expenses and receipts. In the USA city borrowing, while usually subject to statutory limits and referendum requirements, is not guaranteed by higher levels of government. Gaining a high credit rating on the bond markets is thus essential in order to continue to enjoy access at reasonable interest rates. This necessitates not merely policies considered fiscally prudent but the cultivation of a pro-business image and the avoidance of deeds or gestures which might damage investor confidence. In cities with a healthy tax base, this may not impose severe constraints but cities with declining economies may have to cut back on services to the poor and concentrate on measures which enhance the city's tax base. Cities on the point of default may find their decision-making entirely dominated by the financial market (Sbragia, 1983); this happened in the 1970s to New York and Cleveland (Swanstrom, 1988).

In Britain, borrowing is controlled tightly by higher levels of government which then guarantees the loans, so that it is not possible for British local governments to default. Following a number of defaults in the 1930s, Canadian provinces took measures to control local borrowing tightly, so that the situation is now comparable to that in Britain. Consequently, except in the most extreme circumstances (like Liverpool in the mid-1980s), British and Canadian municipalities do not need to worry about their rating on the bond markets. In France, strict accounting rules limit borrowing to capital expenditures amortized by the commitment of revenues. Local budgets can be referred by the prefect to the regional chamber of accounts where irregularities are suspected. Some councils have used their new freedoms to over-extend themselves and provide imprudent loan guarantees to private firms (Conseil des Impôts, 1987), but municipalities are largely prevented from undertaking imprudent borrowing and their credit-worthiness is unquestioned. While borrowing on private bond markets is now permitted, most borrowing is still from state agencies.

Fiscal dependence on higher levels of government can thus reduce dependence on the business sector. Political leaders in more centralized regimes are aware of this, and careful in their demands for more powers. Offered greater powers under the successive decentralization proposals of the 1970s and 1980s, French mayors gave an ambiguous response, welcoming powers but aware that this would expose them to local pressures. A system in which centralization shields them from these pressures, while allowing them to bend the rules in practice, was much more in their interests. American local governments, on the other hand, prefer their autonomy and continue to see the private capital market as a protection against federal intervention (Sbragia, 1983).

Business leaders' motivation to become involved in city government depends on the issues at stake locally. In the USA, the formal independence of cities means that business leaders seeking favourable policies will try to exert influence directly. In more centralized countries, a more fruitful, as well as more economical, way is to pressure higher-level governments so that municipal–business relations are mediated by the intergovernmental network. At one time, it was common for the holders of local economic power also to occupy municipal office, but direct involvement of business leaders in municipal government has declined in all four countries since the late nineteenth century, a trend which has accelerated since the Second World War. This can be attributed partly to the centralization of big business and its later internationalization, as well as to the emergence of professional managers who are mobile and do not have a stake in the local society. Britain and France contain few major corporations which are not headquartered in London or Paris. Nor are there locally-controlled banks as in the USA. Already by the early twentieth century, business representation in local government tended to be from smaller, locally-based industrialists and traders. Since the Second World War, divergent trends have developed. In Britain and France, elective elites have become partisan and specialized; success in business cannot be translated into municipal office. In the USA and Canada, on the other hand, municipal councillors are often drawn from sectors with an economic stake in municipal decisions.

Structural features also serve to make American and Canadian local government more accessible to business interests by containing challenging social forces as discussed in Chapter 3. Running for election at-large requires extensive campaign funds likely to be available only to business-backed candidates, and encourages candidates to stress issues with a broad appeal (like city expansion), and de-emphasize divisive issues of redistribution. Referendums on bond issues or tax rises often require the financial backing and endorsement of business in order to succeed. In Britain and France, partisanship reduces the role of business in electoral politics. British local campaigns are typically inexpensive and business and trade union contributions very modest compared with national elections. In France, the parties have been able to use control of local government itself as a source of finance. Partisan activities are supported on the public payroll (Dion, 1986) while through party-controlled consultancy firms, contributions are exacted from businesses needing planning and other consents, reversing the pattern of dependency in a manner reminiscent of the old American machines. Partisanship also sustains elected city governments, providing organizational cohesion and discipline on councils – and, in some cases, policy initiative. In the absence of such parties, local business groups may have a monopoly of local organizational capacity.

A critical factor in comparative perspective is the absence in American and Canadian local government of an organized opposition with an interest in raising issues and changing the agenda. Private business enjoys an ideological hegemony such that generalized opposition cannot mobilize and individual issues must be addressed within the prevailing framework. There is also the direct suppression of challenges to business dominance. In the early twentieth-century USA, there were periodic eruptions of class conflict, often aimed at locally dominant employers in staple industries dependent on local resources and unable to relocate. The labour movement, unable to mobilize nationally, was suppressed locally, often by force. In Britain and France, by contrast, local struggles connected to national politics. The staple industries which dominated some communities were largely taken into public ownership after the Second World War as a result of the influence of the labour movement at national level. The restructuring of these industries from the 1970s was itself to produce serious conflicts and spark off community mobilization, but these were conflicts in which local business leaders were merely spectators.

The organization of business itself reflects the organization of the state, with greater centralization in Europe and Canada and a greater tendency, especially in Europe, for relations between local governments and business to be mediated by the central state. At the same time, business interest in local government in the twentieth century has become more selective, focused on those items of most direct concern to their enterprises (Barnekov *et al.*, 1989). In the USA, national policy-making is fragmented sectorally while the federal system creates further divisions. Business influence is divided sectorally and territorially with no single national business lobby group. This is not a source of weakness: it is the very dominance of business values and the weakness of the central state which has allowed business to retain an organization which is differentiated but which has considerable capacity to intervene in defence of its interests. Chambers of Commerce exist in all cities, together with a large array of other business-dominated groups. In Canada, by contrast, the greater involvement of provincial and national governments in industrial policies has encouraged peak organizations at those levels.

In Britain, producer groups are well organized at national level with relations of varying intimacy with government. The Confederation of British Industry (CBI), dominated by the larger firms, is professionally organized, well funded and has close links with government. While the CBI has had a regional organization since the 1970s, it has little to do with local government. Local Chambers of Commerce exist in most cities, dominated by small and medium-sized firms. Their capacity varies, but generally they are concerned with offering services to their members rather than with influencing public policy (Stewart, 1984). In recent years, central government has sought to involve them more in urban policy-making, but their role tends to be reactive rather than initiative and, until the nationalization of business rates, focused largely on efforts to keep down local taxes. In France, local Chambers of Commerce are more significant, being legally constituted bodies with compulsory membership and elections regulated by law. They have large service responsibilities in matters such as training and management of airports and industrial zones, and contribute to the elaboration of planning schemes (Paris, 1984). As in Britain, they are dominated by small and medium-sized firms, the larger firms preferring to concentrate on influencing central government through the *Conseil Nationale du Patronat Français* (CNPF). French Chambers of Commerce are considerably more important than their British counterparts, though they retain an air of mystery and are seriously under-researched. In many cities, their integration into territorial administration has tended to reduce them to the status of administrative agents rather than policy influentials. In others, they are a significant element of the local power structure, providing a career route for politicians of the conservative parties and engaged in discreetly conducted but real power struggles with the mayor. In both Britain and France as well as North America, the universal membership of local Chambers of Commerce limits their policy concerns to broad issues such as keeping down local taxation or major infrastructure projects like ports and airports which can be seen as in the general interest of local industry. Policy programmes involving selectivity, preferential treatment of some sectors or areas or new initiatives, are most difficult for such broadly-based groups to deal with. Hence the emergence of specialized business-inspired organizations concerned with redevelopment or change.

Different sections of the business community will have different interests in local government issues and the nature of the task to be performed will affect business' need to organize formally and enter the political process: locally-based and locally-oriented corporations may perceive their interests differently from those based outside. Some business sectors have a large stake in local government decisions, requiring zoning approvals, infrastructure provision or tax incentives. The interest of others is limited to the conditions necessary to expand and make profits. This generally involves supporting low taxes and perhaps a bias in public expenditures to items which foster business development. Some business elites may have an interest in expansion and development of the city as a whole. Others may be largely indifferent to their local environment, trading in national or global markets. Yet other, locally-based, traders may be actively hostile to development with its threat of larger, more efficient competitors.

Molotch (1976, 1988; Logan and Molotch, 1987) argues that American cities are dominated by those sectors of the business community which benefit from growth. This includes local businesses, real estate agents, lawyers, the media and certain sporting and cultural organizations. National and multinational corporations, on the other hand, have no interest in growth in a specific location, though their investment decisions have a major impact on communities. 'Growth machines' dominate local politics and impose a growth agenda which benefits themselves while thrusting the costs onto their fellow citizens. This is legitimized by an ideology of 'value-free development' which holds that markets alone should determine land use and that any increase in economic activity benefits the whole community (Logan and Molotch, 1987, pp. 32–3). In reality, it is not a neutral market but the activities of the growth machine which, within the constraints of nature and multinational capital, determines development. Politicians are rarely able to oppose growth elites, dependent as they are on campaign contributions from developers. Under the name of civic 'boosterism', the growth machine certainly has a long history in the USA. Yet it is a great simplification to reduce business influence in local politics to this. In varying circumstances, different business elites may enter the political process in different ways.

Some American cities are characterized by 'caretaker regimes' which emphasize avoiding challenges to business prerogatives rather than innovating in policy or mobilizing resources (Elkin, 1987). A large employer may dominate politics through anticipated reaction or 'non-decision-making' – that is, the need to retain the business locally may induce elected local governments to refrain from anything which might offend it (Crenson, 1971; Bachrach and Baratz, 1962). This may take several forms. Business interests may control the local media and use this to keep awkward issues off the agenda. In 'reformed' city governments, it is possible for business organizations to approve slates of candidates who will get the necessary finance and support to run successfully. In some cities there is an unwritten understanding that major developments do not happen without the approval of the corporate elite. Influence is so discreet as to be unmeasurable and often takes the form of anticipated reactions, a belief on the part of those who might be inclined to oppose the corporate consensus that they would be wasting their time and energies. In other cases, the diversity of the local business elite may preclude a commitment to precise policies beyond an insistence on low taxes and a minimum of regulation. In some cases, this comes close to a belief on the part of local business elites that all public expenditure is bad and that taxes should be kept to a minimum. This requires little organization and in these cases, business might not be active in policy promotion but remain quite influential.

In other cases, a local crisis or opportunity might lead business leaders to a more proactive role, involving the use of extensive public powers. Business leaders interested in expansion or urban renewal will support spending on infrastructure and the use of extensive public powers in land acquisition and assembly, a task for which the private market is unsuited. Since growth and redevelopment benefit some sectors while disadvantaging others through displacement, competition and extra taxation, they require a different type of business organization to the caretaker regime, equipped for policy initiation and change and not concerned with unifying all business interests. This is not the role of Chambers of Commerce and similar universal associations. In many American cities, there exist 'shadow governments' of business leaders which seek to control the key decisions which affect them while not undertaking the whole business of governing directly. The importance of these shadow governments depends on their own organizational capacity, and on that of potential opponents. In cities where governmental authority is dispersed, those groups with a minimal organizing capacity are at an immense advantage, able to use selective incentives to secure compliance with their proposals (Stone, 1989). In other cities, business organizations have come to terms with partisan city governments, recognizing their mutual dependence. After the Second World War, and again in the late 1960s and 1970s, the needs of urban renewal stimulated business-led development coalitions in a number of American cities. These required both public and private powers and resources to achieve their ends, but sought to cast the partnership in terms favourable to themselves. One of the most celebrated is the Allegheny Conference in Pittsburgh, started after the war by corporate leaders concerned at the degradation of the central business district. With no chance of seizing political control from the Democratic machine, they came to terms with mayor David Lawrence who lent public powers to the urban renewal effort in return for business commitments to remain in the city (Lubove, 1969; Stewman and Tarr, 1982; Coleman, 1983; Weber, 1988). Similar arrangements have been described in Baltimore (Levine, 1987) and elsewhere (Mollenkopf, 1983). In many American cities, powerful business-led coalitions were able to achieve urban renewal on their own terms. In others, the effort foundered because of adverse market conditions or the inability to organize a coherent business leadership and forge the right relationships with local government (Kantor, 1987). The result there was not so much popular control as a policy vacuum and an absence of governing capacity.

In Britain and France, postwar urban renewal schemes were dominated by state planning, against the indifference or hostility of local Chambers of Commerce and local business elites. Central government provided both powers and resources to urban governments for urban renewal while using them as an instrument to develop the welfare state. The influence of business and the development industry was largely mediated by the central state rather than directly applied to local government. Attempts were made in 1980s Britain to establish business-dominated urban renewal groups modelled on the American experience but the initiative came largely from central government. The main instrument was business-dominated special agencies appointed by the central government which made inroads into former municipal responsibilities in land use, economic development, training and education. Local government nevertheless retains crucial powers and resources and urban development corporations have been obliged to cooperate with it (see Chapter 7). In France, a centralized system with a strong local influence prevents business or central government from circumventing local government. It is not true that there is no local business input into local policy-making. Regional *comités d'expansion* bring together local elected elites and business leaders to perform the initiative, innovative function. These, however, have been incorporated by the territorial political network, the president usually being a local political notable.

Business does occasionally involve itself in issues going beyond economic development and urban renewal. There is a debate among business leaders and conservative commentators over 'corporate social responsibility' – the extent to which business should concern itself with wider issues such as the environment and poverty. From the mid-twentieth century, corporate leaders in the USA have preached the need for this, and in the 1980s there were attempts to emulate the tradition in Britain (Barnekov *et al.*, 1989). While right-wing commentators have often criticized this as a distortion of the market, in practice the initiatives have been limited and usually motivated by the need for political and social legitimacy at times of crisis. As the British organization Business in the Community put it, 'strife and decay in the inner cities and associated threats to property carry a high political risk – neglect will eventually impose a high cost on the whole business community' (quoted in Barnekov *et al.*, 1989, p. 207). A business elite demonstrating concern for the community can command greater legitimacy and be better able to resist demands for radical redistribution of wealth and income or restrictions on business operations. It may find it easier to secure support for its own operations where these require public powers and funding; and there may be profit opportunities in public–private urban regeneration initiatives. Faced with specific crises, business leaders may be more innovative. The outbreak of urban riots in the 1960s prompted a renewed business concern with the conditions of American cities and a move by some business leaders into social projects. One of the most elaborate interventions was in Hartford, Connecticut, where the business elite was dominated by the insurance industry, a sector with an obvious concern for property maintenance, social order and long-term stability (Coleman, 1983; Clavel, 1986; Neubeck and Ratcliff, 1988). The social initiatives fostered by this 'corporate liberalism' were not a great success and in the late 1970s business groups largely retreated to their customary, more narrow range of concerns. In Britain, corporate social philanthropy received some attention in the 1980s in similar conditions of urban crisis, but the resources involved were small by American standards and most of the activity symbolic.

The relationship between city governments and business is a reciprocal one since business needs municipal support and cooperation for various purposes. These include provision of infrastructure, education, zoning and land assembly. Whether this creates greater dependence of business on cities or vice versa depends on a number of factors, including the ability of business to relocate. More generally, it creates common interests in development and growth and an involvement of business in local politics and administration. The effect of business entanglement in local politics, however, is to expose it to greater social and political pressures and restrict its freedom of manoeuvre. This is one reason for large enterprises to reduce their direct interventions in local affairs. In France, a tendency has been noted for businesses deliberately to disengage from close links with the territories in which they are situated. This includes the sale of lands and equipment and a policy of reducing the proportion of local workforces employed by them (Plan Urbain, 1986). In the USA, too, local ties of large firms are diminishing. Even in the major corporate centres, the headquarters have been retained but the production facilities have often been dispersed. The shadow governments which were so influential in the past appear to be reducing their detailed influence. In Britain, large industry has shown no tendency, apart from a few isolated philanthropic initiatives, to re-engage itself in local community affairs.

This all reflects the concentration and internationalization of large business. Liberalization of international capital movements, together with free trade in Europe and North America, has increased the mobility of capital, especially in advanced sectors where industry is internationally integrated. At the same time, the opening of European and global markets has weakened the ability of national governments to protect communities through tariffs, subsidies and diversionary policies. Instead, they have become more concerned with national competitiveness in the global economy. In the USA, national urban policies suffered severe cuts under the Republican administrations of the 1980s. In Britain, a similar reduction in support was accompanied by attacks on local autonomy and on the regulatory 'burdens' of business. In France, the decentralization programme was more closely controlled by local elected elites but did have the effect of exposing cities to market forces. This disengagement of national governments, together with the very weakening of business links into communities increases cities' dependence on business. In order to attract and retain footloose industry, cities are increasingly competing to offer a pro-business environment. So business interests can be accommodated with little direct effort on their part, though the form of accommodation is moulded by the local political system and the powers and resources of local governments (see Chapter 7).

At the same time, the ideological challenge to capitalism – always weak or non-existent in North America – has waned in Europe with the failure of the Soviet model and the problems of social democracy in the 1980s. The social democratic project was dependent on the ability of national states to manage their economies so as to provide for both growth and redistribution. The crisis of the Keynesian mode of economic management and the international dependence of national economies has placed this in question. Social democratic parties in Britain and France have now accepted the inevitability of dependence on the international market and the limits which this places on the powers of governments to manage national economies. They have yet to formulate a new vision of the relationship between political and economic power.

The changing competitive context of cities has also affected class relations within them. Traditionally, trade unions were concerned with negotiation and conflict with employers at the workplace and with interventions of varying intensity in politics in order to secure social gains and a favourable climate for collective bargaining. There were marked differences among the four countries. Both membership and involvement in politics were highest in Britain, where the manual unions are affiliated to the Labour Party and exercise considerable influence within it, both at national and at local levels. In France, unions have always been weaker and divided in their political allegiance. In the USA, trade unionism was weak until the 1930s when there was a major expansion. Previously aloof from politics, unions forged local links with the Democratic Party from the 1930s but there was never the organic connection found in Britain. Since the 1950s, union membership has declined again. In Canada, by contrast, membership increased in the 1950s to overtake the American figure. Unions are affiliated to the New Democratic Party but there is not the close connection which exists in Britain.

One factor in common was the tendency for trade unions to take their political concerns to national level. This is because national administrations have often been more favourably disposed, but also because in local confrontations employers can play one location off against another, moving investment or production to where unions are weakest. Internationalization of the economy has increased business' ability to do this, with a consequent weakening of union power. The uneven spread of prosperity and decline have divided national labour movements (Beauregard, 1989), and unions are increasingly concerned with the effects of economic restructuring on local job prospects. Combined with a tendency to decentralization and local bargaining within unions themselves (Edwards *et al.*, 1986), this has brought unions in as active partners of local development coalitions. Labour relations have thus shifted from a focus on bargaining and conflict at the workplace to a collaborative effort at development and economic promotion. The extent of this varies greatly. The French Communist-led CGT continues to emphasize class conflict, though even it has been involved in local efforts to save industries. The CFDT, on the other hand, is more closely associated with the Socialist Party, more decentralist in its philosophy and more inclined to collaboration at local level. In Britain, the unions, weakened by unemployment and legislation in the 1980s, have supported collaborative local development efforts through Labour councils. In the USA, they have joined in local development coalitions, albeit as junior partners, as they have in Canada. The nature of the resulting development politics and the influence of unions within it is discussed later (Chapter 7).

The increased dependence of cities on the international market, together with a certain disengagement of national governments from the fate of cities, has served to narrow the urban agenda. The cooption of trade unions has to some degree restricted it further. Yet this has coincided with an increase in pluralist pressures from the rise of new social movements, creating a major problem for city governance.

URBAN SOCIAL MOVEMENTS

A potential challenge to both political and business elites is provided by urban social movements. This term refers to movements arising from the conditions of urban society. These include the spatial form, which provides the basis for interests and action based on neighbourhoods; and the provision of public services, linking people by their common interests in 'collective consumption'. Unable to find expression through market exchange or political representation, these interests give rise to specific movements with their own agenda. Social movements may also arise *in* cities from the mobilization of groups which find access and influence in national politics difficult, but whose common interests are not defined by the urban setting. These may include ethnic groups, sexual minorities, anti-nuclear campaigners and a variety of other interests.

Pluralist scholars have characterized the urban political system as a competitive struggle for influence among shifting coalitions of interests, downplaying the extent to which the arena itself is structured to favour some at the expense of others. Neo-marxists have examined social movements as a distinct form of social conflict. Castells (1978, 1983) defines urban social movements rather restrictively as groups seeking to challenge the basis and assumptions of the political and economic system, to produce a radical transformation. Like other neo-marxists he has wrestled with the discovery that there are sources of social conflict other than production-based class cleavages, and with the question of whether urban social movements can replace the working class in overthrowing the capitalist system. In the process, marxist analysis has become more pluralist while pluralists have come to accept the reality of structural constraints.

Social movements will be defined here as popular movements to change the urban condition by challenging the existing balance of economic or political power. Movements of property-owners aiming to maximize property values are largely excluded. Owners often resist externally imposed change, such as a disruptive highway scheme or low-income housing, in the interest of preserving private space and the exchange value of their properties. Movements of the propertyless, on the other hand, seek to defend communities and local space as public property, defying the logic of the market which treats space as a tradeable commodity; or seek to expand services in the non-market sphere. The definition of social movements used here also excludes political parties whose aim is to take control of the institutions of urban government, though the distinction is often rather hazy. Social movements comprise a third dimension of urban politics. Their claims to space and consumption are not based on private property ownership but are derived from concepts of community and citizenship. They thus challenge the power of economic and political elites, the nexus of economic and political power and the mechanisms of closure of urban politics examined earlier. To assert use values in space independent of market exchange values is to reject the insistence that all economic development is in the interest of cities. Such claims are accepted as legitimate depending on the cultural values of individual societies and the political structures permitting such claims to be advanced. In the USA, claims of this sort are almost impossible to sustain; in the other countries, they are more often treated as legitimate items for political debate, though private property ownership is so general as to make them difficult to sustain.

Urban movements may be defensive and 'negative', seeking to defend a community or service against change; or positive, campaigning for change. The political logic of neighbourhood defence movements themselves varies. On the one hand is the NIMBY (not in my backyard) syndrome, in which movements seek to avoid developments which might adversely affect them by siting them elsewhere. On the other hand, some movements develop a wider ideology and programme, challenging the need for the development at all and proposing alternatives to unite a broad coalition. A movement to resist highway schemes may simply divide neighbourhoods from each other as each tries to offload the environmental costs of the development; or it may develop into a movement for improved public transport. The development of a broader ideology is a precondition for a neighbourhood defence movement to translate into a wider social movement, but it is not sufficient. Conservation of historic environments may be a goal commanding wide general support in principle but it may divide historic neighbourhoods from those less well-endowed. As high-amenity and historic neighbourhoods are often privately owned by wealthy individuals, conservation may as easily be an instrument for the maintenance of private property values as for the assertion of intrinsic or community value over exchange value.

Defensive or negative neighbourhood movements have arisen at times of change and redevelopment. Typically, these have asserted the value of community preservation or the right of people to continue occupying space against the market logic which indicates that higher exchange values should be obtained by conversion to commercial or high-income residential use. In other cases, they involve the assertion of environmental values to preserve space or historic buildings against the same market logic. Focusing on individual threats of projects, they are usually short-lived, demobilizing rapidly once the issue which has united their members is no longer salient.

Under certain conditions, more positive, constructive neighbourhood movements have developed, often following successful defensive campaigns. In London's Waterloo area, a popular movement was able to impose its own plan against private development interests and an indifferent central government (Brindley *et al.*, 1989). Earlier, community activists had succeeded in recasting plans for Covent Garden to take into account public and popular concerns – though, while the massive schemes of the developers were defeated, the area was to fall prey to gentrification and the loss of the original community (Savitch, 1988). In Paris, community groups in the thirteenth arrondissement were able to defeat redevelopment plans and impose their own ideas (Body-Gendrot, 1987). These cases, however, depended on unusual factors including the presence of middle-class professional support, division among tiers of government and economic change, discussed below.

Collective consumption movements, focused on public services, may also be sparked off by a crisis. A threat to a school, hospital or transport route can unite the users of the service and their sympathisers. Organization may be on a neighbourhood basis or cover the whole city. Again, such organizations tend to be short-lived and rarely survive the crisis. Consumption interests cross-cut each other and other bases for organization and vary through the life-cycle, making long-term organization difficult.

One type of social movement to which it is worth giving separate attention concerns housing, specifically low- and middle-income housing in cities. Neither the public nor the private sector has proved effective in providing affordable housing in major cities in the four countries. The problem, paradoxically, is worst in those cities which are developing most rapidly. Rising land and property prices bar entry into the owner-occupied sector for low- and middle-income households who are not already in it. The price of privately rented accommodation rises for the same reasons. Rent controls can have some effect, but tend to encourage landlords to sell property and realize their improved capital values. Public sector housing schemes, for their part, have been built to minimal standards and often in the cheapest locations on the periphery of cities. Since public housing tenants are in all four countries a minority of the population, it is difficult to mobilize political support for the investment of sufficient resources in the sector. So public housing schemes are often deficient in social and recreational amenities and the housing poorly maintained. Upwardly mobile individuals seek to move out and the public schemes become stigmatized as the home of social problems and poverty. Nor have satisfactory management arrangements been found for public housing. Often public landlords are regarded with hostility, as no different from their private counterparts, but more bureaucratic and often unresponsive. In Britain and the USA, the problem is exacerbated by the system of tax relief on mortgage interest. This provides a substantial subsidy to owner-occupation and fuels inflation in house prices, since prospective purchasers can afford to bid more in a competitive market.

Another type of movement which challenges the logic of market allocation and the political system is the environmentalist movement. There is a long tradition of movements to defend urban spaces and historic quarters, though in many cases it is difficult to distinguish disinterested concern for the urban form from defence of property values and exclusion (Barker and Keating, 1977). In recent years, more radical movements have developed challenging the basis of industrial society and proposing new ways of organizing cities. Some of these have moved into the political arena to contest elections.

Social movements have in some cases been produced by initiatives of central and local governments themselves. The 1960s and 1970s saw a series of national urban policy initiatives in Britain and the USA responding to changing national perceptions of the urban problem and sympathetic national governing coalitions. In Britain, the Urban Programme was launched in 1968, following earlier initiatives in education. In the USA the Great Society programme, including the Model Cities initiative and the Office of Economic Opportunity, was launched in 1964 under Johnson. In both cases, poverty was defined as an urban problem, affecting specific neighbourhoods and requiring the expenditure of additional funds, the redirection of public policy programmes and the mobilization of communities to aid their own development. National resources were provided for new programmes, allowing community groups to challenge local power structures. In both countries, a new breed of professional administrator emerged, the radicalized community worker or planner, committed more to the local clients than to the employing agency and less respectful of traditional bureaucratic and political structures. National guidelines for the urban programmes generally encouraged 'participation' of the local poor in implementing schemes. This was partly a gesture to the fashionable idea of participation, seen as a harmless and consensual process. In practice, participation can range from mere consultation to the handing over of policy-making powers to the community. The ambiguity in official views is indicated by the now famous injunction in the American Community Action Program to ensure 'maximum feasible participation of residents'.

The effects of this were particularly marked in the USA (Kantor, 1988). Many of the anti-poverty programmes were specifically designed to bypass city mayors and provide funding directly to community groups. So non-local resources were available to challenge local power structures and to mount social programmes without tapping the local tax base. The result was an opening of urban politics, an increase in pluralism and a challenge to old patterns of dominance. To some degree, the same happened in Britain, as community activists challenged the local service bureaucracies and the political elite, including local Labour Party establishments. Grants to voluntary organizations by other levels of local government, such as the Greater London Council, helped mobilize community groups, sometimes against their local council.

Urban social movements need to be able to forge coalitions to exercise power within the urban political system. Yet they are divided on several dimensions. Economic interest not only pits property-owners against the propertyless. Cutting across traditional class lines, it may divide owners of capital and workers on the one side from environmentalists and residential neighbourhood interests on the other. Neighbourhood interests themselves may be in conflict. Ideological differences may pit conservative conservationists against radicals wishing to change the social and economic order. In the absence of an over-arching ideology of urbanism, the economic class interests of individuals are likely to take precedence over shared neighbourhood or other values in the long term. This is a serious criticism of the politics of 'rainbow coalitions' which seek to establish common interests among, for example, women or sexual minorities whose class interests may be highly antagonistic. Finally, there is the problem that some demands are more easily concedable than others, allowing political and economic leaders to make staged and modest concessions, splitting off sections of social movements and achieving a progressive demobilization.

By definition, urban social movements lack the economic and political resources enabling them to exercise power within the urban arena. Compared with business elites, they lack economic resources and the ability to use the supply or withdrawal of these as a lever of power. Castells's (1983) concept of the 'urban trade unionism' of collective consumers begs this very question. Industrial trade unionism is based on an economic relationship in which workers exchange their labour for wages, and can bargain over the supply and terms. The analogy with urban social movements breaks down when we observe that there is not the same exchange at work. Urban social movements have no equivalent to the withdrawal of labour except in the housing field, where 'rent strikes' may be used to force public or private landlords to negotiate. Consumer boycotts and political strikes occasionally occur, but these raise the very issue of the division between individuals' interests in urban society and their conflicting class and consumer interests. A more radical option is the use of disruptive tactics, withdrawing the consent which is essential for the urban system to operate, a strategy associated with Saul Alinsky and his Industrial Areas Foundation. This involved organizing communities, initially on the basis of a winnable issue with a clear opponent. Victory could then be used to consolidate the organization as a basis for bargaining with the authorities for further gains.

The problem is that the sources of communities' problems are often not visible, or amenable to local negotiation. In the absence of success, movements may simply fall apart in apathy, or degenerate into random disruption and violence, with residents turning on each other. This was the case in many American cities in the 1960s, when large areas in the black ghettos were burnt out. Castells (1983, p. 71) comments that 'the American blacks consolidated their ghettos against the threat of urban renewal to preserve their social autonomy in a racist society, and to use their free space as a basis for a political challenge to win concessions from the institutional system'. Black political community leaders interviewed in the 1980s saw the episode as distinctly less rational, a tragic turning inwards of the ghettos to self-destruction and intra-community crime. The creation of ghettos and an urban underclass, far from posing a threat to the existing order, is another mechanism for containment and can make the management of poverty a great deal easier. Indeed, a criticism of some of the area-based projects in British and French cities is that they may have the effect of enclosing communities, forcing them to manage their own poverty without access to the resources of the wider urban area (Iion, 1987; Keating, 1988a).

In the absence of economic leverage, social movements need to operate through the political system, using electoral power and access to political and bureaucratic elites. In some cases, electoral mobilization may be possible, to force political elites to adopt an issue, to tilt the electoral balance towards those sympathetic to the movement's interests or secure the election of new challengers. In several major American cities, the black community has been able to achieve sufficient internal coherence to translate its majority or near-majority in the electorate into political office for black mayors. This, however, is a unique phenomenon of the mobilization of a group whose political identity has been forged and reinforced by centuries of discrimination and repression and decades of struggle for equality. For neighbourhood interests, entry into the political arena is dependent on the electoral and party system. In at-large electoral systems commonly used in 'reformed' North American municipalities and all but the largest French cities, election requires a candidate to win votes beyond one neighbourhood and in North America is very expensive. The introduction of ward systems has thus been a key demand of ethnic minorities and other urban social movements. Through state legislatures and by court actions challenging the discriminatory effect of at-large elections, they have succeeded in reintroducing ward elections to a number of American cities, so putting neighbourhood issues on the political agenda and reducing the dominance of downtown business. In Canada, too, urban social movements have attacked elements of 'reform' government and supported ward-based elections. In France, voting is not for individuals but for lists which, except in the small municipalities, are partisan. Before the 1982 reforms, pluralism was restricted by a rule which gave all the seats on the municipal council to the winning list. Now the opposition parties are represented, though the winning list, even where it gains only a plurality of the vote on the second ballot, is guaranteed an overall majority of the seats (Bélorgey, 1984). On the other hand, there is a provision for merging lists between the two rounds of local elections, encouraging social movements to run lists at the first ballot and the major parties to coopt them at the second. In this way, environmentalists have been brought onto socialist lists in several cities – as, more ominously, have members of the racist National Front been brought onto conservative lists.

Mass mobilization is not only expensive and difficult for many social movements to achieve, in some cases it may be counterproductive. Groups campaigning for gay rights or a more liberal penal policy may find that mass mobilization merely solidifies majority opposition. In this case, acting through existing political parties may be more promising, especially when they are ideologically open to the demands of the group while possessing a secure class or national base. Such parties are able to 'carry' a number of relatively unpopular policies as part of a wider programme. In other cases, parties may take on new issues as a means of broadening their support into new social groupings. In the 1970s and 1980s, a variety of urban social activists moved into British local Labour parties weakened by the decline of the blue-collar electorate and disillusionment with Labour's performance nationally and locally. By the mid-1980s, observers were noting a 'new urban left' (Gyford, 1983) committed to a new style of 'local socialism' (Boddy and Fudge, 1984). The French Socialist Party, after its refoundation in 1971, drew in an array of new community activists some of whom had been active in the urban social and municipal reform movements of the 1960s and 1970s. The same phenomenon is observable in the USA. Blacks, feminists, environmentalists, gays and others have worked through the Democratic Party, while religious fundamentalists, anti-abortion campaigners and some racists have worked through the Republicans. The weakness of parties in the USA makes such infiltration relatively easy since the collapse of the great urban machines. The same weakness, however, means that control of the party no longer gives control of the vote. In North American cities where non-partisanship is customary or enforced, social movements are denied that means of access.

Allying with political parties allows social movements to overcome some of their natural shortcomings, depending on the nature of the party system. In Britain and France, it provides a link to class-based alignments and an entry into national politics. Indeed, European social democracy allows a bridging of the 'city trenches' which Katznelson (1981) observes in American cities between work-based class politics and neighbourhood-based residential and ethnic interests. The alliance, however, can be at a cost to the social movements themselves. The ideological structured cadre parties of the European left are more difficult to penetrate than the more loosely organized American parties. If successful in gaining entry, social movements risk losing the distinction between movement and party, and thus their own independence. The way in which the French Socialist (and, to some degree, the Communist) parties were able to absorb the new social movements of the 1970s is one explanation for the demobilization of the latter in the 1980s. Nor is there any guarantee that partisanship will produce the policy results desired. It may be necessary to make too many compromises within the party – and, in office, partisan politicians may be subject to economic and intergovernmental constraints which make progress impossible.

A further problem lies in the weakness of class-based political parties themselves. The European social democratic formula united the interests of workers as producers with the interests of the poor as potential beneficiaries of national welfare policies. A similar idea underlay the American New Deal coalition from the 1930s, though in a less developed ideological form. The interests involved were never identical and some tensions arose from an early stage but the alliance was a major factor in the politics of Europe and America in the twentieth century. Recent decades, however, have seen a loosening of class attachments and a greater volatility in voting. In an increasingly affluent society, the poor are no longer identifiable with the 'working class' but with a marginalized section of it and an underclass which is largely outside the formal labour market. Social democratic parties (and the American Democrats) are forced to compete for the votes of affluent workers attracted by the possessive individualism of the parties of the right. This may mean adopting a more pluralistic vision, as the French Socialist and British Labour parties have done. It may also, however, lead to a downgrading of minority interests and those without obvious electoral appeal.

The capacity for organization and technical skills of social movements are key factors. Body-Gendrot (1987) points to the critical role in the thirteenth arrondissement of Paris of middle-class professionals with the skills needed to deal with state agencies. In Waterloo, skills were provided by a sympathetic local council (Brindley *et al.*, 1989). In the Covent Garden case, on the other hand, the community mobilization which had forced a change of plans was not sustained into the implementation phase of the new plans. There are dangers, too, in successful organization and professionalism. The leaders of the movement may become cut off from their followers and drawn into technical debates about details, allowing the basic policy to go unquestioned. This form of technical cooption can be more insidious than the transparent tokenism of placing community representatives on advisory committees. The penetrability of the governmental system is equally crucial since in the absence of their own financial resources community groups are dependent on public funding in pursuing alternative development options to those favoured by the development industry. In the USA, groups can draw resources and powers from more than one level of government, with municipal, state and federal governments all involved in urban affairs. In Canada, the lack of a federal role reduces this possibility. In Britain, community groups have often been helped by one tier of government against others. The two-tier local government system which existed in London between 1962 and 1986 allowed the development of new types of community involvement where sympathetic Labour administrations were in control at one level.

The absolute control which central government retains over urban political structures, however, means that where it feels strongly enough it can eliminate this factor. In the 1980s, the Greater London Council and Metropolitan counties were eliminated and responsibilities in urban development transferred to centrally-appointed development corporations less subject to social pressures than the municipal councils. While such radical forms of closure are not possible in France, the high degree of integration of the politico–administrative elite makes it difficult for community groups to penetrate (Garraud, 1989).

Social movements are constantly in danger of being coopted into clientelistic or corporatist arrangements with local political elites. In the USA, mayors have succeeded in regaining control over most of the federal urban funds and can use them to reward 'responsible' or co-operative groups. Sometimes this amounts to no more than small side-payments in a strategy where downtown business is the major beneficiary, but it is seen as better than nothing. French mayors, too, have to some degree coopted social movements through official recognition and the award of grants and favours. In both France and the USA the role of the mayor in extracting grants and favours from higher governments may be a source of local political strength, allowing the mayor to deflect complaints towards the inadequate resources available from above and forcing social movements into alliance with city government against the higher level. The growing size and complexity of the social movement and voluntary sector, however, rules out a hegemonic control by party machines of the old type.

Social movements thus face critical obstacles in mobilization and exerting influence in the local political arena. Nonetheless, they have become an increasingly important element in urban politics since the 1960s. Cities face a wider range of demands, and to that extent have become more internally pluralist. Yet their capacity to incorporate or respond to these new demands varies greatly.

URBAN REGIMES

The discussion has examined cultural norms about the scope of government, structural factors, devices for containment, economic pressures and social challenges. It remains to pull these together to characterize urban regimes in the four countries. A regime is a set of arrangements through which policy decisions are made, encompassing formal structures and informal relationships among political and economic elites comprising the governing coalition. Through these arrangements the two principal concerns – the governing capacity of elected local governments and the openness of urban politics to the popular and propertyless interests – can be assessed.

Governing capacity was described earlier in terms of five elements. First, there is political power derived from the possession of local elective office and the legal prerogatives pertaining to it. Second, there is power in the hands of higher-level governments. Third, there is power derived from the possession of scarce knowledge and skills, which may be in the public or private sectors. Fourth, there is power derived from the private control of resources, notably (but not exclusively) in the business sector. Fifth, there is power derived from the ability of certain groups to withdraw cooperation or obstruct change. These powers are exercised within a range of cultural and ideological assumptions which influence their use.

In the USA, city governments possess a substantial formal autonomy sanctioned by statute and the prevailing culture. Their powers are limited by statute while policy capacity is constrained by functional and territorial fragmentation, limited professional resources and the absence of programmatic parties. There is a high degree of dependence on private business, accentuated by the lack of ideological challenge to business-defined policy goals. There is variation in regimes across cities and time periods. Dependence on private business is attenuated where local governments are able to mobilize resources through the intergovernmental network on favourable terms. The existence of two levels of higher government and the fragmentation of the federal system increase the penetrability of the intergovernmental network, but cities find it difficult to mobilize pro-urban coalitions at higher levels.

In Canada, local governments possess a weak autonomy, with no tradition of local home rule. Yet their dependence on private business is attenuated by the stronger role played by provincial governments in urban development. There is less territorial fragmentation than in American cities, but functional fragmentation and the absence of programmatic parties weakens policy capacity. Dependence is increased by the absence of a substantial federal urban policy and the relatively weak leverage of cities over provincial governments. Competition for the urban vote does ensure cities a place in provincial politics, but the partisan parliamentary structure of provincial governments reduces their penetrability by territorial interests.

In Britain, local governments possess statutorily defined powers and substantial bureaucratic resources. Their policy capacity is further enhanced by territorial and functional integration and the presence of programmatic parties. Centralization of both economy and polity reduces direct dependence on business interests, and there is a challenge to business definitions of urban problems. On the other hand, the partisan parliamentary system reduces the penetrability of the centre by local interests while the functional pattern of intergovernmental relations reduces the discretion of local governments. Local government autonomy is constrained by statute, parliamentary omnicompetence and the existence of reserve powers for central ministers. The development of the party system has focused interest on national issues and personalities. The weakness of territorial identity and of territorial power bases further weakens local government, so that in the late twentieth century it cannot protect its own institutional forms.

The French system is characterized by formal centralization, legitimated by an ideology of equality and uniformity, though over recent years decentralist ideas have gained ground. Yet formal equality among communes and departments masks substantial inequalities in governing capacity. Bureaucratic resources and partisan structures make for a distinct style of policy-making in the large cities. As in Britain, centralization helps insulate local elites from direct business pressures. It does not, however, devalue territorial politics, merely changing its form. Territorial elites influence the intergovernmental system, through the accumulation of mandates, the need for a territorial base in national politics, the Senate and the links to territorially-based national administrators. Outside of education, central–local relations are less functionally based than in Britain and are mediated by the prefects and other locally-based central officials. This provides a considerable policy capacity for city governments (though not for small communes), in contrast to the limited formal autonomy.

Formal pluralism in American cities is limited by various devices of closure and containment. Elective office is gained through personal political activity, with candidates dependent on business for election success, especially in reformed cities. The weakness of parties and of mobilizing ideologies discourages stable popular coalitions providing a non-business perspective on issues. Popular movements do emerge, and in partisan cities can often penetrate the weak party structures, but they lack the capacity for *sustained* mobilization and they lack a governing capacity. Interests are disaggregated and business-led coalitions can in these circumstances buy off popular discontent piecemeal through selective material incentives and side-payments (Stone, 1989). Fragmentation as well as statutory provisions limit the scope of government, while the weakness of the public sector technical elite leaves vital knowledge and skills in the hands of the business sector and special-purpose agencies linked to business concerns. The task to be performed does create differences. In 'caretaker' regimes, where dominant elites are content with the status quo, governing involves merely diffusing challenges and pressures for change. Where the task in hand is the promotion of development, activist regimes show more policy capacity but since this requires resources it entails dependence on private business. Populist, anti-business city governments do emerge in declining cities with a lower-class electoral majority but, in the absence of a governing capacity, are soon overwhelmed (Swanstrom, 1985, 1988). One of the ironies of the American experience is that stable progressive regimes tend to be found in a few prosperous middle-class communities without a corporate base. Social movements continue to make claims based on neighbourhood and other interests, but these must harness themselves to the pro-business orientation, seeking whatever side-payments they can obtain.

In Canada, the culture supports broader challenges to business dominance and commercial values. In the late twentieth century, the term 'reform' is applied to the progressive coalitions which periodically emerge to challenge developer prerogatives. Their impact is limited by containment devices such as at-large electoral systems and non-partisanship and the lack of national organization. So reform movements tend to be fragile and rather heterogeneous. On the other hand, the greater centralization within the Canadian provinces means that the stakes in city politics are relatively low.

In Britain, openness and pluralism are encouraged by the wide range of functions and the existence of programmatic parties linked to broader national issues. The latter factor, though, is ambiguous since the major parties have tended to subordinate local politics to their national strategies, with their primary objective being national power. The Labour Party has served as a vehicle for mobilizing lower-class interests in cities and linking this to a national project, and has given distributional issues a place on the agenda. Yet the agenda of municipal labourism itself has been rather limited and unimaginative. From the 1960s, new social movements entered the stage and later penetrated the political system through the Labour Party, broadening the agenda to include radical policies of economic interventionism and social change. With a weak parliamentary opposition, partisan politics came to be played across the central–local divide between a radical right-wing government and these 'new left' councils. There were some notable policy innovations but central government, claiming that left-wing councils had stepped outside the traditional collaborative mode of intergovernmental relations, moved quickly to reassert its pre-eminence.

In France, too, the parties of the left have mobilized the disadvantaged through the local government system. During the 1970s, the Socialist Party was able to expand by providing a home to activists in a variety of social movements, strengthening its commitment to decentralization in the process. Fragmentation of local government provides for the articulation of territorial power but (unlike the situation in the USA) does not close off municipal politics. On the other hand, pluralism is reduced by the power of the integrated political–administrative elite and the at-large electoral system which guarantees majority government. The two-ballot system does encourage the formation of broad electoral coalitions, but coopts social movements and minority parties into governing coalitions. French urban regimes remain relatively closed, but not because of economic and business pressures.

CHANGING URBAN REGIMES

Social change, the rise of new urban social movements and the breakdown of previously monolithic party systems have all served to increase pluralism within the politics of many cities. Mechanisms of political closure have proved ineffective as new movements have used access to the intergovernmental system, entry into political parties and tactics of protest and disruption to press their demands. All this has served to broaden the agenda of urban politics and increase the demands on urban political regimes. Economic restructuring further serves to increase the salience of urban politics since growth and decline, development and plant closures are perceived in terms of their spatial impact and their complex ramifications within spatially defined communities.

Yet at the same time, the ability of urban government to respond to the pressures upon it is reduced by the concentration of economic power and its detachment from place. As competition for business resources becomes first national, then international, cities appear increasingly as prisoners of global forces. Nor can access to the resources and powers of national governments always compensate, since national governments are themselves increasingly limited in their ability to manage territory by the same global forces and by international and regional free trade regimes, including GATT, the European Community and the US–Canada Free Trade Agreement. Cities are thus caught between rising and differentiated local demands and an economic order which poses severe limits on their ability to respond. Stable urban regimes themselves may disintegrate under these competitive pressures. Alternatively, they may reconstitute on new terms as inter-class place-based development coalitions.

National governments, too, have been reordering urban regimes, in response to these trends and to their own preoccupations. In the USA and Britain, radical right governments in the 1980s sought to increase the exposure of cities to market and business pressures, to reduce the role of the state as protector of social interests in cities and to offload fiscal problems onto local governments. The last trend is also visible in Canada as deficits are handed down the governmental hierarchy and functions are 'disentangled'. In the USA, the Reagan and Bush administrations have sought to pass issues down to the localities. Defended in terms of decentralization and local responsiveness, the strategic aim of these measures has been to transfer issues to arenas which are structurally less favourable to social and redistributive demands – namely, the cities. Measures have included cuts in federal support to increase cities' dependence on their local tax bases; cuts in welfare programmes; and the consolidation of grants to allow their allocation to be made in response to the local agenda. Despite rising social pressures, this agenda is dominated by commercial concerns.

In Britain, the Conservative government after 1979 similarly sought to subject cities to market discipline and curtail socially redistributive expenditures. Given the structure of British urban regimes, with their relative openness to non-business interests, this involved taking issues out of the local political arena as well as trying to restructure the arena itself. Central support was cut and cities were forced to rely more on their local tax bases but, in the absence of the market discipline of American cities, local governments responded by increasing taxes. So a series of measures was introduced to reduce local government's ability to set tax rates, culminating in the nationalization of all business taxation. An ambitious attempt was made to restructure the system of personal taxation to make it more difficult for local governments to raise funds for redistributive purposes. The failure of the poll tax to suppress spending demands was characteristically followed by further centralization, as statutory limits were placed on poll tax rates. Housing finance was also subject to close central control and eventually cities were forbidden to use local tax resources to subsidize public housing. In the field of urban development, local authorities were extensively displaced by centrally-appointed development corporations with strong private sector representation on their boards. Those authorities which (as a result of their widely drawn boundaries, large resource bases and light service provision duties) possessed the most discretion to venture into new areas – the metropolitan counties – were abolished.

France in the 1980s, by contrast, experienced an extensive programme of decentralization intended not, as in the American case, to increase the dependence of cities on business but to restructure the system of government itself. Socialist Party control of both levels of government provided the opportunity to undertake a series of reforms which had been much debated in the past, but little acted on. The aim was to reduce the political and administrative load on the centre, to increase local accountability and to shift power from bureaucratic to elected actors. So the remaining veto powers of the prefects were abolished and departments and regions given their own elected executives. This was to clarify responsibilities and ensure accountability. Functions were transferred to all three levels of local government but a large degree of interdependence and joint responsibility remained. Councils were given greater fiscal discretion and some powers to stimulate economic activity. While this was not the primary intention, the effect of decentralization has been to increase cities' dependence on business and stimulate inter-urban competition for investment. There has been some retrenchment in social expenditures as these were decentralized. Under the Chirac government from 1986 to 1988 there was an emphasis on privatization. Yet in contrast to the British experience, territorial elites have retained their influence at the centre in a system where both Chirac and his Socialist successor Michel Rocard remained serving mayors while they were Prime Minister. Resources have been transferred to localities in tandem with their new responsibilities and fiscal equalization has largely been maintained. Decentralization and the opening of the European market have increased competition among cities, but local regimes are still dominated by public leadership. Since 1988, the central state itself has attempted to impose a rationalization of the various development efforts, harnessing them to the needs of national competitiveness. This itself has been only partially successful, given the impossibility of consolidating local governments or even imposing cooperation. Local elites in France have thus maintained a degree of control over the process of regime restructuring as well as urban development. Pluralism has been enhanced by the provision for the opposition to be represented in city councils, but generally the territorial elite has contained the challenge of social movements, where necessary coopting them.

5. Consolidating Local Government

THE CASE FOR MODERNIZATION

The postwar years have seen a debate about the reorganization of local government, specifically, the need to consolidate fragmented jurisdictions into larger units, especially in metropolitan areas. Consolidation has been advocated largely on efficiency grounds, to improve local government's problem-solving and administrative capacity. Yet structures and boundaries also help define problems, frame the terms of political debate and limit the options available. While the argument has revolved around the intellectual case for modernization in terms of efficiency, the outcome has usually been determined by the stakes involved and the pattern of interests.

The issue of reorganization arose after the Second World War in response to the growth of cities, which had spilled over their jurisdictional boundaries, and the expansion of municipal functions. Population movement meant that cities in a functional sense no longer corresponded to urban government units, producing demands for the annexation of suburban areas or the establishment of over-arching units of government to encompass the functional city. This, it was claimed, could enhance efficiency, reduce various types of externality and provide for more effective planning.

The needs of coherent urban and regional planning were critical to the movement for metropolitan consolidation. Urban planning is notoriously difficult to define (Ratcliffe, 1981), covering a variety of activities, from the programming of individual development projects to the comprehensive remodelling of whole regions. In the postwar years, an increasingly synoptic vision emerged, concerned with the relationship of residential, employment and service facilities, the use of resources, and the improvement of the urban environment (Self, 1982). To encompass these, areas needed to be drawn widely to include the major daily travel patterns for work, shopping and leisure and to allow large-scale infrastructure programming. Planning was seen as a goal-oriented activity requiring the coordination of policies and agencies in the attainment of a desired end state. The need to formulate goals and control the resources necessary to their implementation created a strong bias to centralization (Cooke, 1983). So a wide consensus emerged that cities should be planned on at least a metropolitan basis, encompassing the whole built-up area (CED, 1966) or even on a regional scale, including the rural hinterland (Wheatley, 1969).

What was unclear was the status and legitimacy of planning in terms of competitive politics, markets and professional competence, and hence of the sort of urban regime in which planning might be desirable and possible. For some, planning was a device to overcome market imperfections, to make markets operate more smoothly by reducing uncertainty, aiding land assembly and socializing some development costs. This was the basis for what Americans called 'corporate liberalism' in which business and social interests could come together behind agreed policies. For some socialists, planning was a device whereby political choice could over-ride markets. Others saw planning as a mediator between politics and the market. For many planners, however, these questions were subordinated to a technical rationality in which planning was legitimized not by its contribution to markets or politics but through its own professional norms. There was a widely shared assumption that 'rational intervention by an educated elite could produce modifications to the development process which would improve the welfare of all members of society' (Cooke, 1983, p. 87). By the 1960s, there was a wider appreciation that planning was 'political', affecting the allocation of resources and space among social groups and purposes. Urban protests against redevelopment and the increasing tendency of the public to blame the 'planners' for all urban ills undermined the self-confidence of the profession. There was also more appreciation that without authoritative control over resource allocation, plans were unlikely to be fulfilled. So the need for metropolitan planning, previously often seen as a task for professionals, special agencies or intergovernmental teams, gave rise to a need for metropolitan government able to combine planning with the necessary resources and to give the whole a democratic legitimacy. This more political vision, however, continued to sit uneasily beside the purely technocratic view of the planning process. If planning is seen as a democratic political process, then the boundaries of the metropolitan government will determine who is represented and influence the goals selected and the political outcome. If planning is a means for local communities to determine and pursue their goals, these may conflict with those of higher levels of government.

Another 'technical' issue with political implications concerned the efficiency of service delivery and economies of scale. It was argued that many services required specific geographical areas or population bases and that existing local governments were too small to undertake many of the functions entrusted to them, especially those in which technological advances had imposed higher costs. In the early 1960s, the USA had 30 000 independent law enforcement agencies, mostly one- and two-man operations clearly inadequate for round-the-clock service (CED, 1966). 3 000 of the 25 000 independent school districts maintained no schools, functioning mainly as a device to minimize school taxation (CED, 1966). In France, 1 000 communes have populations under 50 and only 30 per cent have more than 700. Reformers in the 1960s wished to eliminate these very small units. It was also argued that larger units were more efficient because of the need to employ specialized staff and to invest in equipment.

More sophisticated theories tried to specify the most efficient population for the various services. It is very difficult to demonstrate that a particular size of unit is more efficient, given the absence of adequate measures of output in public services. It may be possible to show that units of a certain size have lower costs than others, but unless the quality of service is as good we cannot call them more efficient. Nor can we say that a unit is inefficient because its costs are high: it may be delivering a better product, be more responsive to the needs of clients or be paying higher wages as a recognition of employee interests. So exercises in measuring economies of scale in local government services have invariably proved inconclusive (Dearlove, 1979; Ostrom *et al.*, 1988).

Attempts to specify optimum population levels tended in consequence to be highly speculative but, coinciding with the intellectual fashion for 'big is beautiful', they carried conviction where it mattered. The Wheatley Commission on Local Government in Scotland, surveying conflicting evidence about the efficiency of small housing authorities, declared that 'arguments of this kind tend to miss the mark altogether' since they were based on past performance and asserted that in the future large authorities would be needed (Wheatley, 1969, p. 109). The Redcliffe-Maud Commission on England advanced an almost identical argument to defend the prevailing orthodoxy of economies of scale in the face of contrary evidence from its own research unit (Dearlove, 1979). Similarly, the American Committee for Economic Development, conceding that 'the minimum size of a governmental unit ... may be debated at length', insisted that 'The burden of proof must rest, however, upon those who argue for population levels below 50,000' (CED, 1966, p. 35).

A fundamental problem with the argument about economies of scale and the best unit for a particular function is that they constitute just one element in the decision on size of authorities, and cannot be considered in isolation. Crozier and Friedberg (1977) note the errors of the structural contingency approach which purports to relate the structure of organizations to their environment and technology and determine empirically the most efficient. It does not explain why many organizations continue to operate in an apparently inefficient manner; the explanation may be that they have goals other than the maximization of technical efficiency in a narrow sense. Technology is not merely a 'given' but is a resource in a complex political game; its use is determined by political choices. To take the example of water supply, large-scale organization may be appropriate if the policy is for heavy capital investment and an increase in supply, less so if the emphasis is to be put on conservation. If the water function is seen not merely in terms of laying pipelines and pumping but as a subsidiary element of development and planning policy, then it may be appropriate to entrust it to the general planning authorities. It may be more 'efficient' to privatize certain council services, in the sense of obtaining a given output at lower cost, but this may entail a deterioration in wages and conditions or a less equitable distribution of services. If politics is about conflicting goals and interests as well as to how to attain agreed goals, these 'efficiency' arguments are rarely conclusive: as in practice most arguments about technical efficiency concern marginal changes, they are likely to be outweighed by other considerations. Nor can purely technical arguments for a specific size of unit for the delivery of a service ever be determinate, since the choice of unit influences the balance of power and substantive policy outputs. In any case, the 'optimum' unit for one function is unlikely to be optimal for another.

Expansion of service provision in the developing welfare state also provided arguments for consolidation. It was believed, especially in Britain and Canada, that the distinction in needs between urban and rural areas which underlay the traditional system was no longer valid. Not only should urban and rural areas be planned together, it was argued, but they had basically the same service needs, especially in the social sphere. Reorganization could eliminate the anomalous distinction and bring modern services to rural and suburban areas.

Another argument is in terms of power. The fragmentation and functional inadequacy of local government, it is argued, has led to a drift of functions to higher levels of government, an increase of supervision and an undesirable degree of centralization. Consolidation will permit a restoration of the power of local government. Yet, while there is a widespread agreement on the virtues of more 'powerful' local government, there is a critical ambiguity in the theme. Local government may be conceived of as more powerful in a functional sense, able to mobilize local resources and address problems more effectively; or it may be more powerful in a political sense, able to take autonomous policy decisions even in defiance of higher levels. Higher levels of government have an interest in improving the functional efficiency of local government, so enhancing the quality of services while reducing the administrative, supervisory and political burden on themselves. Endowing local governments with political autonomy is another matter. So the Wheatley Commission on Local Government in Scotland argued for 'nothing less than a shift in the balance of power and responsibility between central and local government', adding that some of the most eloquent exponents of the view that local authorities should be strong and vigorous were representatives of Government departments (Wheatley, 1969, pp. 44–5). As one of the civil servants involved has indiscreetly revealed, what central government was seeking was local authorities strong enough to do what the centre wanted (Ross, 1980), to undertake planning and service provision without continual detailed supervision, yet according to centrally determined policies.

A related argument was the need to eliminate specialized ad hoc agencies, seen as inefficient, ill-coordinated and unaccountable. Their proliferation had been partly a response to the deficiencies of local government structure and partly technocratic, a legacy of the belief that certain functions should be treated apart from general municipal administration or handled by professionals. The reformers of the 1960s, unlike those of early twentieth-century North America, sought consolidation of functions in the interests of coordination, transparency and accountability.

More controversial was the debate on the 'calibre' of locally elected representatives. This is another term which is exceedingly difficult to define since one's view of the quality of a councillor will depend on what one wants the councillor to do. The debate has long antecedents, first surfacing in the late nineteenth century, when local social and economic elites started to be displaced by professional politicians as demands for public services were expanding. In the USA, the urban political machine provoked the reform movement to put administration in the hands of technocrats and business elites. In Britain, complaints about the calibre of local representatives were made regularly in the late nineteenth and twentieth centuries (Mill, 1912; Dearlove, 1979; Gyford *et al.*, 1989). In France, the rise of the *nouvelles couches sociales* promoted by the Third Republic was marked by an attack on the traditional territorial notables rooted in the local social and economic structure (Zeldin, 1973; Grémion, 1976). In the 1960s, expansion in the scope of local government again coincided with complaints about the quality of elected representatives. The deficiency was widely attributed to the archaic structure of the system and it was here that a remedy was identified. If city boundaries were drawn more widely, a larger pool of talent could be tapped, while more efficient, powerful and businesslike councils would attract professional and business elements which presently held the system in disdain. These in turn would improve the quality of local administration by focusing on policy rather than on administrative details, taking a longer and broader view of their work and using the latest management techniques.

There are countless tales of municipal worthies spending their time on trivia while leaving the large, long-term issues to permanent officials or higher levels of government. On the other hand, this question, too, cannot be considered in isolation from its political implications. The new needs of local government were couched in terms of planning, economic development and growth. Traditional elites tended to focus on the administrative provision of a static range of services or, on the political side, the politics of distribution and patronage, hence the absorption in administrative detail and individual cases. One of the motives for reform was undoubtedly a desire on the part of higher governments to replace the political elites with more dynamic, growth-minded elites drawn from the professional and business classes. The career officials would also be more managerially-minded and innovative. These new leaders would recast the traditional view of local government, rooted in bureaucratic, administrative rationality (tempered with patronage) into a new dynamic rationality focused on development, planning and action (Grémion, 1976). This new rationality was consistently presented in consensual terms, legitimized by the rhetoric of 'planning' as a technical activity with universal benefits.

Some commentators on the left (Dearlove, 1979; Giard and Scheibling, 1981; Clément, 1988) see the debate about councillor quality simply as a means of reducing working-class representation and putting local government back in the hand of business leaders. Dearlove (1979) draws a parallel with the turn of the century reform movement in the USA with its emphasis on business leadership and professional management. If boundaries were extended to include the middle-class suburbs, local government would again be more concerned with the needs of accumulation than redistribution and genuine political debate muffled. The effect would be compounded by the introduction of modern management techniques, borrowed from the private sector, which would suppress political choice and bias decision-making to business needs.

There was certainly an element of this calculation among some of the advocates of reform. The 1950s was the period when working-class participation in local government peaked in Britain and France. In the USA, black representation increased in city councils in the 1960s and 1970s. Conservatives may well have seen this as cause for alarm. The argument that consolidation is merely a ploy to reassert business control and stifle progressive politics is, however, a great simplification. Traditional local government was ill-suited to economic redistribution – as opposed to individual-level patronage – because of its restricted functions and resource base.

Promotion of equity, indeed, is one of the most important reasons given by progressives to support consolidation. Fiscal equalization could be promoted by taxing wealthy areas to finance expensive city services and social segregation be broken down. The American Advisory Commission on Intergovernmental Relations did not mince its words: 'The near apartheid condition now existing in many metropolitan areas is one of the most insidious consequences of the differing growth patterns that have taken place since World War II in central city, suburban and rural communities' (ACIR, 1973, p. 6). The Wheatley Commission on Local Government in Scotland spoke of 'a very unequal spread of rateable resources' (Wheatley, 1969, p. 33). Ladd and Yinger (1989) show that the spread of suburban shopping malls and the decentralization of employment reduced the capacity of many American central cities to tax non-residents in the 1970s, while the smaller the central city relative to the metropolitan area the larger the costs it had to bear on behalf of non-residents.

Many reformers saw no contradiction between the demands of economic development and those of social justice. Planned growth could accommodate the two, though larger units were a requirement of both. Others supported larger and strengthened local government as a counter-balance to business influence and to promote a new type of politics. They saw in larger units a greater potential for politicization since they would be more socially heterogeneous and would be forced to make policy choices. Fragmentation was seen to promote closure and exclusion, defining issues in narrow terms and encouraging defensive attitudes. The argument for internal management reform similarly has its progressive advocates like Stewart (1971, 1983, 1986), who saw it as a means of aiding political choice and taking strategic decisions. Mackintosh (1968) further argued that in the British case larger units with more powers and resources could encourage the development of territorial political leadership as a counter-balance to the centralization of the British state.

DEFENDING FRAGMENTATION: THE PUBLIC CHOICE SCHOOL

There have always been defenders of small-scale local government, presented as more communitarian, in contrast to the remoteness of large-scale organization. In the 1960s, arguments against reorganization relied heavily on nostalgia and fear of change on the part of conservatives; and the vogue for participation and the 'small is beautiful' philosophy on the left. In the 1980s, a more rigorous intellectual opposition to consolidation was provided by the public choice school of political economists.

Public choice theory is extensive and complex but essentially comprises an extension of the neo-classical model of the market to political life. The basic unit of analysis is the rational, informed individual exercising choice according to market signals. While traditional theories of local democracy focus on the capacity for collective choice through voting, public choice focuses on individual choice through markets: the individual as citizen is replaced by the individual as consumer. In support of this, public choice theorists make two critical claims, the descriptive claim that individuals see public policy only in terms of individual utility functions; and the normative claim that these functions comprise the only possible conception of the public good and thus desirable goal of policy. Like other forms of utilitarianism, it refuses to judge these functions, seeing them as their own justification. In public policy, the key concept is that of 'fiscal equivalence' – that is, that individuals should receive what they pay for in an undistorted market.

Both descriptive and normative claims are open to challenge. In order to make the theory work, individuals are presented as 'asocial, acultural, ahistorical atoms whose self-interested rational calculation produces an ordered and stable form of social organization' (Cooke, 1983, p. 48). So, while ostensibly based on a hard-headed vision of human nature, the approach may require the creation of a new ideal human type. The problems with the claim that collective interest can be derived merely by summing private interests are illustrated by one of the public choice theorists' own examples (Parks and Ostrom, 1981). Individuals are credited with an ability to evaluate the quality of policing, including issuing of tickets for traffic violations, and to make judgements about policy. A cynic might note that individuals almost invariably complain about receiving speeding or parking tickets while collectively they have an interest in enforcement. More generally, individuals' interests and policy preferences, far from being fixed and knowable through undistorted market signals, are both culturally and structurally conditioned. The preferences which citizens might express while working within a given set of parameters (say, a fragmented local government system) might differ from those which they would express were they allowed to change the parameters. The problem of collective action means that it may be rational to make one set of choices in a fragmented system where it is possible to offload costs onto others but another set of choices in a consolidated system. The normative claim that individual utility functions are the only valid guide to policy is often advanced as self-evident. Yet the absence of an external evaluative criterion makes it impossible to weigh conflicting interests in a society characterized by inequality of resources and opportunities.

An early version of public choice was provided by Tiebout (1956) who portrays local governments as seeking to attain the optimum population size to provide the services desired by their populations at minimum cost. Individuals for their part move into jurisdictions which provide the mix of services suited to their individual preferences at least cost. Provided that there is a large number of local governments competing for residents, this provides a set of price and quality signals analogous to those given by retailers in the private market. Metropolitan fragmentation is desirable in order to provide a range of choices for the 'consumer-voter' to maximize his or her utility. The most severe problems with this model are the simplifying assumptions underlying it, notably those of perfect information and perfect mobility. In order to sustain the assumption that individuals are really able to move freely in response to local service patterns, Tiebout has to assume that they all live on dividends so that residence is not determined by the needs of work. Nor does the model recognize that in the USA the existence of multiple jurisdictions does not give all households a choice of residential location. On the contrary, suburbs often incorporate as municipalities precisely to reduce mobility by erecting barriers to people of different social and ethnic backgrounds (Judd, 1988). Tiebout (1956, p. 418n) admits that one motive which individuals may have is the desire to associate with 'nice' people, but sees this entirely in terms of inclusion rather than the exclusion so pervasive in American cities. The creation of homogeneous communities, while satisfying the preferences of those with the necessary resources, can create barriers to the mobility which is an essential element of the model. Zoning regulations and other measures of local policy are used to preserve the exclusiveness of communities, and not merely to reflect community choices (Newton, 1984; Shlay and Rossi, 1981).

The model sees consumer-voters as concerned entirely with qualitative issues, seeking out mixes of services which correspond to their varying preferences. So some people may prefer parks, others schools and others again low taxes. This is no doubt an important consideration in some circumstances and a classic justification for local self-government. Yet in practice, these qualitative issues may be less important than quantitative ones. Most public services are regarded as desirable and most voters would probably like more of everything. The question then is not whether the services are desired but what trade-offs should be made among services, and between services and taxes. Again, this is a matter not merely of qualitative taste but of quantitative need. So families with children need education, old people need special health and social services, people without cars need public transport. The 'preferences' of communities reflect demographic factors, the weight of various social groups within them; and individuals' needs vary according to the stage of their life-cycle. The key question then is not the tastes of individuals but the distribution of resources among social, economic and generational groups. On this issue, Tiebout is silent, though it is difficult to see how his homogeneous communities could address it. Some public choice theorists dismiss the problem by assuming that the question of distribution is being taken care of somewhere else, usually by higher levels of government. This trivializes the whole analysis by taking out of the model one of the fundamental elements of local politics. More recent public choice theorists have admitted that it is difficult to reconcile the public choice principle of fiscal equivalence – that individuals should get what they pay for – with redistribution of resources (ACIR, 1987).

The public choice approach to local government structure gained a great deal of intellectual support in the 1980s. In 1987, the US Advisory Commission on Intergovernmental Relations, previously a strong supporter of consolidation, rescinded its earlier policy and declared for continued fragmentation (ACIR, 1987). The local public economy school (Ostrom *et al.*, 1988; ACIR, 1987; Parks and Oakerson, 1989) build on the Tiebout assumptions about matching individual preferences with service provision through a market mechanism but put less emphasis on the opportunity for disenchanted residents to move to other communities. Instead they focus on the responsiveness of governments supposedly encouraged by the fragmented local government system in the USA. In particular, they reject two propositions of the consolidation school, that larger jurisdictions are needed for efficient service delivery and that fragmentation presents problems of coordination. The findings of public choice researchers on the efficiency of various types of delivery unit tend to be as inconclusive as those of the consolidationists and for the same reason, the difficulty of measuring outputs and in controlling for variations among units other than size. However, while some of them do devote space to attempting to disprove the existence of economies of scale (e.g., Ostrom *et al.*, 1988), this is not essential to the argument.

More important is the distinction drawn between the *provision* of public services – that is, the decision on the quantity and nature of services to be supplied – and the *production* of services. Provision can be organized by small communities to reflect local choices. Since communities of interest may vary according to the service, a single set of local governments would not guarantee fiscal equivalence. A variety of jurisdictions for different purposes is therefore appropriate. Production can be handled by units of varying sizes, depending on the technical requirements of the service. These contract with the provision units. Such a production unit might be a department of the local government, another local government, an intergovernmental agency, an independent public agency, or a private contractor. Ideally, production agencies should compete for the custom of provision agencies. Metropolitan areas are then characterized not as a patchwork of balkananized jurisdictions but as 'local public economies' (ACIR, 1987; Parks and Oakerson, 1989) in which public entrepreneurs and citizens seek out the best ways of providing services in a climate of cooperation and competition within a set of understood rules.

This approach bears comparison with analyses of the complexities of French administration by the organizational sociology school (Dupuy and Thoenig, 1985) (later applied in Britain (Rhodes, 1981) and Italy (Dente, 1985)). An apparently uniform and centralized regime has been disaggregated by pluralist scholars into a complex system of agencies and individuals linked less by formal regulation than by a series of unwritten rules and understandings. Coordination comes about not by hierarchical order but through mutual accommodation and negotiation. Like many systems approaches to political analysis, these often hang uneasily between the descriptive and the normative. If a complex system is functioning in the sense of avoiding breakdown, it is assumed to be working *well*. Yet while public officials may ingeniously accommodate themselves to complex structures and negotiate over items of policy and administration, this can be costly in terms of time and resources. Even if the system is *functioning*, policy outcomes are not necessarily ideal when measured against any specific objective, such as eliminating poverty, maximizing economic growth or improving educational attainment. The model provides no external standard by which to judge the effectiveness of the arrangements. Nor does it guarantee that citizen preferences are able to influence the process.

Indeed, one of the major criticisms of complexity in the French and Italian cases is that it obscures responsibility and reduces accountability. The assumption of perfect knowledge built into the public choice model and the complexity of the local public economy approach imply a large investment in learning the complexities of policy, administration and taxation not borne out by survey evidence. In practice, individuals where possible simplify the process of political choice through parties, ethnic voting or a general judgement on the capacity of rival leaders. The international evidence suggests that where such simplification is possible voter turnout is greater. Where local government is highly complex, with a plethora of specialized agencies, the costs of learning are raised for citizens more than for officials. The result may be a shift of power to public service producers, the very result which the public choice school claims to avoid. In France, where fragmentation of local government is even greater than in the USA, most communes function as provision rather than production units, but there is constant complaint about their subjection to the tutelage of service producers. In the USA service agencies have often been able to build great power and extend their scope beyond their initial functions. In England and Wales, the power of regional water authorities over major public policy decisions has been criticized (Keating and Rhodes, 1981). The problem of producer power is all the greater in the case of services which are natural monopolies, or where there is collusion (including price-setting, market sharing or cartels) among service providers. These forms of market failure, familiar enough in the private sector, are more likely in public services given the smaller number of producers, the high cost of entry into many services, the complexities of the services involved and the difficulties in measuring outputs.

Public choice approaches to local government organization are rooted in the concept of individual utility maximization which, in turn, is assumed to be promoted by arrangements approximating as closely as possible to markets which reflect preferences based on present incomes and opportunities. They are ill-fitted to the achievement of social change or to economic redistribution. It is not true that planning itself is impossible in fragmented areas. It is possible to build highways, to assemble sites, to provide infrastructure, to do most of the things required by economic development, through the cooperation of agencies in defined tasks. What is difficult is to relate the pattern of development to social and political priorities. Policy tends to disintegrate into distinct arenas, each with their own policy communities, meeting at various points but determining their own priorities. There is a denial of the territorial community with an ability to take decisions across functional boundaries or to change the meaning attributed to functions. Instead, it is assumed that problem-solving is possible within functionally-defined homogeneous communities or by cooperation among them. In these circumstances, business influence may be enhanced by separation of the development function into the specialized agencies and shadow governments mentioned in Chapter 4, relieving those involved of concern with the social implications of development. In other cases, the fragmentation of government may give organized private interests enormous scope to construct favourable regimes through their capacity for agenda-setting, coordination and strategic intervention (Stone, 1989).

Some of the most serious consequences of fragmentation concern economic development. In an increasingly open global economy, competition for mobile capital has increased, leading local governments to concentrate their resources on encouraging development. In France and the USA this includes tax abatements; everywhere it involves gearing capital programmes, land policies and selective subsidies to development projects (see Chapter 7). Yet, while competition for investment is increasingly national and global, the powers and resources available to local governments are marginal. Rarely critical in the decision to make a major investment, they may influence the precise site of a development already scheduled for a metropolitan area. This applies to large manufacturing projects and even more clearly to retail developments serving a local market. Metropolitan fragmentation thus leads to intensified competition among jurisdictions *within* a conurbation, producing an under-taxation or over-subsidization of business (compared with what would prevail under unitary government). It potentially reduces the competitiveness of the metropolitan area as a whole in national and global terms by wasting resources on developments which would have occurred in the region in any case. It discourages cooperation on metropolitan infrastructure since this might not meet the test of fiscal equivalence for any separate jurisdiction. Indeed, there is a powerful disincentive to engage in expenditure with external benefits (such as education), even where this might be the most effective mechanism for promoting economic growth.

For similar reasons, redistributive policies are difficult. There is abundant evidence that suburban communities incorporate independently or resist consolidation precisely to avoid redistributive pressures. In St Louis county, cited by public choice theorists as an admirable example of fragmentation (ACIR, 1988), jurisdictions resisting consolidation are motivated above all by a desire to retain tax revenues and seek to annex new retail developments to capture the tax base while leaving out areas expensive to service. Certainly, it is possible to construct public choice arrangements in which redistribution would be technically possible. Parks and Oakerson (1989, pp. 22–3) claim that larger units are not necessary since 'if citizen preferences support resource redistribution to distressed communities within large, general-purpose units, they may also support redistribution to smaller, autonomous units by overlying jurisdictions'. Unfortunately, redistribution does not come about simply because 'citizens' declare a preference for it. Indeed, under public choice assumptions, a preference for redistribution on the part of individual utility maximizers is a mystery, usually coped with by introducing the notion of altruism as an activity from which individuals derive personal gratification. The theory is thus stretched to allow the pursuit of individual self-interest to encompass everything, including its opposite!

In practice, redistributive policies are the outcome of a complex political process, governed by cultural and structural factors. They require a sense of the public domain conceptually separate from private interests, a culture in which community as well as individualist values are important and a sense of solidarity in terms of which redistributive policies can appear rational. They also require structures for policy formulation to allow the key decisions to be taken, political organizations to formulate redistributive policies and integrate them with other policies, and mechanisms for delivering redistributive services. A structure which segregates households into homogeneous communities is unlikely to sustain community solidarity or present choices in an appropriate way. On the contrary, it promotes competition for mobile investment and tax base and municipal politicians must measure themselves against this. Citizen preferences are formed through cultural norms and political choice in a context of political competition among leaders emphasizing different conceptions of the public interest. In a fragmented system, the largest electoral returns go to those leaders who define goals broad enough to include most of their electors, and narrow enough to exclude most outsiders. This encourages a narrow conception of public interests defined in terms of the individual jurisdiction, at the expense of wider metropolitan and regional common interests. So the problem of fragmented local government may not be that it produces a poor 'quality' of leadership but that it produces parochial leadership and defines the political agenda in narrow terms. Political competition is displaced from the municipality to reappear in the form of interjurisdictional competition. Given the need for metropolitan and regional perception of major problems and the mobilization of opinion and resources behind them, this can prove damaging (Altenberger *et al.*, 1988). The encouragement in public choice theory for the most dynamic people to vote with their feet by abandoning communities in decline rather than engaging in action to improve them further weakens urban leadership.

Nor can redistribution be accomplished merely by transferring resources among jurisdictions. Interjurisdictional equity does not guarantee interpersonal equity (Heald, 1983); dominant local coalitions might discriminate against local minorities who have the least opportunity of moving to other areas. Given economic competition among jurisdictions, fragmentation serves to make redistribution within communities more difficult, whether or not there are interjurisdictional transfers, as some authors associated with public choice approaches concede. Peterson (1981) claims that jurisdictions must favour high-income earners and businesses to prevent them moving away and reducing the local tax base. This tendency to favour the better off (and business) will apply equally to locally-raised revenue and to the spending of intergovernmental block transfers. In Detroit, a central city surrounded by competing suburbs, the need to subsidize business through local taxation and federal block grants is seen as so compelling that it is almost impossible to challenge it, despite the city's massive social problems. The only effective way of achieving redistribution in services in these circumstances may be direct provision by larger-scale units.

Fragmentation, then, far from being a neutral mechanism allowing individuals and communities to realize their goals, is another mechanism of closure in urban politics, restricting the agenda and defining issues in narrow, competitive terms. Public choice theorists, consciously or not, embrace a set of values which encourages this. This reading is confirmed by their hostility to collective institutions generally – notably to trade unions which are usually seen as no more than a form of economic monopoly and inherently 'inefficient' (Ostom *et al.*, 1988).

Of course, the mere existence of metropolitan government does not guarantee distributional equity or redistribution. That is critically dependent on the political balance of the metropolitan authority, as well as the taxing and spending powers at its disposal. If the effect of consolidation is to establish a coalition of the better-off, diluting the representation of the poor, redistribution within the larger area may be made more difficult. Again, this depends on what sort of politics emerges, and on the wider political culture and environment. Where the public domain is merely an aggregation of private interests then local government is seen in terms of the defence of private space. Jurisdictional boundaries are fences around private space. There is no role for a specifically political mode of decision-making, separate from the competitive market. The legal equality of jurisdictions and the theoretical possibility of resource transfers among them is seen as sufficient measure of equality. Where the public domain is conceived in wider terms, boundaries may define political communities within which a variety of cooperative and conflictual politics can take place. Social and economic forces sustaining inequality and the unequal political and economic capacities of communities are themselves seen as legitimate items of political concern. This does not necessarily require unitary local government. Consolidation and single-tier local government can themselves produce a closure of local government and a reduction in political competition, especially in relation to planning and land use issues. Two-tier local government, on the other hand, may create competing visions over public interests in the same area of land, bring issues into open political debate and fracture the unity of the technical bureaucratic elite. This, however, implies a degree of vertical competition among governments within metropolitan areas, not horizontal competition over resources.

REORGANIZATION AND INTERESTS

Reorganization cannot be considered purely in terms of intellectual argument. Technical arguments about scale and boundaries are inconclusive, and efficiency can be considered only in relation to what local government 'ought' to do. Empirical tests on the relationship of size and 'efficiency' are undermined when the definition of efficiency is itself contested. Nor is it possible to resolve it on the basis of purely deductive argument, as in the Tiebout model and its derivatives. These are ultimately political questions. The political nature of the issue is further emphasized by the implications which government structures have for the balance of power among social and political interests and for substantive public policies. Consolidation and fragmentation are accordingly supported by competing groups, sometimes using the intellectual arguments surveyed above and sometimes by appeals to the values of community or group solidarity.

In favour of consolidation in the 1960s and 1970s was a large body of intellectual opinion, together with modernizing public sector elites. Often located in higher levels of government, these were committed to a consensual form of planning and an implicit denial of the contradiction between growth and redistribution. All levels of government together with the private sector, it was believed, could come together behind agreed strategies. Senior governments had a further interest, at a time when government was expanding in size and complexity, in devolving the details of local administration – the local management of change – to local elites, as long as these were in tune with the central philosophy of planned growth. Hence the combination of structural change, planning, administrative devolution and a search for new territorial collaborators.

In practice, the failure to find these collaborators often led to bypassing local government structures in central policy initiatives. Nor were all officials in higher-level governments agreed on the need for larger-scale units. While planning was associated with consolidation, other services were seen as more local. In some policy arenas, there are communities of central and local officials who fear a strengthening of horizontal coordination as a threat to their functional autonomy. Education is perhaps the most prominent example of this. Only in Britain is it the responsibility of general-purpose local governments, and even there it clings to its professional independence and links with the central departments. In North America, it is entrusted to separately elected boards which, while being consolidated themselves, have resisted merger with general-purpose authorities. In France, the service is centrally organized, escaping both local political and prefectoral control. Other bureaucratic interests are complex. Elements in higher-level governments concerned with planning and control might favour consolidation, with fewer local governments to supervise. Those responsible for detailed regulation might prefer fragmentation, with a larger number of smaller authorities more dependent on central advice. Some officials in smaller local governments might see consolidation as a threat to their autonomy and status but others might see career opportunities in the larger arena. The same consideration applies to local politicians.

Class interests in local government consolidation vary. Urban areas in all four countries are marked by residential segregation based on income and race. The issue is sometimes presented as one of low-income inner city areas and high-income suburbs. Upwardly mobile middle-class residents forsake the city for the suburbs in search of low taxes, high amenities and social exclusion while retaining access to city facilities. While there is some truth to this in Britain and the USA, matters are more complicated. In France and parts of Canada, the middle classes have not abandoned the cities. In France, it is rather the working class which has moved to the periphery as a result of public housing schemes or the high price of city property. In Scotland and some cities of northern England, too, the poorest sections of the population are found at the urban periphery. In many American cities, white-collar employment has moved to the suburbs, producing inter-suburban commuting. The complexities of geography, however, do not alter the fact of spatial segregation which, coinciding with jurisdictional boundaries, creates new interests in consolidation. Working-class interests and the poor have an interest in enlarging the tax base of their jurisdictions to encompass the wealthy areas. This can facilitate redistribution, force suburban residents to pay their share of city services and may allow residential segregation to be reduced. These effects, however, depend on the mobilization of political forces. If the effect of consolidation is to deprive working-class voters of their majority, they will not be any better off. So in Britain and France small working-class jurisdictions have resisted consolidation. In the USA, the issue is further complicated by race. By the 1960s, a number of cities had black voting majorities or near-majorities and began to elect black mayors. This was important not only within the cities themselves but also as a black power base in national politics. Consequently, blacks have tended to oppose moves towards metropolitan consolidation, preferring the limited degree of power which they have within restricted city boundaries.

In wealthier and exclusively white areas, there is a corresponding set of interests in resisting consolidation with its threat of higher taxes, redistributive measures, low-income housing and the social and racial integration of schools. Within central cities, on the other hand, there is often middle-class support for annexation of suburbs precisely to reduce working-class or black voting strength. By the 1970s, this had been identified in the USA as a ploy to prevent the emergence of black electoral majorities and the courts began to intervene under the provisions of the Voting Rights Act, usually requiring a change to a ward-based electoral system to safeguard black influence in the expanded city (ACIR, 1982). The incorporation of areas as new municipalities can be used to the same effect, allowing areas to retain tax receipts and practise exclusionary zoning while leaving poorer areas unincorporated. In Britain, resistance by suburbs to incorporation into city-based authorities underlay much of the opposition to the Redcliffe-Maud and Wheatley proposals of 1969. The major concerns were higher taxes, social integration and the prospect of low-income public sector housing. In France, too, communal independence has allowed mayors to resist low-income housing development.

Partisan stakes in consolidation are closely tied to social class and race. The Redcliffe-Maud proposals for England in 1969, which built on the cities in which Labour had its power base, were supported by the Labour government and rejected by the Conservatives. The

Conservatives' own reform, building on the counties, was opposed by Labour. Earlier, the Labour Party had put up a strenuous opposition to the dismantling of its power base in the London County Council and its replacement by the Greater London Council. Ironically, it was the determination of a number of Conservative-controlled rural and suburban areas not to come into the new arrangement which allowed Labour to win control of the new Council (which was later abolished by a Conservative government). In Scotland, by contrast, the Conservatives lacked a strong power base in local government and so were prepared to proceed with the recommendations for regional governments, including one covering half of Scotland which could be expected to be under permanent Labour control (Keating, 1975). In France, reorganization of local government was one mechanism used (largely unsuccessfully) by the Gaullists in the 1960s to undermine the power base of their opponents in the localities. For their part, the Communists have defended the institution of the commune, opposing all moves to merger or compulsory cooperation with increasing ferocity as the number of their municipal power bases has shrunk. In the USA, proposals for reorganization have also taken on partisan tones. In the past, Republican state legislatures tried to use it to break up Democratic urban machines. The general absence of parties in Canadian local government has reduced the importance of this factor there, but partisan considerations affected the Manitoba government's decision to reorganize Winnipeg in the 1960s (Brownstone and Plunkett, 1983), while the Quebec provincial government feared the political consequences of antagonizing Montreal's mayor Drapeau in the 1970s (Sancton, 1983).

Consolidation can have a more direct impact on national politics. Higher-level governments, reluctant to establish potential rivals, are wary of endowing capital cities with strong local councils. Paris did not receive its own mayor until 1976 and the abolition of the Greater London Council owed a great deal to its high political profile. In federal systems, state and provincial governments may feel even less secure in the presence of large-scale local governments. Even smaller changes can raise national fears. In France, the opposition to communal mergers can be understood only in relation to the importance of local political office as a power base in national politics. There is a general agreement among members of the political class that no change should be made without their consent, with big city mayors looking after their weaker brethren. In Britain, the interests of individual Members of Parliament are at stake, since the parliamentary boundary commissions take into account local government units in making their recommendations. Merging Labour and Conservative areas for local government purposes thus creates alarm at Westminster.

These political considerations can unite otherwise antagonistic social and political forces in defence of the status quo. Politicians who have come to power in a particular system may be averse to risk and prefer to secure their present position while conceding the same to their opponents. In Britain and France, the tendency for low-income housing to be placed in the constituencies of left-wing politicians reflects more than simply the greater need there. British Labour or French Communist councillors might believe in principle in dispersing such housing but vote with their right-wing opponents to keep it concentrated within left-wing fiefdoms jurisdictionally separated from middle-class areas. Black politicians in the USA can agree with white suburbanites on the undesirability of consolidation, carrying their voters with them. In France and the USA, a sense of solidarity among mayors leads those in large cities to defend their small city colleagues, fearing that any attack on local power bases threatens them all. Sometimes, this is taken as evidence of satisfaction with fragmented government, an appreciation of its democratic virtues and problem-solving capacity (Ostrom *et al.*, 1988). In fact, it reflects the satisfaction of the political elite and an appreciation of the limits of the situation. Whether fragmentation is effective in promoting the interests of all city dwellers is another question.

Business leaders have complex interests in consolidation. In so far as fragmented local governments are in a weaker position to make redistributive demands, and must compete with each other to attract business with favourable policies, business has an interest in fragmentation. On the other hand, business development requires infrastructure, land assembly and coherent policies across metropolitan areas, and the incentives which fragmented local governments offer to business are often of dubious value. Business leaders have supported the elimination of governments in which lack of professionalism, patronage or hostility to business have been seen as obstacles. So activist and pro-development business groups have often endorsed consolidation but worried about the potential of large-scale local government controlled by the left and the redistributive demands which might ensue. In the 1960s, business leaders in Britain, France, Canada and the USA echoed the contemporary demands for regional and metropolitan planning as a framework for growth, though with caveats about the need to maintain business competitiveness and warnings against undue politicization. In other words, they supported development planning informed by the needs of business expansion but resisted the wider conception of planning which links this to social and political objectives.

THE PROGRESS OF CONSOLIDATION

Consolidation of urban governments can take the form of annexation of suburbs by the central city; a merger of municipalities into a new government; or the creation of a two-tier system with an overlying government, directly or indirectly elected. A weaker type of overlying system consists of more or less voluntary cooperation among independent jurisdictions. This is not the place for a detailed account of consolidation but it is appropriate to examine the conditions in which consolidationist forces can succeed, and the strength of the opposition. Systems themselves differ according to whether initiative for change comes from higher-level governments or from localities, and the procedural difficulties involved. In Britain, the formal obstacles are minor. Initiative for change comes almost entirely from national government, there is no constitutional limitation on the changes which can be made and no provision for voter approval or for an individual city to negotiate its own governmental structure. The position in Canada is similar, except that it is the provincial governments which control the system. There is also provision in most Canadian provinces for local initiative on annexation and a greater willingness to tailor local government structures to the needs of individual cities; but nowhere are there referendum requirements (Sancton, 1990). In France, there is no constitutional obstacle to reform but the interlinking of national and local elites creates serious political obstacles. While the national legislature can change or merge local governments at will, both chambers are dominated by the very people most affected. In the USA, there is a large number of procedural devices available to opponents of reform, in the form of state constitutional provisions, home rule charters and referendum requirements. Local government organization is regarded as something to be initiated locally and negotiated, rather than imposed from above.

Annexation of suburbs by the central city was fairly common in Britain and North America in the late nineteenth and early twentieth centuries. Increasing resistance and the reluctance of higher-level governments to force the issue led to a decrease in the practice, and postwar suburban expansion left large areas outside city jurisdictions. In parts of the USA, the separate incorporation of suburbs as cities in their own right became more common as a barrier to annexation, which continued mainly in the south and involved unincorporated areas (Harrigan, 1989). In France, annexation is virtually impossible, given the strength of communal boundaries. In Canada, annexation has encountered increasing opposition. Mergers of cities do take place in the USA, but involving only small jurisdictions. In France, too, communal mergers have been few in number and have involved small, rural areas.

A renewed push for consolidation came in the 1960s with the increased emphasis on planning and service expansion. It focused largely on the creation of metropolitan-wide governments to plan in collaboration with higher-level governments. By leaving a second tier of local jurisdictions underneath, it was thought possible to combine metropolitan planning with the needs of local democracy. Perhaps more importantly, it allowed existing elites to retain their power bases and limit the potential for equalization. Most attempts at metropolitan reorganization, however, have been frustrated or severely attenuated by opposition and a failure to reconcile the technocratic view of planning with political realities.

The most radical reforms were possible in Britain and Canada, where constitutional and political obstacles were smallest. In Scotland, the conditions were present for a major overhaul. Reform was initiated by a cohesive administrative elite in the Scottish Office which had been pressing the cause of regional planning since the 1940s (Smith and Wannop, 1985) and which had become increasingly frustrated in the 1960s with fragmented local government's inability to provide infrastructure to complement central government's regional development strategies (Keating, 1975). Their ideas, endorsed by a Royal Commission (Wheatley, 1969), required powerful planning regions which would control infrastructure and the main spending services to enable their plans to be carried out; second-tier districts would have more limited functions. Though the Labour Party, which had endorsed the proposals, lost office before they could be implemented, the succeeding Conservative government, with little political stake in Scottish local government, allowed the civil servants to proceed. There were some changes. The potential for fiscal equalization and social integration was reduced by assigning public sector housing to the districts and, in response to local pressures, some Glasgow suburbs were allowed to remain outside the city district. The county of Fife successfully made a sentimental case to become a separate region (Keating, 1975). Otherwise, the central administrative elite succeeded in its design for powerful metropolitan regions, notably in the Glasgow area.

In contrast, proposals for radical reform in England were the victim of political calculation. The Redcliffe-Maud Commission's proposal for unitary city regions outside the major metropolitan centres, endorsed by Labour, were overturned by the incoming Conservative government of 1970 in favour of a two-tier system based on existing counties and more favourable to Conservative interests. The cities were subordinated to the counties, though the housing function was kept at the district level. As a partisan measure, the reform was put through over the strenuous opposition of the Labour Party though the proposals of the subsequent Labour government to allow city districts to resume many of their former powers had not been implemented when the government fell in 1979. For the six main conurbations, the Redcliffe-Maud proposals for a two-tier metropolitan system were retained though the Conservatives progressively weakened the powers of the upper tier and narrowed their boundaries as the proposals proceeded to implementation. The metropolitan counties thus emerged as a pale reflection of the Scottish regions, tightly drawn around the urban areas and without the controlling and spending powers needed to make their plans a reality.

What sealed the fate of the metropolitan counties was the type of politics which they sustained. They provided a political base for left-wing opposition to the post-1979 Thatcher government. They also mounted a number of programmes to intervene in the local economy. This was in direct conflict with the views of the central government, which favoured a public choice approach of fragmenting local government, reducing the scope of planning and intervention and enhancing the role of business. The metropolitan counties were summarily abolished in 1986, along with the Greater London Council, established by a Conservative government in 1963.

Canadian provinces face no constitutional obstacles to local government reorganization and the general absence of party politics at municipal level reduces the stake of provincial governments in the issue. On the other hand, there is an awareness of the fiscal stakes in consolidation, and that reorganization can have a political cost. The earliest metropolitan government in North America was in Metropolitan Toronto, established in 1954 in response to problems of planning and infrastructure provision. Afraid of the political potential of a powerful metropolitan government and wishing to carry local elites with it, the Ontario provincial government provided for an indirectly elected council with a chairman appointed by the province. In 1966 the lower-tier municipalities were reorganized into six cities and boroughs. Not until 1988 was the council directly elected. In the 1970s, the principle was extended to the rest of the province, with a proposal for 29 regions to be indirectly elected from existing municipalities, including the formerly independent cities. The new upper-tier authorities were much weaker than English counties or Scottish regions with the existing local elites retaining control not only of the new system (through indirect election) but also having an input into the process of reform. With the incremental approach to change, progress was slow and the political cost so high in relation to the results that it was abandoned in 1975 with only 11 of the intended 29 regions established. In 1990, the province returned cautiously to the issue, taking care to carry local interests with it.

Another notable Canadian case is Winnipeg, where reform proposals were affected by partisan manoeuvring. A two-tier system set up in 1960 was replaced in 1972 by the New Democratic Party provincial government which had long had a major political stake in the city. In its place a consolidated structure, Unicity, was established. While some authors have hailed this as a radical innovation (Brownstone and Plunkett, 1983), others have insisted that the dominance of suburban and business interests and the failure to politicize the system have meant that there has been little real change (Kiernan and Walker, 1983). In Montreal, where the mayor had ambitions to annex the neighbouring municipalities, all that was achieved was a rather weak urban community with some fiscal equalization capacity (Sancton, 1983).

In France, the 1960s saw a series of attempts at metropolitan government, inspired by the needs of planning and the desire of Gaullist governments to outflank their opponents who were entrenched in the territorial power structure. Progress was slow and incremental, especially after the Gaullists themselves put down local roots and many of their leaders became 'notablized'. In 1959, regional coordinating prefects were appointed, joined five years later by corporatist regional development councils (CODERs) appointed from local and central government and regional economic and social elites. When in 1969 de Gaulle proposed to strengthen the regions while abolishing the

Senate's role in representing local interests at the centre, he aroused the opposition of a large section of the political class and the resulting referendum defeat precipitated his own resignation. His successors were more circumspect. Pompidou established indirectly elected regional councils in 1972, firmly under the control of the existing notables. In the course of the 1970s, the Socialist Party was converted to regionalism and promised the direct election of regional councils but in practice their decentralization reforms after 1981 benefited the communes and departments. Direct regional elections were postponed until 1986 when the departments had had four years to consolidate their new position, and their powers remained restricted.

In the urban areas, progress towards reform and consolidation was similarly incremental. Nine urban communities were created in the 1960s, grouping communes for a variety of purposes. While the first communities were compulsory, later groupings have been voluntary, though with financial incentives provided by the state. The councils of the communities are indirectly elected from the constituent communes and, while they have partisan control, they tend to proceed by consensus and avoid bold policy initiatives. Other groupings of communes are special-purpose syndicates either for a single function or a group of functions. The compulsory merger of communes or departments is such a hopeless prospect that governments have long since even bothered to think about it. Compulsory inter-communal cooperation is in the same category and by the 1970s even the provision of financial incentives for cooperation aroused enough passionate opposition to kill the proposals of the Guichard (1976) report. So when the socialists adopted their decentralization programme for implementation after 1981, no changes in local government boundaries and no mergers of municipalities were included. Instead, decentralization benefited the existing units, and fragmentation persisted. The problems which this caused for economic development and planning eventually led the Socialist government to propose a degree of voluntary consolidation in 1990. While compulsory consolidation is still ruled out, the prefect was given power to propose new urban communities. Instead of voting to opt in, communes would be included unless they opted out. Schemes would have to be drawn up for all agglomerations with populations over 100 000, with the possibility of communities as low as 30 000 population. Communes could decide on the list of powers to be transferred but these must include economic development and strategic planning. The *taxe professionnelle* would be equalized throughout the urban community. This was intended to overcome the problem of competitive development, but did not go nearly as far as some members of the Socialist Party would have liked in strengthening the upper tier and equalizing resources.

In the USA, calls for wholesale radical reform were also heard in the 1960s, from bodies such as the Advisory Commission on Intergovernmental Relations and the Council for Economic Development. Yet the American system does not lend itself to sweeping change. Instead, progress is piecemeal and incremental. From the 1960s, the federal government tied some of its urban funding to the creation of metropolitan institutions. A number of proposals have been made to merge cities and suburbs under new over-arching jurisdictions or to bring cities under strengthened county government, but few have succeeded. Notable exceptions are in Nashville, Jacksonville, Indianapolis and Miami. In the 1960s, opposition was strongest in the suburban areas but by the 1970s urban politicians, especially black political leaders, were becoming equally vocal in resistance. By the 1980s, opposition was so general that reformers ceased even to press the issue. In St Louis, where most reformers believe that city–county consolidation is desirable, the issue is considered such a sure loser that the series of reform proposals in the 1980s confined themselves to reducing fragmentation in the county area. In Detroit, where competition for economic development threatens all the municipalities, consolidation is not even an issue. So metropolitan reform in most American cities has taken the weakest form, that of voluntary cooperation, the creation of special districts for some expensive infrastructure services and the creation of Councils of Government (COGs). The latter are often a response to federal requirements for financial support, but reductions in federal urban spending and the relaxation of conditions mean that the federal government is no longer a force for consolidation. COGs themselves vary in effectiveness, but have failed to establish themselves as power centres.

METROPOLITAN GOVERNMENT: A SUCCESS OR FAILURE?

Metropolitan government has not been a success story in any of the four countries. Except in Scotland and parts of Canada, opposition has frustrated its establishment. Even in the British case, where the weak sense of territorial identity together with the power of central government and its autonomy from localist pressures permit radical reform, the very same factors militate against metropolitan government establishing a firm political base. The casual manner in which the English metropolitan counties were abolished in 1986 astonished foreign observers as much as the ease with which the new system had been established in the previous decade. The benefits which higher-level governments may see in reform are rarely worth the political cost of change: this was the conclusion to which the government of Ontario came in 1975. The British Labour government of 1974–9 hesitated in its plans to undo the Conservative reorganization while many Conservatives considered the Thatcher government's attack on the metropolitan councils in the mid-1980s a squandering of political capital.

In the USA and France, local elites have managed to maintain more control of the process. In the USA, this is due to the traditions of decentralization and local home rule. In France, ironically, it is the result of a system of centralization which has forced local elites to secure access to power at the centre. American local elites have maintained their local power bases at the cost of a loss of effective influence, since governmental fragmentation has reduced their leverage over the private sector while changes in the national political balance have resulted in a loss of federal financial support. Wealthy municipalities can conserve their resources and defend their private space, while poorer ones must increasingly manage their own penury. Political leaders in the poorer municipalities still prefer this to a consolidation in which their own power bases would be at risk. In France, fragmentation has reduced local political elites' power in relation to business interests, but the creation of new urban communities will attenuate the effects of this. French local elites have used their high degree of integration in national politics to ensure that the cost of fragmentation is borne by the central state.

Reorganization has not succeeded in one objective, the creation of a new political class of political managers to collaborate in the pursuit of planned development. In France, the decentralization reforms have benefited the existing elites. In the USA, reform has itself largely been frustrated. In Britain, there has been a change in local political elites but not that which the reformers planned. Reform coincided with a politicization of local government. The Greater London Council and metropolitan counties provided a basis for a 'new urban left' committed to major changes in municipal practice and prepared for confrontation with a more ideological, right-wing central government. Partisanship exacerbated central–local conflicts and undermined the consensual approach which was the essence of the planning visions of the 1970s.

Where they have been established, metropolitan governments have tended to be rather weak. Williams (1971) divides services into system-maintenance functions such as water supply and drainage, and social-access functions, such as zoning, schools and housing which influence distributional equity, claiming that it is the former which tend to be taken up to metropolitan level, with wealthy jurisdictions insisting on retaining control of the latter. There is certainly some truth to this generalization. Even in the Scottish case, with the strongest upper tier, public sector housing was retained as a lower-tier function. Establishment of metropolitan government is thus in itself no guarantee of distributional equity, as opponents of consolidation have not hesitated to point out.

Even if strong powers are given to upper-tier governments, the prospects for equalization depend on the political balance there. A metropolis which is merely a federation of municipalities (especially when indirectly elected) may find it difficult to redistribute resources, or to plan strategically, having no metropolitan constituency. In the French urban communities, there is a tendency to *saupoudrage*, the scattering of funds in small amounts to benefit constituent communes equally. A directly elected, politicized metropolitan council such as Strathclyde Region in Scotland, will be less prone to this (Keating, 1988a; Wannop, 1989). Above all, the ability to take strategic planning decisions and redistribute resources (within prevailing economic constraints) depends on a sense of political legitimacy and of social solidarity such that all decisions are not perceived as merely an extension of self-interested individual choice. It is the weakness of such a sense in the American political culture as much as the procedural obstacles which has hindered the attempt to establish effective metropolitan-level institutions.

6. The Politics of Distribution

THE ORIGINS OF REDISTRIBUTION

Local governments are subject to a series of social demands to intervene to alter the distribution of wealth and income. Some of these reflect wider expectations of government in democratic societies; others arise from the workings of the urban and political systems in distributing opportunities. Yet there is a large literature to the effect that local governments cannot redistribute income and wealth since this is in contradiction to their imposed role in facilitating investment and growth (Heidenheimer *et al.*, 1983; Peterson, 1981; King, 1984; Schneider, 1989). The 'limited city' is presented as the prisoner of its environment, reducing the effect of redistributive policies to the purely symbolic.

Before considering how far city governments do redistribute, it is necessary to consider why they might wish to do so. For public choice theorists, redistributive politics remains a mystery which their analytical tools are unable to elucidate. As long as the basic unit of analysis is the self-seeking individual and satisfaction of individual demands the sole criterion of public policy, there is no rationale for depriving anyone of resources to give to someone else. Policy is aimed at creating the conditions in which everyone can satisfy their own present demands given the present distribution of resources and opportunities. The nearest to a social utility function is the Pareto principle that a policy which makes at least one person better off without making anyone else worse off is to be preferred. Policies which advantage some at the expense of others fall outside of this. The best which public choice theorists can do to explain redistribution is to revive the old utilitarian argument that wealthy individuals derive a vicarious but still selfish satisfaction from doing good. Besides being tautological, this defines out of existence the central issue – the conditions under which social entities will produce policies oriented to individual gratification or to wider social goals.

On the political left, class analysis provides firmer grounds for redistribution. According to socialists, private ownership in the economic realm systematically disadvantages classes of people who then seek remedy in the political realm. In European socialism, the disadvantaged are identified with the working class, allowing an aggregation of workplace issues of industrial bargaining, political contestation in the state and urban social struggles. The coalitions of the disadvantaged which formed the basis for European social democracy, however, are breaking down. In the USA such a coalition was never established and in Canada it has been historically weak. Affluence has reduced the have-nots to a minority unable to command national political power except in alliance with better off sections of the population. De-industrialization, particularly in the cities, has decimated the relatively well-paid, organized manual working class, polarized class relations and reduced the weight of labour-dominated coalitions. The disadvantaged in the USA are divided by race and ethnicity, a factor also becoming important in Britain and France, while in all three countries an urban underclass has emerged whose lack of political allies or capacity for mobilization has enabled it to be marginalized.

Redistributional politics is also contingent on cultural and structural factors. In cultures emphasizing solidarity and general interest, the issue is more admissible than in those resting on individual self-gratification as the sole criterion of policy. Solidarity, a term almost unknown in the USA, is prominent in French political debate and exists, albeit contested, in British and Canadian culture. Unlike utilitarianism or public choice, it derives from a view of politics as social construction rather than as mere arbitration of competing interests. In cities with a sense of place, social solidarity at the urban or regional level may exist or be constructed, usually coexisting with other types of solidarity based on class, ethnicity or neighbourhood. This does not, it must be emphasized, require the construction of a common 'city interest' in which other forms of conflict disappear. Rather, it requires a value system in which social solidarity and equity are regarded as legitimate matters of debate and decision. It is then possible for politicians to use the image of munificence to electoral effect (Tymen and Nogues, 1988), albeit balancing this with considerations of cost. In other cultures, by contrast, it is the wealthy and business interests who can present their case as identical with the general good, in a manner reminiscent of Peterson's (1981) analysis.

Structural factors are also relevant. Highly fragmented systems in which jurisdictional boundaries coincide with class and ethnic cleavages militate against social solidarity. This is the case in the USA but markedly less so in Canada. In France, fragmentation also inhibits redistributive politics but this is modified by a stronger national state and sense of solidarity; the fact that communal boundaries are not artifacts of class and ethnic difference but a historic legacy; and the provisions in the decentralization laws which allocate to the department the role of solidarity. In Britain, the value of solidarity is under considerable challenge, especially in England, and institutional restructuring – the abolition of metropolitan counties, the poll tax, restrictions on local spending, privatization – has accelerated its decline. In Scotland, there is evidence that values of solidarity are stronger while consolidated local government provides an institutional forum for its expression (Midwinter *et al.*, 1991).

Internal political structures in cities matter, too. Closed systems, limiting the urban agenda and the expression of social demands, are less likely to generate solidarity than more open systems where broader social issues can be debated in the urban context. In at-large electoral systems, neighbourhood issues will be suppressed in favour of city-wide values. Without a strong concept of social solidarity, city-wide interests will in turn be identified with development. Representatives of minorities and the poor in North America have favoured ward systems to express the interests of the residentially concentrated poor. It does not guarantee that they will be catered for, since in a ward-based city council the wealthy also have their representatives. If the needy are divided by income, neighbourhood or race, they may be unable to go beyond a brokerage system in which each group seeks to exact whatever side-payments it can from the urban regime. Ward elections need to be accompanied by a strong party system if majorities are to be mobilized into coalitions in which redistributive policies have a place. This is the function of the European social democratic parties. In the USA, on the other hand, the Democratic Party, the main vehicle for the urban poor, is weak, divided and ideologically heterogeneous, more attuned to brokerage than to programmatic politics. The same applies to the progressive coalitions which appear from time to time in Canadian cities. Another structural feature is the size of jurisdictions. In fragmented systems, there is little scope for redistribution. In larger jurisdictions, not only is there scope for redistribution but the costs can often be spread so widely as to render them politically acceptable.

There is a widespread assumption in the public finance literature that redistribution is not the task of local governments, which should concentrate on 'non-political' housekeeping functions (ACIR, 1988).

This may be supported by the principle of fiscal equivalence – that households should get back from local governments what they contribute, as in a market exchange. This could rule out any service provision unaccompanied by charges, though it is usually conceded that certain services (such as education or police protection) are public goods with external benefits which people may reasonably be obliged both to consume and to pay for. In a confused manner, this type of thinking inspired the British move to a flat-rate poll tax. Government spokespersons argued that some people were getting services and not contributing while others were contributing irrespective of their use of services. The result, however, was a tax unrelated to either service use or ability to pay. It is also argued that redistribution requires the higher legitimacy of sovereign governments, as opposed to limited-purpose corporations such as municipalities. This concept, conservative in origin, is supported for different reasons by the political left. Favouring redistribution, the left has sought to strengthen higher-level governments with a larger resource base. It has often found it easier to mobilize support for redistributive policies at higher levels, especially at national level, though this is not true of all times and places. Indeed, the rise of urban social movements and the conflict between policies favouring development and growth and the needs of deprived social groups has meant that conflicts over distribution are frequently manifested at the local level, wherever they are finally resolved.

THE BENEFICIARIES

Redistribution can take a variety of forms, aimed at individuals or groups and according to different criteria. Local governments find interpersonal distribution difficult because of the instruments at their disposal: they do not control progressive instruments of taxation or, generally, cash welfare disbursements. Some individual-level discrimination in service provision does occur in machine systems, where favours are traded for votes and support. Some observers have seen in the machine system a functional substitute for a welfare state, others an obstacle to its construction. The fact that this allocation takes the form of an exchange of favours and is not guided by wider social criteria, though, excludes it from a consideration of redistributive politics. The same may apply to forms of collective patronage whereby key groups are accorded favours in return for political support. The distinction between collective patronage and clientelism and the normal electoral competition of democracy is not always easy to make (Graziano, 1984) but conceptually at least it is possible to distinguish allocation made purely according to electoral logic from that guided by the broader policy considerations of combating poverty and reducing inequality.

There is an argument over interpretations of urban inequality and poverty. Some see it as an individual problem, caused by the inability of individuals, because of natural or environmental deficiencies, to compete in social and economic life. Others see inequality as structural, caused by the workings of the urban and economic system and soluble only through radical change. Among those espousing the doctrine of individual failure, some see poverty as a syndrome of deprivations of various types, mutually reinforcing and transmitted from generation to generation. Others see it as a set of problems affecting people at different times and places. These differing analyses affect policy prescriptions but the difficulties of definition, like those of targeting, lead policy-makers towards broad group-based approaches rather than refined interpersonal redistribution.

The group basis for redistribution is also defended on the ground that the urban system systematically discriminates against certain groups. This is particularly so when services are organized according to universal or professionally defined criteria, since these may neglect relevant differences. Rectifying this is thus elementary social justice. For example, it is argued that the middle classes make the most use of the education service, that a property-based view of policing gives more of it to those with property, that transport provision benefits those who travel furthest to work. Support for the idea of group rights and benefits varies according to political culture. It is weak in the USA and France, where the respective revolutionary legacies are rooted in individual rights. In France, this is combined with a collective conception of the state but within the state group distinctions have long been suppressed. In Canada, on the other hand, group rights are the dominant form of political discourse. In Britain, group rights compete with an individualist conception of society.

Groups can be defined in several ways. In Britain (and, to a lesser extent, France) social class is the dominant cleavage. As class is usually defined in occupational terms, it is not always easy to transfer the idea to the urban context, but class consciousness together with the activities of the Labour movement have linked the two realms. In

France, the Communist Party has retained a class view of politics, and seeks to use municipal power to further working-class interests. The Socialists, with a more diverse electoral base, put much less emphasis on this. In North America class-based redistribution is a less important theme in urban politics.

Ethnicity as a basis for redistribution is particularly important in the USA, where urban politics often takes the form of ethnic competition for resources. Blacks, with their historic experience of discrimination and exclusion, are able to make a case for special treatment to allow them to join the societal mainstream. In several cities, they have conquered municipal power, allowing them to translate this into policy, though subject to powerful constraints. In Britain, immigrants from the New Commonwealth (the Indian subcontinent, the Caribbean and Africa) have officially been recognized as a needy group in legislation and in the 1980s urban Labour parties gave more attention to the needs of blacks and Asians as a distinct group. In Canada, native peoples are recognized as distinct as, to some extent, are linguistic minorities. In France, poverty and discrimination among immigrants legitimizes special policies.

Gender is increasingly regarded as the basis for redistributive policies, given the 'feminization of poverty', the problems of single mothers and the difficulties of women in combining access to the labour market with family responsibilities. In other cases, the beneficiaries are defined by age. Helping children is widely supported since they cannot be blamed for their own predicament and can be presented as an investment in the future. Old people are often seen as a key electoral group.

Area is probably the most common basis for redistribution in local government. One reason is that poverty does take a spatial form. Urban social and economic restructuring, the property market, racial and class discrimination and public policy have combined to concentrate the urban poor. In North America, the poor are often found in older degraded quarters of cities vacated by the upwardly mobile. In Britain and France, they are as likely to be found in postwar public housing schemes. Yet a spatial definition of poverty has serious shortcomings, depending on how the evidence is interpreted. Area concentrations of poverty do exist, but in most cases they do not contain a majority of the city's poor and may themselves contain more non-deprived than deprived households. Spatial definitions of poverty nevertheless lend themselves to the urban area, itself defined spatially.

Social demands often arise in a neighbourhood framework. It is also easier, given the nature of urban services, to reallocate spatially than among households or individuals across a city as a whole. An area definition has the added advantage of marginalizing the problem, presenting it as a residual issue in urban restructuring, affecting only the poor areas and amenable to localized and small-scale measures. The issue is thereby contained and insulated from other policy fields, notably development policy. This is a conclusion fiercely contested by those who see poverty as a product either of the workings of capitalist society in general, or of the wider urban economic and political structure.

MECHANISMS FOR REDISTRIBUTION

The mechanisms available to local governments for redistribution are everywhere limited. Local taxation is rarely progressive. Though higher rates of property, sales or income tax will extract more money from the rich than the poor, the proportional incidence may be greater on the poor. Local taxes tend to be non-buoyant and obtrusive, making it difficult to raise them. In Britain, the flat-rate poll tax or community charge, explicitly designed to prevent discrimination by income, was widely seen as in conflict with shared values of social solidarity. In the other countries, there are property taxes whose incidence may be vaguely related to wealth or income, but which are inelastic and politically unpopular. In some American jurisdictions, sales taxes exist, again only loosely linked to income and without a progressive rate structure. Even local income taxes in the USA tend to be levied at a flat percentage rate on all incomes. Generally, though, higher governments have sought to prevent local governments using their taxation powers to redistribute income.

It is argued in the fiscal federalism literature that local taxation is inherently non-progressive because of the possibility of migration by the wealthy, though where jurisdictions are widely enough drawn this does not in practice appear to be a problem (Bennett, 1989). The real problem may be a political unwillingness to provide for progressive local taxation. The lack of progressivity is then used by anti-tax groups to attack taxation as a whole, and with it high levels of spending. In the USA, several states have adopted property tax limitations. In Britain, the result of complaints about the unfairness of property taxes, which did have some progressivity, was the introduction of a tax with no progressive element whatever. In France, on the other hand, recent reforms have introduced progressivity into the property tax levied by departments, the tier explicitly given responsibility for social solidarity and sufficiently large to discourage outmigration. This is done by linking the tax to income levels.

It is possible in some systems to shift the tax burdens from households onto businesses, either by a differential assessment of property values or by differential rates of taxation. This also allows cities to export part of the tax burden to shareholders and consumers outside their jurisdiction. While such tax-exporting is widely condemned in the economic literature (Bird and Slack, 1983) it does permit central city jurisdictions with a large business tax base and with needy populations to extract resources. Some American states permit differential assessment and taxation, as to a very limited extent do some Canadian provinces. A number of American states permit taxation of the incomes of non-resident workers, though others regard this as an unacceptable example of tax-exporting and forbid it or require a lower rate. French municipalities can now alter the balance between taxes to shift the burden. Some councils, usually Communist, take advantage of this, but others are afraid of losing businesses and go rather for business tax abatement. In the USA, too, councils are usually afraid of losing business, though in Canada this seems less of a worry to cities. In Britain differential rating was not possible even before the nationalization of business taxes.

Some local governments use their own hiring policies and those of their suppliers to promote opportunities for particular groups. In North America, there are provisions for the differential hiring of racial minorities, which have had considerable effects in some parts of the USA. Indeed, the proportions of blacks in senior administrative positions is one of the most significant changes made by black mayors. Minority hiring policies are also imposed on private firms contracting with cities. In Canada, a series of policies exists to increase the proportion of women in public employment. In Britain and France, the lesser salience of race in political life has meant that the issue has had less prominence, though there have been efforts by ethnic minorities in Britain to use access to local government as a means of expanding group opportunities.

There are several problems in using public hiring as a mechanism for social equality and redistribution. Favouring members of historically deprived groups may achieve a form of intergroup justice at the expense of interpersonal injustice. Nor are all group claims compatible. For example, a policy favouring the hiring of women may discriminate against male members of minority groups and vice versa. Yet it is difficult to be more sophisticated in positive discrimination since the policy can operate only on the basis of visible differences – meaning, in practice, gender, race and possibly language. The scope for achieving major change through municipal hiring policies is limited, given the small numbers of people involved. Sometimes, it is no more than tokenism, a symbolic gesture to disadvantaged groups, if not always to the most disadvantaged individuals within them. In other cases, the aim may be to alter the way in which local government operates by introducing greater concern for groups in administrative practice. Given the power of bureaucracies and their operating cultures, this may be an important goal. It is not always clear, though, that changing the composition of the bureaucracy will change major decisions, given the constraints under which local governments operate. There is an additional danger that differential group hiring policies will degenerate into patronage reminiscent of the old urban machines.

Most policies for redistribution therefore concentrate on spending decisions and the possibilities for spatial and/or social targeting. Much of local government consists of purely housekeeping services like refuse collection or traffic management organized according to professional, technical criteria. Others are public goods like clean air or law and order which are impossible to allocate selectively. Yet other services (such as social service provision) are explicitly selective, intended to redress social and economic inequality, while others (such as education or planning) can potentially be so used.

At one time, local governments had extensive social welfare responsibilities. Since the interwar period, income support has progressively been taken over by higher levels of government. In the USA major shifts in responsibility occurred between 1967 and 1982 (Ladd and Yinger, 1989). Local governments themselves have been eager to rid themselves of a function which is costly and brings few political benefits (Levitan and Taggart, 1976) and in only two states do the localities remain the dominant welfare provider (ACIR, 1982). In Canada, cities retain a role in welfare payments but subject to close provincial regulation and with limited discretion to pay higher rates. In Britain, local governments have had no role at all in welfare payments since the Second World War. The move to national provision was supported both by conservatives fearful of Poplarism – the payment of high welfare rates by left-wing councils – and by socialists desiring equality and uniformity. In France, most cash assistance is administered by central government but departments and cities have long had a role in certain types of payment, subject to a national minimum (Bélorgey, 1984). Since 1982, departments have assumed responsibility for welfare payments and there are some marked differences in social spending among them (Fayolle, 1989). In the 1980s, several cities anticipated the national minimum income scheme through provisions of their own. Most cash payments, though, are at national level and the minimum income scheme has now been incorporated into a national programme. There are common reasons for the upward drift of responsibility: the fiscal burden, especially in the interwar depression; the increased mobility of the population; the growth of national welfare states; and the lack of appeal to local politicians of a function which divides the population and brings few votes. In other respects the politics differs among countries. In the USA, conservatives have been more favourable than liberals to local welfare provision, since the local arena is less amenable to redistributive demands. In Britain, conservatives have favoured centralization through a fear of the strength of local redistributive demands and socialist councils.

Local governments retain wider responsibilities in non-cash social services. In the USA, where there is no national health service, local governments may provide hospitals giving access to groups who otherwise would lack health care. Local governments have varying roles in the administration of social work and community development, which is provided directly in Britain but elsewhere often undertaken by special agencies and voluntary organizations. Whether or not they run the services directly, they have the ability to spend money in the field. Financing these functions out of local tax revenue has an undeniable redistributive effect.

Other local government services may be targeted to specified groups, depending on the nature of the service and its mode of distribution. Many local services are demand-led, available to those who choose to take them up. In the case of post-compulsory education, libraries, highways and certain types of cultural activity, these are often disproportionately the better off. Bureaucratic and professional routines are another obstacle. Professional and technical criteria for resource allocation and the routines of service-delivery agencies often do not easily accommodate criteria based on broad socially redistributive principles. Redistributive policies and anti-poverty programmes may thus require an attack on bureaucratic power structures and professional standards.

This is not always easy, especially where professionals are strongly entrenched, control their own service-delivery agencies or are insulated by legal provisions or higher governments.

Transport spending has a major social incidence. It can concentrate on highway building or on public transport. If the latter, it can concentrate on capital or revenue and be targeted to needy areas or follow demand. In practice, transport spending is often regressive, benefiting long-distance commuters, though efforts may be made to change this. One French Communist council decided to abandon the apparently socialist policy of free municipal buses once it became apparent that it was mainly benefiting the middle class (Schain, 1985).

Education has been seen as a means of achieving social and class integration and equality of opportunity. It permits policy to break into the cycle of deprivation at an early stage and can be targeted spatially, given the neighbourhood focus of schools. In Britain, comprehensive education, intended to break down class barriers and benefit working-class children by eliminating selection at age eleven, was introduced by Labour-controlled local councils before becoming national policy. Some of the earliest experiments in inner city policy focused on Educational Priority Areas. Several British councils provide additional teaching resources to needy areas. In France, where matters of curriculum and teacher recruitment are the responsibility of central government, local councils have extensive spending responsibilities in education, and left-wing councils have used these to increase spending levels and promote equal opportunities. In both Britain and France, though, the use of education as an instrument of social integration has been frustrated by the pattern of residential segregation. Neighbourhood schools thus come to be dominated by members of one social class or racial group, while the perception of this in turn leads more parents to move out of the school attendance area. The British experiment in comprehensive education was to a large degree frustrated by this, with schools becoming in some respects more socially segregated than in the old selective system.

In North America, education is usually entrusted to separate school boards which, while elected, are at one remove from city governments and politics. It is more difficult, therefore, to use them as an instrument of broader social policies. Matters are further complicated by the fragmentation of school districts in the USA, allowing education, like municipal government generally, to be used as an instrument of social and racial exclusion (Harrigan, 1989). After legal segregation in education had been struck down by the Supreme Court in 1954, *de facto* segregation remained and was reinforced by residential segregation. It required a further series of court rulings in the 1970s to force school boards to bus children to achieve racial mix in schools. This policy, besides being highly unpopular, stimulated more white families to leave city jurisdictions while attempts to get courts to enforce cross-district bussing have had limited success.

In recent years, there has been a retreat from education as social policy towards a more economic conception of its purpose. The emphasis is less on social equality and integration, more on the promotion of economic competitiveness and vocational skills. This reflects both national priorities and the view of local elites that this is the major requirement of urban development.

Urban planning may also be used as an instrument of social equality, curtailing market advantages in property, providing access to public facilities and land uses to those on low incomes. This requires an expansive conception of planning and of the public interest in land use. In France, extensive powers exist to control land markets, to retain land for public use and to provide public access to major facilities. In the USA, on the other hand, planning is seen essentially as a means of arbitrating among competing private claims and zoning (the most common form of planning) was introduced as a mechanism for preserving private property values. The constitutional protection of private property weakens the public power in land use matters while fragmentation of government militates against employing planning powers as an instrument of social integration. In the USA, and to a large extent in Canada, the limited nature of the planning system means that social gains can be extracted from development only in exchange for concessions to developers. Linkage policies have been introduced in some American cities, requiring developers to provide social facilities or low-income housing in return for planning concessions. In Canada, density bonusing allows developers to exceed prescribed density levels in return for similar provision. The problem with this is that the social benefits tend to be rather small in relation to need, and bear a heavy cost in terms of the environmental concessions made to secure them. Where linkage policies are routine, they may become simply a means for developers to purchase zoning consent, further weakening public power. In Britain, the planning system is stronger but has been weakened in recent years. Successive attempts by Labour governments to capture for social use the profit in rising land values accruing from planning decisions failed, and the relevant legislation was repealed by the Conservatives. In the 1980s, planning restrictions have been relaxed while in certain cities the development planning function has been taken over by development corporations largely closed to social considerations. More generally, the emphasis on urban development and competition for investment has led local governments everywhere to de-emphasize social considerations in planning, albeit to varying degrees. The growth of public–private partnerships in development policy and the insulation of development from other policy arenas has had the same effect (see Chapter 7).

More radical approaches to redistribution have focused on encouraging the urban poor to exert influence in the local political arena. Community development combines measures to improve matters using local resources and help in building community structures. The theory is that the urban middle classes are advantaged by their superior political skills and familiarity with administration, allowing them a disproportionate share of benefits. If poorer areas can develop such skills, the balance might be redressed. A series of community development strategies has placed an emphasis on getting the urban poor to participate in the solution of their own problems. Yet there are dangers and problems in the approach. Like other area-based approaches, community development risks a marginalization of the question of inequality, as something amenable to small-scale ameliorative projects. Effort may be concentrated on the neighbourhood when the real problem is elsewhere, in the wider urban or economic system. Community leaders may be coopted into urban strategies by being rewarded with small-scale payments which they are able to distribute as patronage. Neighbourhoods may be divided against each other in the fight for resources. So, without a strong neighbourhood and spatial concern within city government as a whole, community politics may be another measure of closure and containment.

CONSTRAINTS ON REDISTRIBUTION

The major obstacle to using local government powers for redistribution remains the open nature of the system. Any serious attempt at raising local taxes to redistribute to the poor will lead the wealthy to migrate and so be self-defeating. The more decentralized the system, the more local government becomes the prisoner of its economic environment. The more cities compete for investment, development and increases in their tax base, the less able they are to redistribute. Whether redistribution and development are really incompatible or not, they are widely perceived as being difficult to reconcile. In the case of conflict, those urging priority for development are likely to have the stronger case, since they can present it as in the interests of the whole city. Minorities and those perceived as the 'deserving poor' are less able to appeal to shared values. The more cities are seen as competing with each other for development, the stronger this constraint becomes. The poorer the city, and thus the more need for social expenditure, the stronger the imperative is felt to engage in growth politics.

There is evidence for this effect both from the USA and from recent changes in France. The extent, however, differs according to the structure of local government and the allocations of functions within it. In highly fragmented systems, where people can choose among local governments while continuing at the same place of work, the incentive to migrate is larger. Both Britain and Canada have relatively consolidated systems of city government (albeit largely lacking in over-arching regional structures). In the USA and France there is great fragmentation. The decentralization of welfare expenditure and social services to the French departments, to be borne on their local tax bases with the help of block grants, has dramatically limited the growth of expenditure (Tymen and Nogues, 1988; Guengant and Uhaldeborde, 1989). Fearful of attracting additional poor, departments have defined eligibility restrictively, though without drastic cuts in provision. Fears have been widely expressed that decentralization will increase social inequality and force poor areas to manage their own penury (Iion, 1987; Preteceille, 1987). The dilemma between growth and redistribution, however, is reduced by the fact that these are the responsibility of different levels. Fragmented suburbs in the USA do not cut social expenditures to keep out the poor because they do not have such expenditures to cut (Schneider, 1989). In turn, American counties and French departments which have welfare functions are not able to zone out the poor, since it is the lower-tier municipalities who have the zoning and urban development function. It is the unitary city government, with responsibilities for both development and social services, which faces the most acute dilemma.

Difficulties in using local government powers for redistribution stem from analytical difficulties, structural constraints and political problems. Programmes to tackle poverty or redistribute resources, while rooted in local politics, have thus often to be taken into the intergovernmental sphere in order to circumvent them.

INTERGOVERNMENTAL APPROACHES

Taking issues of redistribution to higher levels reduces the opportunity cost of social intervention, by providing resources and by allowing existing programmes and routines to remain intact. National urban policies are commonly prescribed as the solution to urban decline, especially by American liberals. Yet they depend on a favourable balance of forces both at central level and in the intergovernmental system. Representatives of the wealthy can also take their concerns into the national arena, as happened in Britain in the 1980s. For much of the postwar period, American federal policies encouraged surburbanization, dispersal, and regressive urban renewal policies (Kantor, 1987; Judd, 1988). Redistributive national urban programmes will come about only if progressive urban leaders possess the requisite political weight and skills. National policies must be informed by a spatial concern which itself is the product of the territorial power structure. Otherwise, national policies will merely reproduce the problems already analysed at local level.

Since the 1960s, Britain and the USA have had a series of national programmes for selective social initiatives in declining cities. French programmes dating from the 1970s were expanded in the late 1980s. These are new funds, reserved for specific purposes and protected from hostile local political influence. Relatively small in scale, they are intended to show what might be done, and influence cities to change their own ways of operating. The early British and American programmes were also inspired by the idea of community development – that is, encouraging neighbourhoods to frame their own demands and programmes. In this way, the local political and bureaucratic arena would be reshaped and deprived communities given a greater say in policy. This did not go down well with existing elected officials. Nor did the latter take to radical community workers employed in national programmes. Requirements for local participation and community development were steadily reduced, but the new generation of community workers and activists were to be a force in the more radical Labour politics which developed in British cities in the 1980s. Levering resources for social programmes, however, requires a will at national level. Civil disturbances such as happened in the USA in the 1960s and Britain and France in the 1980s might appear a sufficient threat to the state to provoke a reaction, but there is more to it than this. Urban riots also undermined support for urban policies in the USA. In Britain, the first initiatives came in the 1960s, and while it is true that some observers were haunted by the American experience, serious urban disturbances did not come until the 1980s and at that time produced a different response. The national ruling coalition is also critical. While political alignments favourable to urban social programmes existed in Britain and the USA in the 1960s, they have given way to administrations and legislative majorities less sensitive to urban social interests and concerned to promote development and the private sector. The Conservative and Republican parties respectively now have little stake in the major cities and have been increasingly unreceptive to demands for urban social programmes (Barnes, 1990). In France and Canada, on the other hand, the cities are the object of serious contestation in national (and provincial) elections. So in Britain and the USA urban programmes have been reduced in scope and geared more to investment promotion and economic development. This has been accompanied in the USA by a relaxation of controls on spending, putting federal urban grants back into a local political arena dominated by development interests. In Britain, a similar effect has been achieved by the addition of controls on urban programme spending and the diversion of substantial amounts of it into urban development corporations (see Chapter 7). In France, on the other hand, local elected elites have largely retained control of the new urban expenditures.

The most ambitious ideas in all four countries were to establish comprehensive national urban policies, bridging the dimensions of physical renewal, social intervention and economic development and involving all levels of government. These encountered formidable analytical difficulties in defining problems and designing policy instruments. In practice, national programmes tended to be seen as add-ons to local spending. Where higher-level governments provide funds for specified social programmes, the effect can be to marginalize those programmes and relieve cities of the need to bend mainline programmes and policies to social needs. As national funding is typically limited in time, local governments in Britain and the USA have often retained separate budget headings for these items so that the programme can be shut down if necessary. Where grant systems are complicated, as in the American urban programmes, local policy-making comes to revolve around 'grantsmanship', levering as such as is available out of higher-level governments rather than devising local corporate strategies. Local political leaders may even see national programmes as a threat to their control over local resources, and as an invitation to vexatious demands.

In Britain, the earliest attempts at selective national policy for cities were housing initiatives and Educational Priority Areas, aiming to break into the cycle of deprivation through early education. In 1968, the Urban Programme was launched as a series of special grants to distressed urban areas. Also in the 1960s, government established the Community Development Project (CDP), an action–research programme in which specially recruited teams were sent into selected distressed areas to explore ways of attacking poverty. The reports of the CDP teams, (especially that in Coventry), concluding that the problem was rooted in capitalist society and could not be solved by marginal, ameliorative efforts, did not commend them to government and the project was discontinued. A series of Inner Area Studies produced a major initiative in 1976. Inner City Partnerships were established in major distressed cities, bringing together central and local government and relevant public agencies. Later, Programme Authorities and Designated Districts were declared in which special funding was available without the whole partnership machinery. Funding was increased substantially and the 'traditional' urban programme remained alongside the new scheme. The objective of the initiative was to mount a coordinated attack on urban deprivation, mobilizing the resources of all agencies concerned. In Scotland, the GEAR project for Glasgow's East End was based on similar principles, but led by the Scottish Development Agency (Keating, 1988a).

From the late 1970s, the urban programme was oriented increasingly to economic rather than purely social goals. Under the Conservative government from 1979, funds were diverted towards capital rather than revenue projects and to private sector activity. In 1983, Urban Development Grants, borrowed from the USA, were introduced for private sector projects. These were replaced in 1988 by the City Grant. Most local governments proved willing to adhere to the new emphasis on development rather than social intervention, though some did express misgivings (National Audit Office, 1990). More opposition was expressed to the decision in the 1980s to establish Urban Development Corporations (see Chapter 7) with an explicitly developmental focus, to which Urban Programme money was then diverted. Between 1984 and 1990, Urban Programme expenditure declined from £380 million to £220 million ($737 million to $426 million) while expenditure on Urban Development/City Grant and Urban Development Corporations increased from £125 million to £550 million ($242 million to $1067 million) (National Audit Office, 1990).

In the USA, Democratic administrations in the 1960s coincided briefly with a liberal Democratic majority in Congress to launch the Great Society and War on Poverty initiatives (Mollenkopf, 1983). In 1964, the Economic Opportunity Act established the Office of Economic Opportunity, with a programme of job training, pre-school education and small business assistance. A Community Action Program was intended to by-pass local governments and involve the urban poor themselves in the development and management of initiatives (Barnekov *et al.*, 1989). Like the British Community Development Project, this was to antagonize both central and local officials and its radical features were soon dropped. The 1966 Model Cities programme was a coordinated attack on physical, social and economic problems in distressed urban areas, managed by local governments in partnership with the federal government. By the late 1960s, the Department of Housing and Urban Development, established in 1964, presided over a bewildering variety of programmes and funds to relieve urban distress. The liberal, pro-urban majority in Congress had now disappeared while disillusionment with the complexity of federal programmes had emerged. The Nixon administration after 1968 sought to reduce the federal role and return social programmes back to the local political arena through reducing and consolidating federal grants (Judd, 1988). General revenue sharing was introduced, allocating federal money with no strings attached. A Comprehensive Education and Manpower Act rolled a series of federal–local contracts into a single system. The 1974 Housing and Community Development Act consolidated seven special-purpose grants into a single one.

Grant consolidation was generally popular with mayors, since it apparently gave them greater control over federal programmes. It was unpopular with representatives of the poor and congressional liberals who feared, correctly, that money would be diverted from social programmes in distressed areas to development. Though the 1977–81 Democratic administration of Jimmy Carter did attempt to mount a new national urban policy, most initiatives were mired in congressional opposition and the thrust to development promotion and private sector initiative was maintained. The President's National Urban Policy Report in 1978 endorsed the emphasis on development and the retreat from social policy while the Urban Development Action Grant (UDAG), one of the few urban initiatives which had little trouble in Congress, was explicitly aimed at encouraging private sector development projects in distressed areas. By 1980, the President's Commission for a National

Agenda for the Eighties was advocating an end to place-based policies in favour of encouraging people to move where jobs were available. Direct financial aid which peaked at 25 per cent of cities' own revenue in 1978, declined thereafter (Ladd and Yinger, 1989). Retrenchment and consolidation were continued by the Reagan administration. General revenue sharing was eliminated altogether while Community Development Block Grants (CDBGs) were cut and further decentralized to states and cities. The result has been a diversion of CDBG funds to development rather than social programmes (GAO, 1983). Comprehensive Employment and Training funding which had provided for public service employment, was terminated and large cuts made in federal housing support (Wolman, 1986; Judd, 1988). The UDAG programme, slated for elimination each year by the Reagan administration, was finally deprived of funds in 1989. Overall, federal grants to state and local governments fell from 3.4 per cent of gross national product in 1980 to 2.4 per cent in 1989 (ACIR, 1989a).

France has not experienced the scale of urban distress found in Britain and the USA, and it was not until the 1980s that a distinct set of urban programmes was adopted. In 1981, the new Socialist government created the *Commission de développement social des quartiers* under mayor Dubedout of Grenoble. This was responsible for a series of neighbourhood initiatives bringing together central and local government with the low-income housing authorities. Expenditure was divided among central government, the region and the city in the proportions of 2:1:3. A *Conseil national de prévention de la délinquence* was set up after disturbances in Lyon reminiscent of American and British experiences. When the Socialists again returned to government after the 1986–8 Chirac administration, urban policy was adopted as a priority. A *Conseil national des villes* was established to absorb the existing agencies, bringing together local elected officials, ministers and outside experts under the presidency of the Prime Minister, with a government and an opposition mayor (who both also hold national mandates) as vice-presidents. A *Comité interministériel pour les villes* was set up to coordinate government policy on cities and distribute the *fonds social urbain,* increased to the still modest sum of F440 million, to which were added line items in individual ministerial budgets for a total of around F2 billion ($400 million). A *Délégation interministérielle à la ville* was established as the executive arm of policy, in charge of local initiatives, and associated with all items in the finance law which concern urban policy.

The urban programme in France remains small, but is increasing. While the sums available through the *fonds social urbain* are modest by British or American standards, the programme has not been mounted in a context of general cutbacks in intergovernmental aid. Nor have social moneys been diverted to support development projects. More revenue sharing among rich and poor communes has been introduced and regulations tightened to ensure priority for low-income housing. A national minimum income has been established, jointly financed by central and local government. Ministerial statements, in contrast to Britain and the USA, are replete with warnings about the dangers of neglecting social priorities and deprived neighbourhoods in the quest for development. Rather than treat urban poverty as a separate policy issue, the emphasis is placed on integrating cities into the mainstream of national policy.

There has been little by way of national urban policy in Canada. In 1970, the federal government established a Ministry of State for Urban Affairs. Launched in the hopes of establishing a comprehensive urban policy for Canada (Frisken, 1986), this assumed rather vague responsibilities for coordinating federal policies affecting cities (Cullingworth, 1987). Unlike the British, American and French schemes, this did not represent a response to the discovery of urban poverty or to pressures from city elites for federal support. Indeed, the Ministry did not command a grant programme at all. Rather, it stemmed from a desire within the federal government for a larger role in urban planning and an enthusiasm for techniques of rational forward planning and coordination. Lacking its own programmes, apart from those of the Canada Mortgage and Housing Corporation over which it assumed authority, and resented by the provincial governments as an intrusion on their jurisdiction, the Ministry languished and was abolished in 1979. Since then, urban affairs have remained the almost exclusive responsibility of provincial governments.

HOUSING POLICIES

Of the policies available to local governments to redistribute income and opportunities and to secure social integration, housing is among the most important. Access to housing, its costs and its condition are central issues of urban policy everywhere. Yet not only have governments failed to solve the problems of universal access to affordable housing, some policies serve to make the problem worse. Britain and the USA have national programmes to subsidize owner-occupation through tax relief on mortgage interest, which are socially regressive since relief rises with the size of mortgage and is at an individual's highest marginal rate of tax (though this has now been limited in Britain). It is debatable how much benefit new buyers receive since, housing markets being competitive, the effect is to drive up prices and reduce access to those lacking capital. In Britain, national policy has been to increase the mortgaged stock by forcing up rents for public housing while allowing tenants to purchase at a discount. The abolition of domestic rates left housing as one of the few untaxed forms of consumption, giving a further stimulus to prices. Mortgage subsidies have few friends among economists or urban policy analysts and stand in stark contradiction to the professed beliefs of the national administrations in both the USA and Britain, but they are now so widely available that they have become politically untouchable.

The price of owner-occupation puts it beyond substantial numbers of people. Successful urban growth and development policies, ironically, make matters even worse by pricing low-income housing out of the land market. Some relief may be obtained through rent controls, which prevent landlords exploiting market shortages. In Britain and France, national programmes of rent control have existed for some decades while local schemes are available in some North American jurisdictions. The long-run effect, however, is to reduce the quantity of rented property, especially if buoyant property markets permit landlords to sell out. Security of tenure laws and restrictions on change of use can limit this, but at the cost of under-investment and a neglect of maintenance. In the long run, regulation of the private market has proved no substitute for measures to provide more low-income housing. This task has usually fallen on local governments.

The most extensive system of public housing is in Britain, where municipal councils in the interwar period acquired the duty to build and maintain rental housing. After the war, the sector grew steadily, to peak at around 30 per cent of housing stock, rising to over 50 per cent in Scotland. Both parties encouraged the growth of council housing but it was Labour-controlled cities which were associated with the largest programmes and with a policy of subsidizing rents from local rate income as well as central grants. In France, *habitations à loyer modéré* (HLMs) were built by special agencies, using both central and local funds, though the system was less extensive than in Britain. In the USA, low-income rental housing was also provided by special agencies, drawing funds from both local and higher-level governments. In Canada, it was initially built by the Canada (originally Central) Mortgage and Housing Corporation but was later taken over by provincial agencies.

Subsidizing low-income rental housing from local tax revenues, with support from higher-level governments, is one of the most effective methods available to local governments to redistribute income. On the other hand, a policy of low rents in the midst of a market-based system can cause problems of its own. When combined with pressure to build ever more units, it leads to a decrease in the quality of housing. The search for low-cost solutions has also led to building low-income housing on the cheapest, most easily worked land, producing high-rise developments and large public housing schemes at the periphery of cities. Housing provision was frequently divorced from wider planning considerations or access to employment, shopping and leisure facilities. Social segregation has been reinforced, deprivation and social stress concentrated.

Indiscriminate subsidies to buildings are also a blunt instrument for redistribution, especially in places like the west of Scotland, where up to 80 per cent of the housing stock in some towns came into public ownership. Instead, access to council housing served as an instrument of individual and collective patronage. While political patronage in house allocation in Britain was gradually removed through professional housing management, house building was rarely undertaken without an eye to the electoral consequences. In both Britain and France, the left sought council house building to reinforce its electoral base while the right was equally keen to exclude it from jurisdictions which it controlled (Guglielmo and Moulin, 1986). The result in both Britain and France was further segregation. Jurisdictional boundaries and the allocation of the housing function to the lowest tier of local government have tended to reinforce this.

Public sector housing thus came to be stigmatized as housing for the poor, who could not afford access to owner-occupation. In North America, it tends to be occupied by the poorest and by racial minorities. In France, HLMs were initially occupied by lower-middle-class and skilled working-class families but, as these moved into the expanding owner-occupied market, they were replaced by immigrants (Iion, 1987). By the 1980s, Communist councils, which had previously welcomed the *grands ensembles* turned against them when they needed renovation. Immigrants do not have the vote, and several Communist municipalities maintained quotas for immigrants (Dion, 1986); others cut back renovation funds and bulldozed immigrant quarters to save money and appease racist sentiment among the native working class. In Britain, advocates of council housing had originally envisaged a thriving rental sector and council tenure came to be the norm for a large part of the working class. Quality varied considerably, with waiting lists for the most desirable stock. In the 1980s, however, central government introduced the right to buy at a discount for sitting tenants, resulting in the sale of the best stock and with the aim of transforming council tenure to a residual category, as in North America and France. At the same time, councils were progressively banned from subsidizing council rents from local tax income, forcing up rents and increasing the attractions of owner-occupation. Needy tenants were eligible for housing benefit to help with rents, though the value of this was steadily reduced. As public sector housing, in all the countries considered, becomes a residual category, used only by those who have no other tenure choice and spatially segregated from other neighbourhoods including working-class ones, it becomes more difficult to sustain political support for it, and housing budgets come under further pressure. Unable or unwilling to spend large sums on maintenance and rebuilding, public landlords are regarded by their tenants as little different from private ones. The bureaucratic style of public housing management, criticized as excessively remote, insensitive and paternalistic, does not help.

These problems have led many to advocate an end to public housing provision, with tenants instead subsidized directly through cash allowances paid by national government (Heidenheimer *et al.*, 1983). Indiscriminate subsidy would be removed and tenants given freedom of choice. This has been done in Britain through the housing benefit system but, as a selective subsidy, this has proved vulnerable to cutback. In France, the move in 1977 to individualized subsidies gave HLM managing agencies an interest in attracting the poorest households, as sure clients (Ronai, 1986), maintaining the pattern of segregation.

The experience of new towns in Britain and France, on the other hand, suggests that, with adequate funding and a commitment from national governments, more balanced communities can be created and housing provision planned in relation to employment, leisure and other activities. In France, there have been experiments in integrated rental housing in high-amenity areas, the most spectacular being the Antigone at Montpellier. Planned initiatives such as these require the ability to mobilize large-scale public funding and to control land prices. Cities cannot do this on their own but must rely on higher-level governments. In North America, the lack of powers and resources forces city governments to rely on linkage arrangements with developers whereby low-income housing is provided as a by-product of development. Yet development can itself exacerbate the problem. This is shown by the British experience with urban development corporations (UDCs) and the Scottish Development Agency, based on the American model of urban renewal. These have concentrated on urban regeneration through the stimulation of property markets but, as public agencies, were intended to carry social responsibilities including the provision of low-income housing. The responsibility was particularly sensitive politically since, at the same time as establishing and funding UDCs, central government was cutting back on support for council housing. The evidence shows, however, that low-income housing was consistently neglected and priced out of the market (National Audit Office, 1988a, 1988b; Committee of Public Accounts, 1989).

Voluntary housing associations in Britain have come to occupy a larger role since the 1970s. These are locally-based, more sensitive to tenants' needs and concentrate on the refurbishment and management of older housing, conserving existing communities. There have been experiments in cooperative management of housing by council tenants, extending to the transfer of ownership to the tenants collectively as an alternative to individual house purchase. Housing associations and cooperatives are of major importance as a means of breaking the political deadlock over housing, since they appeal both to Conservatives (as an alternative to council control) and to Labour (as a form of collectivism). They are not cheap, requiring substantial amounts of public money, but their ideological acceptability makes this easier to obtain. Their impact is, however, limited since they account for only a small section of the market and may not always reach the most deprived.

REDISTRIBUTION AND URBAN REGIMES

Redistributive policies at the local level are not impossible, but require the presence of a series of cultural, political and structural factors to be viable. A rationale for redistribution in terms of generally accepted values is needed. A local political system which allows redistributive demands to be articulated and aggregated within a progressive coalition is necessary. Local bureaucratic and professional obstacles need to be overcome. Finally, the intergovernmental system must permit an opening of urban politics, its integration into national politics and the mobilization of resources from high-levels of government. These conditions are found in Europe to a greater extent than in North America, but everywhere are being questioned by the increased emphasis on development and inter-urban competition, the subject of Chapter 7.

7. The Politics of Economic Development

WHY INTERVENE?

Local governments are inescapably involved in their local economies. They have substantial spending and taxation powers, plan and build infrastructure and are responsible for planning and zoning and in some cases education. Protective services such as police and fire are equally essential to business. None of these functions is exclusive to business, and each could be supplied in various ways to benefit different categories of user. Recent years, however, have seen a growth of local government policies explicitly aimed at economic development. Given that this is not one of their statutory responsibilities and that there is widespread doubt about their abilities in the field, this needs to be explained.

Peterson (1981), like many other observers, maintains that cities are engaged in a zero-sum competition for growth, given the porous nature of their economies and the mobility of capital and individuals. This imposes policies favourable to business interests and wealthy households who will otherwise remove themselves, their incomes and their capital, to the detriment of the city as a whole. Cities are seen as engaged in a competition for a fixed amount of capital, the gain of one being the loss of another. Peterson draws attention to a series of powerful influences and constraints operating on city governments. Yet the attempt to present the economy as imposing specific policy imperatives rests on a number of unproven assumptions and underestimates the influence of politics. Comparison of the USA with the other countries shows how different institutional structures alter the nature of the constraint. Peterson himself recognizes that the dependence of American cities on attracting business and wealthy residents may not extend to European countries with fiscal equalization provisions and guarantees for local debt. Yet the proposed solution to the American problem – to extend these European devices to the USA – itself ignores the *political* reasons why this has not been done, reasons rooted in the closure of urban politics examined earlier. Nor is it true that national states, centralization, fiscal equalization and debt guarantee insulate European cities from economic influence. They attenuate the effect of economic factors in city politics but, in a world where cities are increasingly competing internationally, do not eliminate it. It is necessary therefore in each urban regime to examine the balance of economic and political influences, the dominant assumptions within the culture and the way in which economic and political pressures are perceived and mediated.

A fundamental problem with Peterson's analysis is the reification of the city and its 'interest'. It is asserted that all citizens of the city have an interest in economic growth and development policies, even if some individuals personally do not benefit. This removes the fundamental issue in growth politics – namely, that not all benefit equally, and that some individuals may be better off in a stagnating city. The postulate of a common city interest in growth begs the question of why citizens should recognize common interests, or why that of the city should take precedence over class, ethnicity or neighbourhood. Common interests can neither be assumed nor arrived at by deduction. Rather, they are a form of social construction which takes different forms at different times and places.

The assumption that growth is a zero-sum competition and takes place only through the attraction of wealthy residents and the awarding of favours to business is questionable as a universal assertion. This depends on the specific economic and political arrangements, and on the strategies for growth. National and regional planning systems are based upon the assumption that growth in different places may be complementary, and one of the arguments for metropolitan consolidation is precisely to encourage this awareness. Mobilizing local resources and extracting resources from higher levels of government may also be alternatives to beggar-my-neighbour development. Indeed, there is abundant evidence that municipal policies to attract businesses to cities through tax and subsidy incentives at the expense of social programmes are rarely effective, except across small distances within metropolitan areas (Wolman, 1988). Nor is the attraction of capital synonymous with economic growth or enhanced social welfare.

It may be argued that city governments do have one compelling interest, in the maximization of their tax base, which in turn requires them to cater to business and wealthy residents whose resources they need. This argument, too, is complex. The fiscal health of the city is related to, but not identical with, its economic health. Ladd and Yinger (1989) find that improvements in the economic health of American cities lead to increases in expenditure need, the balance varying from one city to another. Improvements in the economic health of city residents, on the other hand, lead to lower expenditure needs in several services. The relationship between city economic health and residents' economic health is determined by whether the benefits of growth (in terms of jobs and dividends) are going to city residents. Economic growth will improve fiscal health only if taxable residents are the beneficiaries of growth, or if tax burdens can be exported to non-resident property owners. It is also necessary to ask in whose interest the tax base is being maximized. A city controlled by lower-income interests may wish to impose high taxes on wealthy residents and businesses in order to provide services for the poor. Peterson argues that this is self-defeating since the wealthy will merely relocate out of the jurisdiction. Yet, since inducing them to stay would require the municipality not to tax them, the city government might argue that it had little to lose through their outmigration, especially if this reinforced the electoral base of the local politicians. Institutional arrangements are again critical. Where local government is fragmented, municipalities will compete for shares of the local tax base. In a more consolidated system, this is less so. Where there is resource equalization among local governments, the size of the local tax base is less important.

While it cannot be demonstrated that 'cities' have a determinate interest in growth, it is true that global economic change and the restructuring of urban regimes have led elected local governments increasingly into the field. The very internationalization of the economy, the mobility of capital among locations and between sectors (which at one time was thought to herald the disappearance of local politics) has in practice increased the political salience of territory. It has intensified the competition for global investment while reducing the ability of national governments to control it. At the same time, it has exposed a gap between the global rationality of corporate decision-making and the spatially-bound rationality of urban and regional policy-makers. The global rationality of a large corporation may indicate restructuring and plant closures which, from the point of view of the corporation, are marginal. The effect on individual places, however, may be devastating. For the traditional, locally-based one-plant firm, on the other hand, survival and location may be identical, creating a shared interest with those sections of the local community which depend on it for employment. To point out this contrast is not to reintroduce the notion of determinate common city interests criticized above. It is merely to point to spatial communities as one basis for the construction of common interests in economic change and of strategies contrary to the logic of the global market. Mobilizing resources to pursue such strategies is another matter.

Local governments have also adopted economic development policies because of the run-down of national spatial anti-disparity policies. These were widely adopted in the 1960s for a variety of political and economic reasons. Politically, governments were concerned to maintain support in declining regions, and to demonstrate national solidarity. Economically, they were concerned, in times of overall full employment, to bring into use idle resources in underdeveloped and declining regions without overheating the economy as a whole. From the late 1970s, emphasis shifted to the promotion of national competitiveness in the global economy. International agreements through the General Agreement on Tariffs and Trade (GATT), the European Community and the US–Canada Free Trade Agreement further limited the power of national governments to intervene in the spatial economy through subsidies and tax preferences. This coincided, in Britain and the USA, with the 'discovery' of the urban economic problem, with the de-industrialization of older cities and the abandonment of large amounts of industrial land in inner city and waterfront locations. Spatial economic disparities in Britain and the USA, and to some extent in France, were redefined in urban rather than regional terms and, in the absence of comprehensive national policies, local governments stepped in to fill the gap.

Ideology also plays a role, on both left and right. The 1980s saw the emergence in Britain of a 'new urban left', committed to radical change in the cities. While this was to some extent a reaction to the poor prospects for Labour regaining power nationally, together with disillusionment about the performance of Labour governments in the 1960s and 1970s, there was some philosophical development. Small-scale and locally-based businesses, along with cooperative and municipal enterprise, were presented as a distinct mode of development. With local government using its statutory and financial powers and institutional devices such as local enterprise boards, it was believed that local social control over the economy could be achieved. In France, a similar long period of opposition for the left produced a flurry of ideas on locally-based development in the 1970s, presented not merely as a substitute for diversionary policies but as part of a break with capitalism itself (Keating and Hainsworth, 1986). On the right, a parallel philosophy of local development can be discerned, focused on low taxes, deregulation and privatization as a means of liberating local energies.

Another political motive is the utility of the development theme in political mobilization. Economic development can be presented as in the interests of the city as a whole, the ultimate non-zero-sum policy. Even where it is recognized that development generates a pattern of winners and losers, it is argued that growth should allow losers to be compensated so that everyone can benefit. In practice, the very conditions under which development takes place may preclude this. Yet to argue against growth as such appears irrational, and opponents are often reduced to supporting whatever growth strategy is chosen in the hope of extracting limited benefits from it. Development has the further attraction that failure is intangible and difficult to assign while success is highly visible and prestigious. Even development initiatives which merely displace local activity and employment can have a political pay-off where the new development is visible and the displaced activity dispersed. Physical development is particularly attractive, hence the 'edifice complex', in which political leaders strive for the most impressive buildings on which to hang their reputations. Development can thus be presented as a consensual policy area in which a general interest exists and is knowable. This then allows all manner of initiatives and policies to be legitimized where they can be claimed as part of development. Subsidizing such leisure facilities for the rich as marinas, which would be regarded as regressive considered purely as recreational or social policy, can be justified if presented as 'development'.

Politicians may be more inclined to emphasize development as a mobilizing theme where politics is personalized, as in North America or France, or where they lack a stable political base in a party, class or ethnic group. In France, Britain and the older cities of the USA, class and party alignments are weakening, tempting politicians to seek mobilizing themes which can incorporate the whole population. French mayors have long sought, despite the increase in partisanship under the Fifth Republic, to broaden their appeal as the protectors of the population as a whole against the rigours of the state and market. This humanistic, social role has to some degree been supplanted by the theme of development and change, but with the same unifying political logic. If the city is presented as in competition with others, this can consolidate support for the leadership and the growth strategy. Emphasis on development may further allow city leaders to tap business support, providing a range of benefits from financial assistance in elections, to wider legitimacy, to abstention from backing rival candidates.

A final reason for cities to engage in policies for economic development is that everyone else is doing it. City governments take a long time to learn what instruments are available, what are effective and how resources should be allocated. The academic literature itself is uncertain on what causes some cities to grow more than others. In their ignorance, cities are tempted to try almost everything once or to smother the problem with initiatives, haunted by the idea that other cities may be stealing a march on them. Gradually, out of the experience of different cities in different contexts, a body of wisdom might be emerging as to what policies are effective, what the costs of various policies are, and how resources may best be deployed.

POWERS AND RESOURCES

Local governments' capacity to influence the local economy is extremely limited. Not controlling trade, exchange rates, credit or monetary creation and obliged to balance their accounts in specified ways, they have few of the means of which national governments still dispose. Lacking control of credit and money supply and interest rates, they can practise neither local Keynesianism nor local monetarism. Nor can they be sure that any increase in economic activity generated locally will be captured for local purposes rather than flowing out in dividends, profits or the wages of non-locals.

One mechanism is negative, the maintenance of a pro-business image and a low tax burden. Others are more positive. Municipal councils everywhere have a role in infrastructure provision and can bias this to economic development. Education spending can be increased to provide a better-prepared labour force and curricula can emphasize entrepreneurial and industrial values. Councils' own purchasing can be used to favour local business. Most councils also have powers to assemble land for industrial development and to provide buildings, sometimes on favourable terms.

These are the traditional functions. In addition, councils in some jurisdictions can make loans or give tax breaks and subsidies to firms. Many American states permit local governments to abate taxes on existing or incoming businesses to lure or retain investors. In Canada and Europe, this type of subsidy is controlled by higher governments to prevent local bidding wars and protect local finances, though local governments can provide cheap land and buildings and some forms of financial help. In France, local governments can provide loan guarantees and, under national regulation, remit part of the *taxe professionnelle*. In Britain, councils' powers to aid business were formalized in 1989. While in principle they are fairly wide, in practice they are tightly controlled by regulation. In both France and Britain, local subsidies in cash and kind to business are also subject to scrutiny by the European Commission which has increased the rigour of its competition policy in preparation for the internal market in 1992.

Local governments' powers to provide investment finance for industrial and commercial development are everywhere regulated, but a number of devices have been invented to avoid the legal and financial barriers. In the USA, wide use is made of the Industrial Revenue Bond. To evade rules on direct involvement in business investment, the arm's-length company is widely used in all four countries. These may be publicly owned or represent partnership with the private sector, the balance of power varying from one case to another. Investment moneys have been mobilized in many cities by using employee pension funds, though this poses the question of whether these should be placed where they will gain the highest return or whether fund managers have a duty to promote local development in the interests of local wage earners and long-term prospects for the community.

Local governments provide a variety of advisory services to business while many have encouraged research application and technology transfer through science parks. There is also a long tradition of municipal trading. Much of this dates from the nineteenth century or the Reform era in North America, and involves matters of collective interest such as abattoirs, transport undertakings and energy utilities, though there are examples in Britain and France of municipal restaurants, bakeries and workshops. Generally, municipal trading has declined since the Second World War as undertakings have been privatized or taken over by national governments. The main examples remaining are transport systems and North American water and energy utilities. The scope for using these to promote economic development is limited, especially as they are often removed from political control.

Local governments can also press their other functions into the service of development. Education can be reorganized to provide particular types of manpower, encouraging vocational training or entrepreneurial skills. Land use zoning can be made more favourable to developers, and planning used to promote specific land uses. Cultural and leisure facilities can be planned in such a way as to make the city more attractive for managers and owners of capital, or to attract high-income patrons from outside.

OBJECTIVES AND POLICY CONFLICTS

Economic development covers a multiplicity of strategies with multiple objectives. If the wealth of the locality is to be increased, this cannot be done merely by redistributing incomes and employment within it, though a great deal of local economic intervention does just this. It can be done only by innovation, increasing the community's exports to other communities or replacing imports from other communities, or attracting inward flows of capital. This insight is the foundation for export-base theory, according to which cities can grow by increasing exports or replacing imports just as countries can, to their mutual benefit.

It can also sometimes be used as a justification for policies aimed at maximizing capital inflow for its own sake. Either it is seen vaguely as 'bringing in money' from outside; or it is assumed that other objectives will flow automatically from capital investment. Enhancement of local land values may also be sought in order to attract capital or to allow the disposal at profit of publicly owned land, with the surplus applied to other purposes. This technique has been widely applied in waterfront locations, with large amounts of publicly owned derelict land and the potential for high-value use. Public investment in clearance, improvement and land assembly are used to enhance the value of the land, which is then disposed of for higher-value uses such as marinas, exclusive condominiums and leisure complexes. Attracting the maximum capital leads, especially where local authorities face a fiscal squeeze, to an emphasis on projects with the highest 'leverage ratio' of private to public capital, rewarding the wealthiest investors rather than the neediest communities. Given the de-industrialization in Britain and the USA, the highest ratios are usually found in high-value commercial, retail and residential development. This not only diverts public resources from other purposes; by pre-empting space and raising urban land prices, it excludes other uses, including manufacturing and employment creation initiatives. In recent years, downtown commercial development and high-income residential and commercial development on abandoned industrial waterfronts has been encouraged as providing the most immediately visible results. Leverage policies, while maximizing capital mobilization, entail a loss of control over the type and location of development. A similar process is visible in Canada where the transfer of infrastructure costs onto developers through lot levies makes it more difficult for municipalities to refuse or guide development.

Enhancing the local tax base is a common objective, which is often confused with increasing land values. The most important source of local taxation is property tax. While this is levied on capital values or notional rental values, it is paid out of income. So a genuine increase in the tax base requires either an influx of new taxpayers or an increase in the economic activity of existing taxpayers. Inflating the assessment base is functionally equivalent to raising the tax rate, since the tax continues to be paid out of current income. There is a net benefit to the city only if the result is to tilt the assessment balance towards externally owned businesses, allowing a proportion of the tax burden to be exported. In the USA, even municipalities who are aware of this have been forced to inflate assessed values where state legislation has limited permissible increases in rates. In jurisdictions with local sales taxes, such as some American cities, there is a strong incentive to attract retailing at the expense of neighbouring municipalities.

One objective listed in nearly all local development policies is the creation of employment. Even this is problematic, since many policies create new employment while destroying existing jobs. Other strategies aim at employment creation more indirectly, by creating the conditions for capital investment, seen as a prerequisite to employment creation; or insist that only jobs in private business count at 'real'. Sometimes the objective is not the creation of employment but the reduction of unemployment. This implies not merely job creation but the targeting of job opportunities to those currently unemployed rather than incomers. Qualitative considerations may also come in. Some strategies aim at any jobs at all, seeking to compete with depressed wages and conditions; others at high-wage jobs or long-term jobs. Raising the tax base may suggest highly-rated, high turnover business with low employment levels. If there is employment involved, this will be high-wage jobs for individuals who will also pay high personal taxes. Maximizing employment, on the other hand, may lead to an emphasis on lower-paid jobs.

More sophisticated strategies have aimed at diversification of the local economic base, strengthening the local economy to face future cyclical downturns. This implies a selectivity in intervention and the elaboration of sectoral strategies. Sometimes, this is linked to an emphasis on technical development and productivity improvement. Encouraging innovation and technical progress may conflict with job creation, given the role of technology and productivity in reducing manpower. Such employment as is needed in advanced technology enterprises will often be brought in from outside where the skills are available, leaving the pool of local unemployed untouched. Providing work for the latter is a quite distinct goal, as is increasing opportunities for disadvantaged and immobile groups. Other strategies have aimed at linking economic intervention with social objectives, targeting growth to specific neighbourhoods or providing employment to women, ethnic minorities or the long-term unemployed.

Development policies are not free of the conflict between the goals of policy and the need to raise taxes to implement it. Funds available to local governments are limited everywhere and tied to the performance of statutory services. Development, while a high-profile activity, is not one for which large resources are available. Other conflicts arise with environmental protection, provision of affordable housing and the construction of public facilities, especially if intervention has stimulated land markets and raised land prices. The use of education as a development tool may conflict with the goal of social integration and liberal intellectual development. The promotion of high culture to raise civic prestige and attract wealth patrons may conflict with the broader role of culture in enhancing citizens' life experience.

DEVELOPMENT STRATEGIES

It is impossible, then, to reduce development to a single objective, to see all city residents as having the same interests in it or to demonstrate that cities are under a compelling obligation to adopt a particular strategy. Economic conditions, structural factors and political choices and assumptions incline cities to behave in particular ways. To simplify greatly, we can identify three types of strategy: a civic mercantilist strategy aimed at maximizing capital inflow; a strategy based on planning and controlling development; and the partnership model.

Civic mercantilism (by analogy with the precapitalist doctrine that nations must compete to acquire a fixed amount of wealth) presents the issue as one of capital accumulation, maintaining that the other objectives will be fulfilled if only capital can be attracted. As most available investment is held in the private sector, it follows that facilitating private capital markets is the main requirement of policy. To describe this as a market approach would be too simple. A pure market approach would involve keeping taxes low and minimizing planning restrictions. Yet the lower the taxes the less resources will be available for infrastructure and other services, and there is little evidence internationally to show that differential local tax rates are a major influence on business location except in marginal cases between neighbouring jurisdictions (Crawford *et al.*, 1985; Conseil des Impôts, 1987; Wolman, 1988; Wassmer, 1990). Experience of British enterprise zones and American urban renewal schemes suggests that spatial planning, including the regulation of incompatible uses, land assembly and infrastructure provision, is important. In practice, the strategy relies on the manipulation of markets by public agencies. This implies making matters as easy as possible for whatever mobile capital is around, including minimizing burdensome planning restrictions while retaining the capacity to assemble land quickly and the application of selective subsidies. The key measure of success here is the 'leverage ratio' – the amount of private capital attracted to a project for every unit of public money. In fact, leverage ratios are a quite meaningless measure of policy success without a separate measure of the objectives for which the capital is being invested. Yet often the ratio itself becomes the policy, its maximization the goal, leading to the subsidization of capital and the diversion of public resources into ventures which would have occurred in any case.

Some of the problems with this have already been noted. There is no necessary connection between capital accumulation (which often takes the form of property speculation) and employment and production. The approach creates a bias to financial subsidies, overt or disguised, and to physical development, since other measures are difficult to localize. For example, improving education may attract inward investment to take advantage of better manpower, or it may simply make it easier for people to leave. Improving the environment may attract incomers and firms; or it may simply attract residents who commute to work and resist local development. Capital subsidization, on the other hand, provides a spatially immobile product. Cities pursuing this type of strategy will seek activities with a high monetary value and low revenue costs. Convention centres are the classic example, since they are frequented by people with relatively high spending power who stay a short time and then leave, making few demands on local services.

Retail developments, attracting people from other jurisdictions, would be another example.

Since the competition is for a fixed sum of mobile capital, development is at the expense of the urban system as a whole. Since location incentives are powerful only over short distances, much of the fiercest competition occurs within metropolitan areas, so that unless we define the city restrictively to correspond with the local government jurisdiction it is hard to say that the city as such has any interest in bidding capital away from its rivals. Convention centres may have a national or international market and be able to bring in outside money, though at considerable cost (Judd, 1988). Retail developments serve local markets, displacing local competitors. Indeed, the displacement effects of retailing, some types of service and even manufacturing are so marked that they are likely to affect the sponsoring municipality itself. Such policies are often accompanied by an insistence that the days of manufacturing are over or that the transition to a tertiary economy is a natural, market-led development. Yet the process, far from merely following the invisible hand, is being given an enormous boost by interventionist public policy. The payment of financial subsidies to incoming investors involves a regressive redistribution which is difficult to achieve in a democratic and participative system. It may then require local political restructuring to suppress distributive demands or coopt potential dissidents into the strategy.

Social inequalities and redistributive issues will be kept off the political agenda or assigned to the separate realm of 'social policy'. The term 'social economy' is sometimes applied to strategies for neighbourhoods or groups which involve an element of subsidization or protection from wider market forces. This term, as well as being slightly disparaging, allows this type of intervention to be assigned to social policy, with economic policy proper confined to activities which promote market or inter-urban competitiveness (though these, too, may be subsidized). Development policy may be insulated through the creation of special agencies, earmarked funds and general secrecy. The distribution of economic benefits is left to the market and trickle-down, though the very form of development may prevent this, or the resolution of social problems through diverting public resources, pre-empting land uses and inflating land prices. In spite of all this, civic mercantilism remains widespread, especially in the USA, since it appears to unite the city electorate behind a common interest, is rather simple to operate and offers tangible results. Social discontent is managed by small-scale side-payments to individual groups or the argument that only the capital accumulation strategy will provide the resources to assuage it.

A second type of approach attempts to secure local economic planning and social control of the economy, as proposed on the British urban left in the 1980s and in France in the 1970s. Such strategies have been rare in North America. Occasional attempts in the USA to assert community values against the market-based logic of corporations have faced formidable ideological barriers (Portz, 1990). In the social control strategy, local political power is mobilized, along with the powers and resources of local government, to exert a dominant influence on the local economy, shifting development priorities away from property investment and retailing and towards employment. Social and distributive considerations are placed at the centre of the economic strategy and the aim is to maximize the use rather than the exchange value of land. The emphasis is less on attracting inward investment than on mobilizing local resources, including resources which would otherwise escape, such as pension funds.

This approach, too, suffers from serious problems. Local governments lack the powers, the resources and the information to engage in local economic planning. Even with pension funds, the capital is minuscule in comparison with the needs of development. Private capital is increasingly mobile and could not be constrained by local government even if it possessed stronger powers over the direction of investment. So it must be accommodated and compromises made. Legal restrictions everywhere limit what local governments can do and higher-level governments jealously guard their monopoly of economic powers. Nor has the ideological climate of recent years been favourable to directive economic strategies. Even on the left, the hegemony of market ideology has removed local economic planning from the political agenda. Even if social control of capital were a reality, multiple objectives would still compete in framing development policy.

The third approach is captured in the word 'partnership'. While civic mercantilism has cities doing whatever is necessary to attract all and any capital and the local planning approach has capital subject to local political control, partnership recognizes the mutual dependence of business and city governments. City governments need business to provide investment, employment and taxes while business needs government to provide services and to zone, reclaim, assemble and service land. While the notion of partnership sounds reassuring, it assumes an identity or compatibility of goals which may not always be present, given the divergent logics of spatially-specific need and global corporate competitiveness. Formulating goals and strategies is thus a matter of political negotiation. Partnerships may be of equals, or they may be tilted to one side. The balance will depend on the needs and resources of each party, the nature of the task and the institutional and political structures within which policy evolves. Most cities face an imbalance of information, with business corporations knowing more of their affairs than they do of the corporations'. This imbalance can be used to extract a 'corporate surplus' in the form of higher incentives than would be necessary in a world of perfect information (Jones and Bachelor, 1986). Depressed cities, starved of investment capital, may need to make greater concessions to investors than buoyant ones, unless they are capable of mobilizing political power to extract resources through the intergovernmental system in the form of fiscal support or diversionary national policies. Institutional arrangements may take the form of special agencies insulated from the wider political process and social demands and operating to commercial criteria. Partnership may then degenerate into an open-ended series of concessions and subsidies to investors. This in turn may lead to the use of public money to subsidize the projects with the highest leverage ratios, often downtown commercial and retail development, irrespective of their wider utility. Partnership thus degenerates into civic mercantilism. In other cases, it may be possible to attract capital and apply some of the increment to socially useful purposes. It is necessary, then, to examine individual urban regimes to see what the power balance is, and how this affects the development policies which emerge.

These models are ideal types. There are few examples of cities which have no development priorities other than capital accumulation and advocates of local planning have usually been aware of the wider constraints. In practice, urban regimes have adopted various forms of partnership, but these have inclined to one extreme or the other. Development is a complex phenomenon, with multiple objectives and a range of winners and losers. These objectives impinge on decision-makers in ways which reflect the prevailing political culture and value system, and the institutional arrangements. In turn, the policies themselves can, in a reverse of the usual process, mould politics, creating assumptions and shaping alliances and strategies. Systems closed to social and political pressures but open to business influence will generate a narrower development agenda, though rarely entirely conflict-free. Within the business community, there may be conflicts between existing small businesses looking for low land prices and rents, low taxes and depending on local markets; the property industry seeking high land values; and the interests of mobile capital. Open, politicized systems of urban government are subject to a wider range of social pressures, the multiple objectives articulated in debate and producing social and political conflict. Where development is seen in terms of mobilizing the maximum of investment capital, the result is increasing social inequality within the city.

Generally, an emphasis on economic development in all four countries, together with the competition for globally mobile investment, has tended to narrow the local political agenda to exclude objectives which might damage investment. Development is presented as a consensual policy area, requiring wide social cooperation and long-term stability of objectives and instruments, reducing the scope for partisan, class, ethnic and ideological conflict. Along with this depoliticization comes an enhancement of the influence of private business. Urban development coalitions have emerged, uniting the political parties representing lower-class and blue-collar populations and local business leaders, displacing lines of political cleavage, and pursuing policies to encourage growth. Social democratic parties and labour interests have moved from their old strategy of confronting capital at the workplace to extract wage benefits and seeking to capture political control of the central state towards place-based coalitions in collaboration with business interests aimed at capturing mobile capital and extracting whatever resources are available from higher governments (Keating, 1991b). Opposition to the prevailing trend of development becomes very difficult to sustain in these circumstances. It is hard, except in the most prosperous and congested cities, to appear 'anti-growth'. Those concerned about the uneven urban development or the social distribution of its benefits will often include elements of the urban bureaucracy, less concerned with prestige projects and less dependent on mobilizing wide political support, neighbourhood groups and social movements. Yet they can modify policy only by accepting its broad lines, and seeking a share of any surplus.

Development politics has also altered the conduct and governing ethos of local government as municipalities are drawn into the world of business, governed by secrecy, competition and the ethics of the market place, rather than the political and bureaucratic worlds of open debate, equity and professional standards. The restructuring of local political systems has reinforced this trend, with decentralization in the USA and France forcing cities into closer partnership with the private sector. In Britain, the same effect has been achieved by the selective displacement of local councils with Urban Development Corporations (UDCs) responsible to central government and business, together with a reduction in disposable resources. There has been a new closure of local politics, as critical decisions are moved into agencies and development separated from wider social pressures and considerations. National differences do, nevertheless, remain to modify these general trends. Since the test of governing capacity is the ability to perform difficult tasks rather than simply accommodate global economic trends, the discussion of national trends concentrates on policies for distressed cities.

NATIONAL TRENDS

In the USA, city governments must extract resources from private investors in a market-based system in which, as explained in Chapter 3, they are the weaker party. There is a tendency in distressed cities for city hall to take the lead in framing development strategies, while in growing cities, the private sector takes the initiative (Carlson, 1981). This reflects the pressure on mayors to do something about economic decline and to unite lower-class residents and business interests so as to ensure his ability to govern and his chances of re-election. In both depressed and prosperous cities, however, resources must be levered out of the private sector. Shortage of resources and dependence on private investment encourage city governments to concentrate their own resources on the most buoyant sectors of the local economy, downtown commercial development. This has the further advantage of being relatively easy (compared, for example, with sectoral intervention in manufacturing) and to maximize visual impact and prestige (the edifice complex). Federal policy has encouraged the trend. The federal Urban Development Action Grant (UDAG) introduced under the Carter administration was aimed at development projects which otherwise might not have taken place. It typified the selective economic and commercial renewal policy of the 1970s and 1980s, focused on downtown commerce, but it had friends in Congress and survived until the late 1980s. Under the Reagan and Bush administrations, federal funding has been further reduced. UDAG was eliminated and Community Development Block Grant (CDBG) cut. Together with relaxations on the use of CDBG, this led cities to put even more emphasis on levering private capital and

CDBG moneys were increasingly used for high-value commercial development. Another way of tapping federal support for investment is the Industrial Revenue Bond (IRB) which, because it is floated by a municipal government, is free of state and federal taxation. The proceeds are then turned over to commercial and industrial developers. Because repayment of the bond is tied to the proceeds of a commercial project, the IRB is usually able to avoid state and municipal rules about voter approval for borrowing or limits on indebtedness. The high cost to the federal treasury of IRBs in the 1980s finally led Congress to limit their amount and restrict them to infrastructure projects. This has left cities more dependent on their own resources to lever capital. In many cities, tax abatements and subsidies are freely deployed or tax increment areas created in which new taxes generated in a commercial development are retained within that area rather than swelling the general tax base. Special agencies and public–private bodies are used to insulate development policy from political influence.

There are differences within the USA. In some cities, business-led development politics is unchallenged or there is an insistence on 'trickle-down' theory, the idea that downtown development will benefit everyone as its benefits diffuse throughout the city. Trickle-down theory is usually more of a hope than a rigorous model of development, and in many cases the conditions of downtown development – with tax increment districts, subsidies and political insulation – are precisely such as to prevent benefits being captured for the wider city. In other cities, opposition has emerged, focused on the issue of 'neighbourhoods', low-income areas outside the commercial city centre which do not enjoy the benefits of subsidized development. Progressive coalitions have been established to challenge business dominance. Yet, lacking a secure partisan or class base, these are ephemeral and easily unpicked by the selective incentives available to business-backed development coalitions. Progressive urban politics in the USA, outside a few professional middle-class communities where resources are large and problems small, involves extracting piecemeal benefits from developers. Some cities have adopted linkage policies, requiring developers to provide social facilities or low-income housing as a condition of being allowed to develop prime sites. In Canada, 'density bonusing' is used to similar effect. Developers are allowed to exceed zoning densities in exchange for providing social facilities. The concessions are usually small and illustrate the weakness of the public authorities, obliged to surrender one of their few instruments of control in order to exact social benefits from development.

Unable to fight or challenge the logic of development politics, American mayors have usually joined in enthusiastically, to extract whatever benefits they can. The fragmentation of the system maximizes competition for growth and isolates declining inner city jurisdictions. So mayors in poor inner cities, including many black mayors, become the most enthusiastic supporters of development politics and of the subsidization of business (Ferman, 1989), creating serious tensions with their own supporters; yet in the absence of a real alternative policy, political rivals are reduced to criticizing while recommending more of the same thing. The organized working class, too, is affected. While levels of trade union organization in the USA are low, in the older industrial areas, trade unions join the development coalitions, abandoning their previous confrontational attitudes.

The predominant style is mercantilist, attempting to mobilize investment capital in competition with other locations. There are certainly efforts to promote sectoral strategies, to mobilize local entrepreneurship, but these tend to be a minor theme, given the high cost of such ventures and the difficulty of attracting investment. Political opposition has also produced neighbourhood development corporations with the task of fostering locally-based business and targeting economic development programmes to the poor and unemployed. Chicago in the 1980s provided a notable example of mobilization of non-corporate interests in development and neighbourhood-based policies (Giloth and Mier, 1989). Generally, however, community development corporations have been poorly funded and reliant on a diminishing pool of federal aid. They cannot demonstrate the high leverage ratios of city centre commercial projects and tend to be regarded as part of the social economy, a way of attenuating the impact of economic change rather than a contribution to mainstream economic development.

In Canada, there is some of the same emphasis on growth politics. In the absence of parties or strong class identities, the urban agenda is often occupied by a consensual vision of growth. Progressive or anti-growth coalitions are short-lived and easily unpicked. An example is the campaign over Toronto's bid for the 1992 Olympic games. Opponents charged that further development in the most congested Canadian city would divert public resources, cause environmental damage and further price out affordable housing. The response of the city leadership was that only with the Olympics could affordable housing be provided, since some of the anticipated surplus could be devoted to social purposes. Waverers, including the provincial NDP (the social democratic party) thus drifted into the pro-Olympic camp, with the hope of extracting some social benefit. In several cities, development corporations have been established by the federal and provincial governments, leading to a displacement of social by development objectives and increasing secrecy in operation (Leo and Fenton, 1990). Yet both the severity of the task and the means available differentiate the Canadian case from that of the USA. Canadian cities generally have not yet experienced the mass poverty, de-industrialization and obsolescence of their older American counterparts. They are protected by more interventionist higher-level governments, which prevent them indiscriminately subsidizing development or diverting moneys from social budgets. Competition for development is further muted by the lesser governmental fragmentation in urban areas.

In Britain, economic development efforts have taken several forms. Most cities responded to the recession of the early 1980s by increasing traditional activities such as building factories and advertising their attractions to inward investors (ADC, 1987). The number of district councils giving grants for economic development increased from 16 per cent in 1982 to over 33 per cent in 1987, though legislative and financial restrictions kept total spending to just over £3 million; only a few councils in the most depressed cities spent the full amount permitted under Section 137 of the Local Government Act (ADC, 1987). Priority for development was given in corporate and physical plans and new activities such as business advisory services, science parks and local purchasing schemes launched.

Some councils went a great deal further, to establish elaborate strategies for locally-based regeneration and transformation, the best known being in Sheffield, the West Midlands and Greater London. This was part of the 'new urban left', initiatives by Labour councils to promote radical transformation through local government (Gyford, 1985; Boddy and Fudge, 1984; Lansley *et al.*, 1989). Rather than rely on mobile capital, the emphasis was placed on mobilizing local sources through pension funds and the revenue and capital budgets of local government. While some councils established arm's-length enterprise boards, others (such as Sheffield) retained direct control. Rather than attempting to attract all and every type of capital, strategies were based on local needs and the promotion of employment. Investment was seen to involve not merely the owners of capital but the community and the workforce, so schemes for participation and democratic control featured widely. Firms to be aided had to sign planning contracts promising to deliver specified social benefits, including jobs, trade union recognition and local investment. New types of enterprise such as cooperatives were encouraged. 'Contract compliance' clauses were also inserted in contracts between councils and their suppliers, stipulating matters such as trade union recognition, equal opportunities or local purchasing. Apart from these common features, there was a wide variety of experience. Some councils saw their economic initiatives as the basis for a radical transformation of society, breaking down the distinction between social and economic policies. This was notably the experience in Greater London, where emphasis was placed not merely on employment but on its distribution, in particular the needs of ethnic minorities and women. Investments were to be subject to social as well as economic accounting. In the West Midlands, on the other hand, a more conventional view of economic activity was taken, with distributional questions assigned to the realm of social policy. The aim here was to make capitalism more responsive to local needs, including employment and manufacturing and to the long term, rather than to achieve total social transformation. The emphasis was on the large- and medium-sized firms capable of providing the largest employment. In Sheffield, radical policy aims were combined with a realistic assessment of the limitations of the locality. The council aimed less at socialism within one city than at showing what could be done should a radical Labour government take power nationally.

The new urban left initiatives were formulated in the context of Labour's Alternative Economic Strategy, an ambitious if somewhat vague programme for state-led, autarkic national regeneration outside the constrictions of the European Community (Jones and Keating, 1985). The collapse of Labour support in the early 1980s followed by the abandonment of the Alternative Economic Strategy removed the promised external support for the new urban left strategy. It was further undermined by the national Conservative government's abolition of the metropolitan counties, financial restriction, liberalization of planning regulations and outlawing of contract compliance. Nationally, the Labour Party moved to the centrist position previously occupied by the Liberal–SDP Alliance while sharply reducing left-wing influence in its ranks. Equally important are the changes at the local level as cities learnt more about economic development and the limitations on their own powers. Unable to exercise a leading role in the local economy or to extract resources from the centre, councils and local enterprise boards sought to lever capital from other sources and to forge closer relationships with the local business community. Increasingly conscious of the shortage of mobile investment, they saw themselves engaged in the national and international competition for growth. Rather than wait for the arrival of a new Labour government which would shower them with resources, they have concentrated on doing what they can locally. The language of partnership and cooperation has come to replace that of confrontation or socialist transformation (Audit Commission, 1989; Shaw, 1990; Seyd, 1990). The enterprise boards which survived the abolition of the metropolitan counties moved into closer partnership with the local business community, which came to accept them, shorn of the more radical rhetoric which had characterized the London board, as useful adjuncts (Cochrane and Clarke, 1990).

Central government under the Conservative administration sought explicitly to encourage a move to the American model of urban partnership, with business playing a dominant role. This involved changes both in policy and in the local political structure to limit the scope of development politics and close it to non-business influences. Privatization and deregulation have weakened the local public sector while reductions in central financial support have increased dependence on private sources of investment. General support for local government has been reduced while the selective financing under the Urban Programme has been increasingly directed by central government instructions to economic development (Committee of Public Accounts, 1986; National Audit Office, 1990). In 1982 the Urban Development Grant, based on the American UDAG system was introduced for development projects in cities; later it was replaced with the City Grant, payable directly to developers without the need for local government mediation. Although the conservative initiatives were introduced with a great deal of free market rhetoric, the reality, as in the USA, is less an unregulated market than a new form of planning, more aligned to commercial objectives and business needs.

Selective financial help was provided in demonstration schemes. In the early 1980s, a series of enterprise zones was established, ostensibly to show how an unregulated market and low-tax regime could regenerate inner urban areas. Despite the ideological basis of the scheme, Labour councils (with the exception of Sheffield) rushed to apply for enterprise zones, seeing them as a source of scarce national resources. In one sense they were right. Government, to ensure that its experiment worked, pumped large amounts of public money into the zones, which were also the site of major public interventions in land assembly, clearance and preparation. So far from demonstrating the case for deregulation, they showed what could be done by public intervention and subsidy. On the other hand, they proved an extremely costly form of job creation, at some £30 000 on average (National Audit Office, 1990), with most of the jobs representing transfers or displacement rather than new job creation. Indeed, the experience represents an example of capital subsidization comparable to some of the American urban renewal schemes. Another demonstration policy was the Technical and Vocational Education Initiative (TVEI), in which the central government, through the Manpower Services Commission, persuaded urban local authorities to bid for extra resources for vocational education programmes, despite their incompatibility with the liberal comprehensive education which Labour had been pursuing since the 1960s.

In 1989, central government moved to rationalize the system of local intervention with the Local Government and Housing Act. This for the first time provided local governments with a formal power to engage in economic development, a provision generally welcomed by councils, but subjected it to controls on capital and revenue expenditure. Subsidies and grants are limited by regulation and confined to nationally defined development areas. It also closed off the possibility for local governments to use arm's-length companies to evade capital controls by counting their expenditure and debt as that of the parent authority.

In several cities in England and Wales, central government went further, displacing local government in the development role by appointed urban development corporations (UDCs), responsible to central government and with strong business representation on their boards. In Scotland, the agency style of intervention had begun earlier, with the Scottish Development Agency increasingly taking the lead in urban redevelopment projects (Keating and Boyle, 1986; Lloyd and Newlands, 1990). Urban development corporations, like enterprise zones before them, are less a testimony to the virtues of the unfettered market than a new form of planning (Brindley *et al.*, 1989; Griffith, 1990). In this vision, economic development is defined more narrowly than before, with the lead role assigned to the private sector and central agencies which in turn are less amenable to local political pressures to emphasize social considerations. Both the functions and the areas of the UDCs are restricted, to focus attention on the immediate issue at hand, but their powers are extensive, including the right compulsorily to acquire land, give planning permission for development, build infrastructure and undertake physical development. Finance is provided by central government grant, together with profits made from land and development. In a time of general retrenchment, the funds thus made available are considerable. In the period 1989–92, the government grant for the eleven UDCs was set at £1 413 million ($2 741 million), of which £600 million ($1 164 million) was for London Docklands. Funding for the Urban Programme, which includes social as well as economic projects and is administered by local government, was set at £496 million ($962 million) for the same period (CLES, 1989), having declined steadily since 1984 (National Audit Office, 1990). UDCs also benefit from enterprise zone benefits in London, Tyne and Wear and Teesside. Additional grants for infrastructure include £100 million ($194 million) from the Welsh Office towards the £113 million cost of the Cardiff Bay Barrage, intended in turn to enhance property values in the UDC area; and City Grants such as the £50 million ($82 million) towards the £150 million cost of the Hartlepool marina on Teesside.

Initially, there was considerable hostility to UDCs on the part of local government. In the London Docklands, local councils refused to take the seats offered on the board of the corporation. The UDC, in turn, pursued a policy of massive, subsidized commercial and high-income residential development to the exclusion of low-income housing, social amenities and creation of jobs for local residents (Employment Committee, 1988). While this caused a great deal of political opposition and vocal criticism, experience with the other UDCs has been less conflictual (CLES, 1989) as councils and UDCs realized their mutual dependence. UDCs saw the need to cooperate with local governments in order to secure their own political legitimacy and the complementary services which local governments supply. Councils appreciated that UDCs were the only means through which new central government resources would be made available for regeneration. Personality and the fact that chief executives of some corporations have come from the public sector with its traditions of cooperation and a search for common goals, also helped. There was also, though, a change in the attitude of Labour local governments, more attuned to the competitive, commercial ethos represented by the UDCs and anxious to obtain resources from wherever they might be available. So by the end of the 1980s, most city councils were eager to receive UDCs, with their resources, powers and central government commitment.

This apparent consensus should not obscure the change in thinking which has occurred, or the underlying differences on the meaning and future of urban regeneration. UDCs, which have a limited life, have tended to focus on activities where their powers and resources can produce swift results. This has involved the mercantilist model of development, concentrated on property operations and high-income residential and leisure developments in waterfront locations. The amount of capital brought in and the leverage ratio is the most common criterion of success, with reliance on trickle-down to diffuse the benefits. Local governments often complain that UDCs have merely taken up ideas which were in the pipeline but which they lacked the resources to pursue. More seriously, they complain that UDCs have chosen the easiest projects, at which they have then thrown money, leaving local government to manage the social implications of change, including the management of unemployment and the targeting of jobs. The pursuit of high land values, especially since central government has instructed them to sell their land for the highest possible price, has effectively excluded a range of uses, including manufacturing industry, low-income housing and public social facilities (National Audit Office, 1988b; Employment Committee, 1988). There are complaints about the style and mode of operations of UDCs, their greater willingness on occasion to consult business leaders than local government, their lack of accountability (CLES, 1989; Coulson, 1989). Their limitations, too, had become apparent by the end of the 1980s. In the absence of wider metropolitan development strategies, the overall impact may be limited to bringing derelict sites into use somewhat earlier than otherwise. Even this may depend on the state of the local property market which in the 1980s enjoyed a boom, starting in the South East and rolling through the country. Already, in 1990 there were strong signs that the end of the land and property boom was threatening the property-based redevelopment model and that those regions which had retained a significant manufacturing sector were bearing up better.

Central government has also sought to encourage the emergence of local business leadership, the weakness of which marks twentieth-century Britain off from the USA. In the early 1980s, business leaders sympathetic to the Conservative Party founded Business in the Community, an organization aimed at showing that social concern for urban problems can be good business as well as improving the image of business as a whole. Business-led organizations like Glasgow Action, emerged with government encouragement (Keating, 1988a). In the absence of a strong locally-based business sector, these remain pale imitations of their American counterparts but they mark a new willingness to recognize business prerogatives in development policy. In 1990, a radical reorganization of the former Manpower Services Commission devolved many of its functions to Training and Enterprise Councils (Local Enterprise Councils in Scotland), funded by central government but organized and run by local business. Labour city administrations have sought to work with the new bodies in developing local business and attracting capital in competition with other cities. In Birmingham, the Labour city council, in order to stave off the threat of a UDC, proposed its own alternative, a development organization under private leadership, a proposal welcomed and supported by both local business and the trade unions. More generally, the climate created by UDCs and other central initiatives has altered the assumptions of local actors and their mode of operation. Cooperation with the business sector has become not merely a means of extracting resources but a mechanism for bestowing legitimacy on what local governments do in terms of the prevailing ideology (Thornley, 1990; Barnes, 1990).

So British cities have witnessed the emergence of a new type of cross-class development coalition, uniting local business leaders, Labour city councils and the trade unions, dedicated to civic promotion, growth and competition with other locations. Development has assumed a new priority, with reduced emphasis on distribution or environmental issues such as green belts. The abolition of the metropolitan counties has intensified competition and, despite the existence of some conurbation-wide committees and coordinating mechanisms, has intensified the determination of each city to accommodate growth within its own boundaries. This represents a significant change in local Labour politics, from a concentration on confrontation with capital to extract benefits at the workplace (on the part of unions) and the pursuit of power in the central state combined with distributive politics locally (for the political wing of the movement).

The terms of partnership and the style of growth politics vary among cities. In some, leaders are entranced by the image of the post-industrial city, pursuing prestige projects and enticing downtown developers in a manner reminiscent of North American experience. In others, especially where manufacturing trade unions remain influential within Labour Parties, there is a commitment to manufacturing industry and an attempt to tap incoming capital for social purposes. Officials continue to criticize UDC operations for displacing small businesses in the manner of the redevelopment programmes of the 1960s while pricing reclaimed land out of the manufacturing market.

Labour's national party programme, with its emphasis on markets, has encouraged this move. There is no commitment to a return to national planning and only rather vague proposals for regional government to rationalize local development efforts. On the other hand, the party generally supported the provisions of the Local Government and Housing Act of 1989 which formalized the power of local councils to encourage economic development. Indeed, Labour spokespersons in Parliament criticized the restrictions placed on local governments' ability to subsidize business development (House of Commons, Standing Committee G, 16 March 1989), suggesting an even firmer commitment to the American model of competitive development. It must be assumed that this demand was made in ignorance of the effects of such permissiveness in the USA.

France, too, saw an explosion of local development efforts in the 1970s and 1980s, much of it from Socialist mayors seeking to combat the effects of the free market strategy and reduced regional aid of the Giscard d'Estaing government between 1974 and 1981. In time-honoured fashion, ingenious ways were found to circumvent legal restrictions, often with the connivance of the prefects. In the 1970s, the Socialists became increasingly attached to decentralization, though never adequately resolving the relation of decentralized political to economic power. Instead, they talked vaguely of a third way between the free market and the statist–centralist approach of soviet systems. Strong regional and local governments would plan their economic future within a decentralized national planning system. This would comprise part of the rupture with capitalism to be achieved by a front of all progressive forces including small and locally-owned businesses, excluding only large corporations. While the Socialist Party was a strong supporter of European integration, no reference was made in the discussion of decentralization to the implications of European competition for a decentralized economic order. Nor was the potential contradiction between the plans for large-scale nationalization and economic decentralization resolved.

When the Socialists gained power in 1981, they were caught between competing pressures, from regionalists who wanted powerful, large-scale units, notables seeking consolidation of the powers of departments, and mayors of large cities. Unable to choose among the three tiers, they proposed strengthening them all though attempting some differentiation by function. The communes would be responsible for local planning and urban development, the departments for social solidarity, and the regions for economic intervention and planning. The legislation after 1981 was strongly influenced by the powerful presidents of departments and big city mayors, and much of it simply legalized existing practice. Subsidies were to be rationalized and regulated through strengthened regional governments which would have the prime role in local economic development. They in turn would negotiate with the central government through a revived National Plan. Distinctions were made between 'direct' aid and 'indirect' aid, such as cheap land and buildings and advice. The former was to be tightly regulated and confined to the regions; the latter was less strictly regulated. General economic development was separated from emergency provisions to save firms in difficulty, safeguard the interests of the population or provide essential services in rural areas. In practice, these vague distinctions have proved virtually impossible to enforce (Douence, 1988). The regions alone were empowered to subsidize industry directly in the form of three grants devolved from central government and subject to central controls on the amount and criteria for distribution. Regions were empowered to make loans, advances and abatements of interest within conditions laid down by the Ministry of Finance. Departments and communes could participate in these only with the region and subject to regional ceilings such that communes and departments could make up only the shortfall between the region's contribution and the ceiling. All three levels could make loan guarantees within conditions laid down nationally.

Abatement of the *taxe professionnelle* by local governments is possible under two schemes, one applicable everywhere and limited to two years, the other confined to development regions and available for five years, with safeguards to exclude firms restructuring or moving to take advantage of the tax break. Councils were able to provide firms in difficulty with all forms of aid, subject to two conditions – that the firm be genuinely in difficulties and that a contract be signed specifying the council's commitment and the steps to be taken by the firm to redress its accounts.

All aid is subject to three principles: respect for the central government's competence in economic matters; respect for the principles of freedom of commerce and equality of citizens before the law; respect for the principles of *aménagement du territoire* (a term encompassing regional anti-disparity policy and planning) laid down in the National Plan. Regional plans would be produced alongside the National Plan with a complex process for exchanging views on priorities. Then the central state would adopt its plan with its investment priorities. Regions would be free to adopt other priorities as long as these did not conflict with those of the state. Planning contracts would be negotiated between the state and the regions.

There was a consequent explosion of efforts to attract industry. By 1988, local governments were providing F6.4 billion ($1.28 billion) in direct and F2.4 billion ($0.48 billion) in indirect aid, up from F3.4 billion and F1 billion respectively in 1982 (Némery, 1989; Ministère de l'Economie, 1990). Forms of aid have largely broken the bounds set to establish coherence and hierarchy, and figures are not always reliable or consistent. It appears that about half of all aid is provided by communes and a third by regions (Deves and Gouttebel, 1988; Cour des Comptes, 1987; Ministère de l'Economie, 1990). Only a few regional councils spend up to the ceiling on aid, most leaving some scope for departments and communes, though the extent to which the latter take advantage of this varies greatly (Keating, 1991a). Some regions and departments started out with clear sectoral priorities and plans for restructuring the local economy, but most have ended up supporting employment-creating investments of whatever sort.

Tax exemptions have been very widely used as a development tool. By 1986, tax exemptions under the two-year scheme had been granted by 2 554 communes, 22 urban communities and intercommunal syndicates, 55 departments, eight regions and 57 Chambers of Commerce at a total cost of F56.3 million ($11.2 million). More important was the second type of exemption, the five-year scheme. By 1985, this was operated by 1 736 local governments at a total cost of F573.5 million ($114.6 million), though a change in the rules had reduced this from a peak of F669.5 million in 1984. The average value of the two types of exemption was F27 800 ($5 600) and F214 550 ($42 800) respectively (Conseil des Impôts, 1987). In some areas, this constitutes a severe burden (Keating, 1991a). Indeed, some councils do not know what the budgetary effect of tax abatements is going to be until too late. There has, partly as a result of this policy, been a transfer of the local fiscal burden from firms to households. The proportion of local tax receipts accounted for by the *taxe professionnelle* fell from 52 per cent in 1981 to 44 per cent in 1987 (Prim, 1988), though this was also affected by central government measures to reduce the impact of the tax (Guengant and Uhaldeborde, 1989).

Local governments, forbidden to take stakes in private firms, operate through special administrative authorization or through the creation of development companies. The *sociétés d'économie mixte* sector has expanded considerably over the years, with development companies operating in the private sector but with public funds.

Loan guarantees have been used by the larger councils. The survey by the association of French mayors showed that 2 per cent of the communes under 7 000 population had used them, against 19 per cent of those between 30 000 and 80 000, though none of those over 80 000 had done so (Steib, 1987). A survey by the assembly of presidents of the departments showed that 42 per cent of departments were making loan guarantees (Steib, 1987). Most regional councils had loan guarantee funds before 1986, though many of them subsequently abandoned the policy (Cour des Comptes, 1988). Councils at all levels have also advanced loans at low interest and, while this is in principle subject to control, there are many ways of circumventing it.

The clause allowing intervention in favour or firms in difficulty is potentially very broad, but has been approached with great circumspection. After a number of such interventions mayors realized the enormity of the problems of industrial restructuring and the inadequacy of their financial means, and sought to pass the burden to the regions (Deves and Gouttebel, 1988). The political pressure to intervene is often greatest in small communes, where a single firm may be the dominant employer and there is a strong sense of community responsibility focused on the mayor. Yet these are the communes in the weakest position to act effectively, and a number of communes suffered serious financial losses in failed attempts to keep local employers in business (Cour des Comptes, 1987).

Non-financial incentives have also been used widely. Communes now are free to adopt their own local land use plans, and have done so in order to attract industry. They have also been prepared to change their plans to accommodate the needs of investors. Where there is an approved land use plan, the mayor has the right to grant development permission, a power previously held by the prefect.

The effectiveness of much local development aid has been widely questioned, by business leaders, central government, academic observers and the auditing agencies, the Cour des Comptes and Conseil des Impôts. The Conseil des Impôts (1987) found no difference in the increase in the number of firms nor in the tax base between communes applying tax abatements and those not doing so. The Cour des Comptes (1987) noted that there was little evaluation of aid nor even any attempt to add up all the types of aid given to a particular firm. Grants were often seen as a reward for creating jobs rather than as an incentive for development, and regions were often unaware of the failure of aided firms. Surveys showed a higher rate of failure than was recorded in regional council statistics and employment creation was usually below target. There is a failure to reclaim aid from firms failing to fulfil their promises, for fear of causing more unemployment. Loan guarantees have also been criticized by the Cour des Comptes (1988), since they have tended to go to firms in difficulty rather than to new enterprises, and they have resulted in public subsidization of shareholders. The Economic and Social Council also noted a tendency for banks routinely to demand council guarantees for loans to firms in difficulty, so pushing risks onto the taxpayer (Conseil Economique et Social, 1987). There is evidence of firms taking advantage of local government subsidies merely to relocate, and examples of apparent blackmail of councils as a condition of remaining in place (Prim, 1988; Plan Urbain, 1986). The Cour des Comptes (1987) cites several cases of councils being exploited by firms which have benefited from subsidies or favourable land deals and then failed to produce any jobs.

The limited role of the regions and their absorption in their new statutory functions in training and education has left the initiative in many cases to big city mayors and presidents of departments. Often, the maximization of status and prestige has been the dominant motif, with mayors seeking to establish *technopoles* and using leisure and cultural facilities as a development tool. Urban areas continue to be fragmented among competing communes and any attempt at coordination is vigorously opposed by mayors fearful of losing their power bases. Within conurbations, territorial and political rivalries can be intense and the device of the intercommunal charter, specifically designed to enable cooperation in development, has been little used. Yet, as in other countries, the marginal nature of the incentives means that the competition is not among regions which might be able to equip themselves for the increased competition after 1992 but among communes within conurbations, to the neglect of measures to improve the conurbation economy as a whole (Plan Urbain, 1986).

The increase in inter-urban competition for development, together with the decentralization of planning and development assistance, have tended to weaken the public power in development decisions, and increase that of the private sector. A tendency has been observed for large corporations to disengage themselves from communities, insulating themselves from social and political pressures which might force social considerations on them. They have sold land and plant, reduced the proportions of local workforces dependent on them and their participation in the capital of local firms, as part of what has been described as a *rejet d'un certain enracinement local* (Plan Urbain, 1986). This has only increased the pressure on local governments and locally-based businesses to attract mobile investment through economic incentives or measures appealing to business executives. As it is the better off and better equipped localities which have the means to do this, there has been an increase in inter-urban inequalities. The smaller cities may be suffering as a result. There is also some tendency to seek high-income residents and zone out low-income housing, especially public housing occupied by immigrants.

In principle, local government leaders of the right disclaim the desire to intervene, preaching the virtues of the market. A 1983 survey of 200 mayors by the Institut de Sciences Economiques of Brest showed 80 per cent of left-wing mayors in favour of aid to firms in difficulty, against 40 per cent of those on the right (Steib, 1987). Employers' organizations tend to be opposed to intervention in principle. In 1986, the vice president of the CNFP, the main employers' organization, insisted that public intervention at all levels must be subsidiary *(Le Monde,* 3 October 1986). The private enterprise group of the national Economic and Social Council warned in 1987 against 'the artificial maintenance of activity in condemned firms, the loss of independence in assisted firms, the blow to competition, the development of an assistance mentality and above all the cost to public finances' (Conseil Economique et Social, 1987). Equally strong opposition is found from the Communist Party, which objects to subsidizing capitalist enterprise as a regressive form of redistribution. The Communist line is that local governments should continue to tax industry to provide social services and that, where firms are in difficulty they should support the workers' struggles for jobs but not the firm itself. Strongest support for the idea that local governments do have a role in economic intervention comes from the socialists, committed neither to the free market nor to the overthrow of capitalism. While they did devote some effort in the 1970s to providing an ideological wrapping for this attitude in terms of the virtues of the local economic sector of small firms, their attitude in practice owes a great deal to more immediate pragmatic considerations.

There is much evidence, indeed, that for local governments as a whole it is the local circumstances which determine the decision to intervene, with ideology conditioning only the mechanism. A survey by the association of French mayors found, in contrast to the Brest survey, that just 10 per cent of mayors refused economic intervention in principle in the name of private enterprise. Much more important was the size of the commune, with pressures to intervene increasing with the size of the city (Steib, 1987): in the smallest, most demand for intervention is reported from the general public, while in the largest it tends to come from firms themselves.

The new growth politics has led to changes in the local power structure. Development coalitions are emerging in the major cities, grouping local political, bureaucratic and business elites, cutting across previous alignments. In contrast to the American case, though, control tends to remain in the hands of the political–administrative elite. This varies from one city to another, according to the social and political cohesiveness of the governing coalition. Le Galès (1990) shows how in Rennes, a modernizing Socialist mayor was able to build on a collectivist tradition inherited from Christian Democracy and civic identity to forge a development coalition with privileged links to the state. With the increasingly technical nature of government, a new type of notable again has been identified, a technocrat who is able to deal on equal terms with the local bureaucracy, the state administration and the private sector. Local elected officials are increasingly drawn from the ranks of the public service (Garraud, 1988) and base their power not only on their position within the administrative structure but on their command of technical language and norms (Gaudin, 1988). These norms are common to the public and private sectors and the networks of committees and quasi-governmental bodies linking local government and the local business community. Yet the structure of demand, from firms and communities, has tended to ensure that attention is focused on job creation and retention rather than simply capital mobilization. While French mayors are not immune to civic mercantilism, the concentration of leadership in political hands reinforces the concern with employment.

These arrangements do not work everywhere. In cities with a highly fragmented local government system where there are political rivalries among notables, the retreat of the central state as a result of decentralization has led to a planning vacuum. Cities without the capacity for social mobilization and coalition-building have tended to lose out in the competition for growth. In some cases, the vacuum has been filled by local private development committees. Great admiration is often expressed for the local development coalitions of American cities such as Pittsburgh and Baltimore, together with laments that France lacks this tradition (e.g., in Greffe, 1989). Yet without political leadership and links to the central state, the private sector-led model of development has little prospect of success.

The integration of this political–administrative elite in national politics has largely prevented the isolation and closure of city politics characteristic of the USA. Cities collectively have continued to extract substantial resources from central government. Despite inequality in the capacity to mobilize for growth, the national welfare state has attenuated the social consequences of development politics, though an underclass has emerged largely comprising disenfranchized immigrants. Above all, the central state continues to attempt to rationalize the system to attenuate the effects of inter-urban competition. Already under the 1981–6 Socialist administration, there were warnings that cities should not over-extend themselves. The brief conservative government of Jacques Chirac (1986–8) put the emphasis on privatization and curtailed the powers of communes to intervene. Since 1988, the emphasis has again been on rationalization and tapping local development energies in the effort to increase French competitiveness within Europe. Proposals for communal groupings put forward in 1990 were deliberately intended to reduce bidding wars and to ensure coherence in local development. Central government launched its own urban economic initiative under the prefects while the Minister of the Interior warned that local initiatives must not prejudice the preponderant role of the state in economic development. The revived regional planning system has surprised observers by its success as a vehicle for intergovernmental exchange. The state–region planning contracts were by and large fulfilled and in 1989 the government announced a new round. There is some evidence, too, that councils are becoming more cautious in their interventions and reluctant to assume responsibilities which belong to the central state, notably in rescuing firms in difficulty.

France, then, is characterized by conflicting pressures. Development politics and inter-urban competition lead to greater inequality among (and, to some extent, within) cities. Yet the effects of this are powerfully mediated by national and intergovernmental politics. The national state remains committed to promoting national development and competitiveness in collaboration with the territorial elite. The system provides a continuing capacity for integrating urban and national politics and policies, while the collective weight of territorial elites in national politics ensures a continued flow of resources to all cities.

COMPARING GROWTH POLITICS

The result of economic restructuring together with changes in national policies has been a series of local political realignments on both sides of the Atlantic. New development coalitions have emerged, transcending traditional divisions. By a development coalition is meant a place-based, interclass development effort, aimed at enhancing the economic competitiveness of a city. It will comprise the local political leadership together with local business interests. Class conflict is attenuated in favour of business and trade union collaboration to promote inward investment. Partisan divisions are attenuated similarly in the defence of place. Intra-urban political competition and conflict is partially displaced by inter-urban competition for growth. A development coalition in this sense is not the same as Logan and Molotch's (1987) growth machine. The growth machine is dedicated to a narrow view of growth as the enhancement of land and rental values and is socially restricted. It is a specifically local phenomenon, though operating in an open market economy. A development coalition may be more or less inclusive, broad or narrow in its policy focus and social project. It is rooted in individual places but includes national agencies operating in space and may be supported by national governments.

There are some common tendencies. Development politics has blurred partisan and class divisions. Representatives of the urban working class in the Democratic, Labour and Socialist parties are heavily involved in collaboration with private business. European ideas of a radically different economic order, to be implemented from a local and regional base have been abandoned in favour of participation in the capitalist order. Ideology is muted. Public–private partnerships blur the lines of politics while commercial norms of secrecy and selectivity challenge public notions of accountability and equality. Policy is determined by location as much as by choice so that ironically those parties with the strongest working-class and lower-class base are often most favourable to the subsidization of private capital.

Another common trend is towards inter-urban and intra-urban inequality. Some cities are better equipped to face competition than others, especially in relation to new technology (King, 1990). Within cities, the pursuit of growth imposes costs in terms of social and spatial priorities. There are winners and losers, though the capacity to compensate losers varies. Cooption of working-class based parties into development coalitions leaves an urban underclass without adequate political expression. In the USA the conquest of civic power by black mayors has not radically changed the logic of development politics despite the social and financial cost. In Britain, an underclass remains trapped in inner cities and peripheral housing schemes, electorally loyal to the Labour Party but increasingly alienated. In France, the underclass consists largely of North African immigrants, excluded from electoral politics and largely segregated in low-cost public housing schemes.

Also common to all the cases is the marginal effectiveness of much intervention. Arguably the main effects of the commitment to growth are on the urban political structure and the priorities of local governments rather than on local economic performance.

Yet institutional and political differences do differentiate development politics in the four countries, making any general 'growth machine' model inappropriate. In the USA, development coalitions involve direct partnerships between local governments and private actors. Given the mobility of capital and the weak power of local governments to act directly or through the intergovernmental system, business has a privileged role. It would be misleading to characterize this as a neo-classical market system. Urban restructuring takes the form of planned interventions by public–private partnerships aimed at maximizing investment. There are, of course, differences among cities, depending on the strength of local political mobilization and the market position of cities. Stone (1987) characterizes regimes as 'corporate' ones, in which private interests dominate and the central concern is to promote the interests of downtown corporations; progressive regimes in which there is a challenge to corporate power; and caretaker regimes dedicated to preserving the status quo and the interests of established business. Given the economic dependence of American cities, progressive regimes do not emerge where there is the greatest concentration of deprivation but in middle-class professional cities relatively independent of the corporate sector (Clavel, 1986). In Canada, many of the same features are present (Magnusson, 1990) but the larger role of provincial governments in spatial planning and fiscal equalization attenuates its effects.

In Britain and France, local governments have increasingly sought partnerships with the private sector yet urban restructuring remains dependent on central state intervention. Despite the rhetoric about markets, the weakness of the locally-based private sector means that the partners are not always available. This has disappointed admirers of the American model. It has also disappointed some individuals in the Labour and Socialist parties who still see locally-based capital as a potential ally against the central state. Some British local leaders emphasize common interests in fighting the emphasis on the London-based finance sector, in supporting manufacturing and opposing an over-valued currency. A similar idea in France underlay the Socialists' idea of the 1970s that localities could sustain a progressive alliance including locally-based business, against the Parisian nexus of the central state and large corporations. The problem remains the weakness of the local business sector. In Britain, central government has had to intervene through development corporations to simulate a strong business input to development decisions. In both Britain and France, any locally-based business organization would still face the need to go via the central state to mobilize resources and resolve problems. Local development coalitions must therefore continue to work through the central state. Attempts to by-pass it by going to Europe are of more symbolic than substantive importance. This, together with the relationship to global economy and external dependence, conditions the terms of the new partnerships.

In France, territorial elites are better able to influence the terms of their relationship with capital via the central state. An integrated national political and administrative elite discourages the separation of national and urban policies while local networks sustain a sense of place. A commitment to national competitiveness attenuates urban competition while the state retains a capacity to rationalize local initiatives and harness these to national development. Integration of the political system and the leverage of local elites over national politics prevents unilateral restructuring of power relations or the abandonment of cities by the state. In Britain, by contrast, spatial development policies have been largely uninformed by any coherent strategy for national competitiveness. Rather, cities have been expected to adapt themselves to the new international division of labour.

Displacement of social by business priorities also varies. In Britain, France and Canada national political competition and values of social solidarity have ensured that national welfare states have survived the 1980s largely intact. In all four countries, social movements have challenged the new definition of the city interest and postulate a different type of place-based politics.

8. Conclusion: The Progressive City

> The inhabitant of New England is attached to his municipality because it is strong and independent; he is interested in it because he helps to direct it; he loves it because he has nothing to complain about; he places in it all his ambition and future; he is involved in all the incidents of municipal life; in that limited sphere which is within his reach, he tries to govern society; he accustoms himself to forms without which liberty can only advance by revolutions, imbues himself with their spirit, acquires a taste for order, understands the harmony of powers and finally gains clear and practical ideas on the nature of his duties and the extent of his liberties (de Tocqueville, 1986, p. 92).

The previous chapters have examined urban regimes in terms of the governing capacity and openness to social interests. They have assessed the power of urban elected elites to mobilize resources, allocate them, shape the development of the city and distribute opportunities within it. It has emerged that urban politics is to a greater or lesser extent closed to popular influence and largely confirmed the conventional belief that city government is limited by the intergovernmental system and by the private control of resources. It has, partially, confirmed the view that city governments are caught between the need to defer to the owners of capital with anti-egalitarian policies, and the desire to achieve social justice. Yet the analysis has shown that these are not determinate factors but constraints, not constants but variable across time and space. It may not be possible to return to the simplicities of early nineteenth-century New England celebrated by de Tocqueville but, within constraints, there is room for an urban politics. There is even room for a progressive urban politics with some ability to reconcile governing capacity with openness and pluralism, growth with social justice. This requires improvements in policy capacity, in the analysis of problems and the search for solutions, but there is more involved than this. It is dependent equally on a broader set of conditions in the political system itself: these are derived from the categories of culture, structure and political choice.

It is not the intention here to set out a blueprint for a progressive urban politics. The task at hand is political analysis, not social engineering. Different societies necessarily combine elements of political life in different ways; this is the essence of a genuine local politics. On the other hand, it would be indefensible to take refuge under the blanket of 'political culture' and conclude that societies will be different because they are different, because they have been different. There is a complex interplay between culture preconditions and action. It was noted in Chapter 1 that cultural beliefs are important in shaping political activity, providing the premises on which rational judgements are made and setting standards of legitimacy. Yet culture itself is formed by political action, historic events and the more or less accurate memories of them. The circularity of this mode of explanation can be broken only by examining historic experiences in specific places. The importance of nation-building in forging political beliefs, institutions and modes of action has been noted earlier. Yet cultural and ideological dispositions are continually being remade, either by catastrophic events which force a new appraisal or by gradual change. The effects of the interwar depression and the Second World War on assumptions about national welfare in the USA and Britain respectively are examples of the former. The secularization of western European societies in this century provides an example of the latter.

Structures similarly constrain the scope for political choice, while being themselves malleable in the longer run. Structural factors also shape individuals' perceptions of their self-interest and their shared interests. At the same time, they encourage modes of individual or collective action which become assimilated into cultural and ideological assumptions with a weight of their own. Culture, structure and choice are analytical categories which clarify aspects of social reality but are mutually dependent and inextricably connected in individual places. Rather than analyse them separately as in Chapter 1, the following discussion looks at some of the interplays between culture, structure and choice which might encourage the emergence of a progressive urban politics, with some commentary on their presence or absence in the cases examined.

THE PUBLIC DOMAIN

A precondition for a progressive urban politics is a broad conception of the public domain, encompassing the worlds of production and distribution. Linked to this is a vision of the citizen as stakeholder in city politics, with no special prerogatives for property owners. Only then can a conception of public interests be forged in which the public interest is not identical with economic development (however defined); in which economic development is not identical to the aspirations of business leaders; and in which distribution is as important as accumulation. This is not to claim that there is an identifiable 'public interest' in every issue, awaiting revelation; public interests are themselves political constructs. What is important is that they be constructed in an arena characterized by the equality stemming from citizenship rather than by the inequality stemming from property; and where publicly-oriented or universal claims are accorded higher legitimacy than privately-oriented ones. Lest this appear utopian, it is worth noting that in all the societies considered here publicly-oriented claims do enjoy some special status with greater persuasive power. That is precisely why business groups take such pains to present themselves as custodians of a social interest in economic growth and production, rather than emphasizing their sectional claims. Yet culture and political institutions themselves are critical in sustaining a publicly-oriented politics, without violating rational self-interest. De Tocqueville was aware of this. After commenting on the instinctive love of country found in primitive societies, based on tradition, he goes on:

> There is another [love of country] more rational than this; less generous, perhaps less ardent but more fecund and more durable; this one is born of enlightenment; it develops with the help of laws, it grows with the exercise of rights and finishes by somehow becoming identical with personal interest. A man understands the influence which the wellbeing of the country has on his own; he knows that the law permits him to contribute to producing this wellbeing, and he concerns himself with the prosperity of his country, first as something which is useful to him and then as his own work (de Tocqueville, 1986, p. 230).

Institutions play an important role in forming civic consciousness and a sense of the public good. Even public choice theorists, while purporting to describe hard reality, are frequently engaged in a quest for institutions in which people will be encouraged to behave as the self-interested maximizers which their theory assumes. John Stuart Mill, though a utilitarian and believer in the individual's right to maximize his or her personal utility, was more aware of the role of local institutions in 'the nourishment of public spirit and the development of intelligence' (Mill, 1912, p. 365). Elsewhere he claimed that 'The first question in respect to any political institutions is, how far they tend to foster in the members of the community the various desirable qualities, moral and intellectual' (Mill, 1912, p. 167). Emphasizing the individual as the unit of analysis, American scholars, on the other hand, have played down the role of institutions in defining the character of individuals themselves (Dyson, 1980).

The formulation of a public interest in cities is dependent on a sense of place and of community. It is incorrect to impute a unitary interest to reified cities and a liberal democracy requires a domain of private rights. Yet this does not mean that cities cannot constitute political communities in which common interests coexist with internal differences. These common interests cannot be discovered by the crude reductionism of the public choice school. Rather, they are a political *construction*, in specific conditions. Place as public space must be distinguished from the defence of private space or the purely market-based conception of place as commodity. These two conceptions are constantly in competition. Structural changes in the polity can affect this. In Britain and the USA recent national policies have sought a deconstruction of place (Warren, 1990), the reduction of space to an element in the exchange economy. Structural economic trends may have the same effect. Global economic restructuring and the increase in inter-urban competition are putting local social solidarity under great strain. Yet place-based politics are, in some respects, becoming more important, and new solidarities are possible.

One common spatial interest can be derived from the idea of spatial rationality – that is, that it may be rational to act jointly within one set of spatial constraints but individually faced with the same issue in another spatial setting. So a community, faced with a plant closure with major ramifications on the economic base and quality of public life, may consider it rational to mobilize to prevent it. For the multinational corporation, the closure may be consistent with a broader, global market rationality. For the individual household, in the absence of a collective action, the rational response may be to relocate or accept wage cuts, a strategy in which, if generally applied, all households will lose. There is more than one rational and optimal way to allocate resources, dependent on whose perspective one adopts.

Common interests based in civic consciousness can in turn sustain institutions. An example is metropolitan government. Metropolitan governments may not evoke the sentimental loyalty of the affective community but they can help formulate a public interest. In fragmented local government systems, citizens may feel themselves in competition and define their interests accordingly. If problems are taken to the metropolitan level, perceptions change and common solutions may emerge. These may prove positive-sum, yielding more to most citizens than competition. Other common interests may be discerned in development. Some (though by no means all) types of economic development might be in the wider urban or metropolitan interest, though this can be appreciated only if they are placed in the appropriate context where social as well as private benefits can be evaluated and external costs included in the calculation. The creation of a stable, just society can also be seen as a general, public interest where this is conceived in social rather than purely individualist terms. At the appropriate spatial level modes of problem-solving which combine social solidarity with economic efficiency may be possible. In turn, these may help shape civic consciousness and trust in government, leading to further cooperative solutions. There is not just one such level but a series, which may or may not correspond to institutional forms: the neighbourhood; the city; the metropolitan region; the province, state or historic region; the nation. The concern in this book is with the city in its regional and national context, but other levels of territorial rationality exist, with their own logic (Keating, 1988b).

Local conditions are important in the construction of public interests. A sense of place is the product of history, culture and the capacity of the system to forge common interests and solutions. The quality of local democracy is measured by levels of voting and other forms of participation, but also by the degree of social solidarity and the extent to which solutions and policies are accepted as legitimate; not all urban policies can be presented as matters of common interest. Cities are also the locus of conflict and competition, and it is important that local governments should have a capacity to provide a forum for debate and the resolution of conflicts. They can do this more easily in some respects where local government is closed through cultural bias and structural manipulation, so that the agenda is limited and choices restricted. Then local politics, operating within narrow parameters, is manageable. Where the agenda is broadened, conflict resolution becomes more difficult. This is the real limitation of local government, and can be resolved only by placing urban political systems within their broader context. The critical issue is thus not autonomy but how to sustain a viable local politics together with a governing capacity in the city. Local governments resolve few problems autonomously. Within wider economic and political systems, their capacity may be increased.

POLITICS AND MARKETS

A critical issue remains the relationship between politics and markets. While state control – and, *a fortiori*, local state control of the economy – is an impractical proposition in the modern world, simplistic formulations about private market solutions are equally so. Urban governments are inescapably involved in local economies because of their responsibilities for land use. As business corporations are well aware, urban land use planning is equally inescapable. The only question is who will plan, and in whose interest. The basis therefore exists for a balance of public and private power, the terms of which will vary from one situation to another.

State–market relationships are governed partly by ideological presuppositions, as the comparison of different cultures shows. They are also affected by government structures. If local politics is often the politics of private development, this is because of ideological and structural factors which have served to limit the urban agenda. More consolidated local governments will generally be less vulnerable to business pressure. The involvement of national parties in local politics opens up the political agenda. More centralized systems of government may similarly protect cities from dependence on the market. This belief underpins the conclusions of many American texts on urban politics which call for a national urban policy as the solution to the dilemma of the cities. Often this is invoked as a *deus ex machina* to rescue cities from the bind which the analysts have discerned. It is not clear, however, just what a national urban policy might include, or that greater centralization would provide an answer to cities' problems. If the central regime were unsympathetic to urban problems, as the British experience shows, centralization would achieve little. On the other hand, if the central regime were sympathetic, then presumably we would have appropriate national urban policies already. What is needed is not merely a policy shift but a regime change to an intergovernmental system in which urban interests are articulated in national policy-making. Only then can state–market relations be put on a more equal footing, though admittedly international capital mobility weakens the capacity of the nation state itself. In this respect, the French system exhibits a larger capacity than the American one, despite the high degree of decentralization in the USA, and the presence of a locally-based business sector.

POLITICS AND POLICY

These problems of capacity to define issues, formulate policies, gain legitimacy and implement solutions are greatly increased by the new roles and relationships with which city governments are confronted. They are no longer merely service providers or more or less passive servants of business development needs. Rather they are at the centre of a series of conflicts among rising social demands in a context of increased inter-urban economic competition. Cities are becoming internally more pluralist as new social movements emerge, old political alignments fragment and new issues reach the agenda. At the same time, economic restructuring and capital mobility have increased the external dependence of cities on a private capital which follows its own logic. Place-based politics has become more important to environmentalists, labour movements, ethnic minorities and a variety of popular movements, while the viability of place-based politics is undermined by global economic trends. For the traditional marxist, this represents a 'contradiction' ultimately fatal to the system. For some neo-classical political economists, it can be resolved by reducing all issues and relationships to market ones. For others, it points to a need for structural reform, with the social issues taken to a higher level (Peterson, 1981). In practice, matters are more complex and the reconciliation of the social and economic dimensions of policy is something which must be accomplished at all levels at all times. Cultural factors greatly influence the way in which the issue is perceived in different places. Structural conditions may help or hinder the task. Equally important is the matter of learning capacity. If these issues are new or are changing in shape and incidence, it is not surprising that the search for solutions is lengthy.

The problem is posed acutely in economic development and anti-poverty policies. There are certainly difficult policy choices here, and there may be a trade-off between efficiency and equity. It would be wrong to assume, however, that this is always the case: there may well be policies which can achieve both sets of goals. Part of the problem is that in these key policy areas we still do not really know what works. Cities have rushed into the economic development role under the impetus of events with little knowledge or understanding. They have ridden the latest fashions, imitated each other in often highly inappropriate ways. The perceived imperative of economic competition in a homogeneous world market has led to a homogenization of space as all cities strive for the same things, convention centres and shopping malls one year, science parks and waterfronts the next. A particularly pervasive idea has been that of the 'post-industrial city'. Extending the truism that industrial employment no longer accounts for the large proportion of jobs which it did in the past, policy-makers have imagined that industrial production itself is redundant or that all cities can share in the new service economy. In reality, cities are very differently placed to share in service development which itself is limited in quantity; and a large number of services are devoted to servicing manufacturing industry itself. The cultural contempt for manufacturing, which has long roots in Britain, is increasingly encountered in the USA. In both countries, it has been fostered by national governments which, nominally committed to sound finance and production, have based their electoral fortunes on consumption and cheap imports. Urban development strategies, in turn, have tried to cater for this through encouragement and subsidization of cities' consumption functions, geared towards the rich. Though Harvey (1989, p. 48) may be right to note that 'the argument that the only way to preserve jobs for an increasingly impoverished underclass is to create consumer palaces for the rich with public subsidies has at some point to wear thin', it remains pervasive.

In the confusion as to what makes economic development work, there has been waste of public resources, subsidization of developments which merely displace others and a tilt towards property development as the sector which produces the quickest and most visible results. Cities have chased mobile investments by multinationals with whatever incentives they can muster, often without serious cost–benefit analysis. In the new form of civic boosterism, all development comes to be regarded as beneficial, almost regardless of regressive social effects. Politics itself has been affected by the perceived imperatives of the new order, with the consolidation of place-based development coalitions incorporating the representatives of the have-nots.

The extent of this new politics varies from one place to another, and is affected by cultural traditions and structural variables. The scope for cities is tightly limited by the economic conditions which they face, but even in the most unfavourable environments there is some room for political choice. Much of what cities do by way of economic development policy is ineffective. They have little direct leverage over the global economy or the investment decisions of multinationals. Where they attempt to negotiate with the largest corporations over incentives and conditions, they are seriously outgunned in knowledge, resources and options. Their resources rarely run to undertaking the most grandiose development projects or assuming a commanding role in them. Subsidizing business investment and functioning is usually ineffective as well as regressive, reversing the proper relationship in a market economy in which the private sector is the source of resources which governments devote to social purposes, rather than vice versa. Similar criticisms can be directed at strategies to socialize development costs and investment risk, responsibilities which again properly belong to the owners of capital. Yet it is 'progressive' city (and to some extent national) governments which are most associated with this strategy. Social democracy, in particular, has allowed itself to justify widespread subsidization of private industry, creating a 'reverse welfare state' in contradiction to its original beliefs. The 'partnership' of public and private sectors in development has led to the slow but steady absorption by public decision-makers of private values and criteria and of the private canons of secrecy and selectivity in place of the public canons of accountability and universality.

Despite the strong political and environmental pressures, this is a matter of political choice. If economic development policy measures are ineffective, then it cannot be argued that local governments are forced by the imperatives of growth and competition to adopt them. Urban governments can refuse to subsidize development projects, often without damage to their economic interests. They can insist that spending must be justified by a wider social welfare function, and that development is not always its own justification. They can resist the temptation to become subordinate partners of developers in the hope of obtaining side-payments. This does not mean abandoning a concern with the local economic environment. Local governments cannot command their economic environment, but they can manage their relations with the global economy. Many of the things which local governments can do are inexpensive or not in contradiction with wider social objectives. These may use the sense of place and the characteristics of territories as an element in the development process. Large multinationals may be beyond the scope of city government but entrepreneurship and growth are activities which happen in specific places with particular combinations of physical, social and cultural characteristics. So, instead of reducing all territories to the same homogeneous commodity which is assumed to be necessary to feature in the global economy, some of the most successful areas have exploited those characteristics which make them different and which cannot be reproduced.

Far from encouraging territories to retreat into local protectionism, this can provide a means for them to enter fully into the global economy. Another area in which local government can make a contribution is in establishing a degree of consensus on growth policies. This is not to remove the politics from the process of consensus-reaching, but to recognize that economic development does have characteristics which differ from those of other policy areas – notably the need for stability and some continuity. In these conditions and with the right encouragement, inter-firm linkages can develop into networks in which competition is tempered by the existence of cooperation and common interest, motivated by rational individual and collective self-interest. What Nanetti (1988), in the Italian context calls 'social capitalism' can develop. Studying the conditions in which political decentralization and local growth have supported each other in Italian regions, she emphasizes that 'the society must have the ability to use public resources for promoting broad, socially-based rather than narrow individual gain ... there must be a sense of the public interest well rooted among politicians and members of the bureaucracy as well as society at large. Otherwise, public resources will be siphoned off for private production as in the case of graft and corruption, in which case the nexus between the social–historical fabric and institutional decentralisation will be broken' (Nanetti, 1988, p. 9). Ritaine (1989), examining the same phenomenon, notes that external linkages can provide external economies of scale to replace the internal scale economies of the large corporation, while preserving flexibility.

Given their limited resources, local governments must concentrate on low-cost initiatives within their capacity. This requires a learning process. Given the needs of economic development, it also requires a new kind of local government official, at home in both business and government, able to talk on terms of equality with business leaders without entering into their assumptive world. Such a profession is slowly emerging. Business advice, fostering inter-firm exchanges and technology transfer, promotion of the characteristics of the territory, the *image de marque*, are areas in which a local agency has much to offer. There is also a limited role in improving local capital circuits and retaining local savings for investment. This requires more than the presence of locally-headquartered banks which may be more effective in channelling savings out of the locality than retaining them. Publicly-managed pension funds may also be a source of capital for viable ventures. Small-scale business operations and cooperatives, lacking easy entry into the business world and financial circuits, are also targets for local intervention.

On the other hand, local government subsidies to business investment or current operations would rarely be justified. They involve regressive transfers from taxpayers to the owners of capital; they are not usually effective in increasing local output and exports; and they encourage other localities to compete. (National regional development schemes, which alter the conditions of national markets, are another matter.) There may be a territorial rationale for intervening to sustain industries threatened by a national or global recession such as that of the 1980s in order to retain capacity for the recovery. Many local governments in Europe and North America were brought into the economic development field through such measures, and are only just beginning to distinguish between emergency measures and a permanent economic strategy. This is particularly noticeable in France, where the 1981 decentralization legislation contained a clause, potentially deadly for municipalities, allowing them to intervene in favour of firms in difficulty.

The local enterprise boards set up in Britain – in the West Midlands, Greater London, West Yorkshire, Merseyside and Lancashire – provide examples of institutions which have succeeded in achieving a degree of consensus. While these have differed in their strategies, their resources and their target groups, they have demonstrated that there is a role for local institutions in the development process. While the boards never succeeded in posing a challenge to capitalism as some had dreamed, they have brought a local dimension to economic and industrial policy. The first three have become sufficiently part of the local economic landscape as to survive the abolition of their sponsoring councils in 1986. After periods of learning and experimentation, these have had some success in mobilizing local capital and in stimulating enterprise (Mawson and Miller, 1985; Cochrane and Clark, 1990), though at the time of writing there was a question mark over their future. In France a number of local initiatives have served to reconstitute networks of decision-makers, stimulating enterprise and sustaining it through infancy (Arocena, 1986). More broadly, local governments can focus on those responsibilities which are theirs already. Providing good education, high levels of environmental amenity and quality public services may not have the immediate political pay-off of economic development but is probably more effective in the long run, not only in promoting development but as a direct contribution to social welfare.

Distributional issues are often posed as in contradiction, either with the need for economic development and capital attraction, or with the needs of private consumption. In practice, it is usually less a matter of contradiction than of more or less manageable conflict. Local governments cannot achieve a radical shift in the distribution of wealth and income, so the question of whether this is a legitimate objective hardly arises. On the other hand, the elimination of poverty is an objective that can mobilize wide support, depending on how it is approached and just what the opportunity cost is. Again, cultural and structural constraints are important, and a sense of community helps to sustain the social solidarity necessary for anti-poverty programmes. Given these, political choice is possible. It is not necessary to reduce support for anti-poverty measures to a form of self-indulgence, a vicarious pleasure derived from doing good. Nor is it necessary to conclude that no-one will ever vote for such measures if they cost taxes. The experience of western European countries in particular shows that voters will often support such measures because they think that they are *right*. The emergence of an urban underclass is not merely an aesthetic annoyance or sporadic threat to public order. It is an affront to any notion of citizenship with a substantive social or economic content. Support for anti-poverty measures can also be bolstered by linking them more closely to economic development. Trickle-down approaches to the solution of poverty, relying on the automatic effect of development to solve the problem, have proved an illusion. Policies to ensure that the poor benefit from development can be self-reinforcing, helping to increase the legitimacy and acceptability of policy in both social and economic spheres. It is precisely in this linkage of the social to the economic that public intervention has an important role distinguishing it from market rationality. For local governments to devote themselves to imitating or stimulating markets is to ignore this vital distinction.

The progressive local government therefore depends on all three elements of culture, structure and choice. A value system is needed which will sustain the notion of a public sphere, public interests and public spaces separate from private interests. A structure is needed which will present issues in such a way as to facilitate public-oriented rather than purely private choices, allow government to negotiate with private capital rather than being subject to it and capture a large share of the external benefits of policies. Fragmented local government systems are ill-suited to this. Structures at the metropolitan level are necessary, as are systems of intergovernmental relations which prevent cities being thrown back on their own resources. Political parties play a crucial role. They must be able to articulate local preferences, sustain political competition within the city and at the same time open up local politics to larger national questions and national politics to urban issues. Finally, a form of local politics is needed which recognizes the limitations of city government, mobilizes electors and is able to learn from experience.

City governments do not simply require autonomy if this exposes them to unbridled private business influence. Nor is more centralized government in itself the answer, as the British experience shows. American liberals are prone to advocate a national urban policy as the solution to urban ills. Yet the comparative analysis shows that the choice is not between strong national government with a strong social concern, and decentralized government subject to the market. Business is itself critically dependent on government, both central and local. The free market is a theoretical construct not found anywhere in reality. National governments can be subject to both local and business influence. Both national and central levels therefore need to reconcile the social and development dimensions of policy. A progressive urban regime requires not strong autonomous central government but a national policy system responsive to urban needs.

These are stiff requirements, made the more demanding by the scale of the problem facing some cities. Prosperous cities favoured by the global market will have spare resources both for social initiatives and for the promotion of development. Declining cities are less well-endowed and face more difficult tasks. National governments therefore have a role in equalizing conditions and fiscal capacity. American traditions of self-government are an important element in the democratic inheritance. Yet local politics is closed and governing capacity limited. Western European systems provide more governing capacity than do North American ones, yet centralization in the British case and the weakness of popular participation in France reduce self-governing capacity. Only by combining elements of each can a true local democracy be built. This cannot be reduced to some simple formula or an exhortation to local or national governments to change their ways. It requires sustained political action to change attitudes and restructure institutions, as well as serious examination of the nature of policy problems and their solutions.

Bibliography

ACIR (1973), Advisory Commission on Intergovernmental Relations, *Substate Regionalism and the Federal System*, vol. 1, *Regional Decision Making: New Strategies for Substate Districts*, Washington: ACIR.

ACIR (1977), Advisory Commission on Intergovernmental Relations, *Regionalism Revisited: Recent Areawide and Local Responses*, Washington: ACIR.

ACIR (1980), Advisory Commission on Intergovernmental Relations, *Public Assistance: The Growth of a Federal Function*, Washington: ACIR.

ACIR (1982), Advisory Commission on Intergovernmental Relations, *State and Local Roles in the Federal System*, Washington: ACIR.

ACIR (1986), Advisory Commission on Intergovernmental Relations, *The Transformation of American Politics. Implications for Federalism*, Washington: ACIR.

ACIR (1987), Advisory Commission on Intergovernmental Relations, *The Organization of Local Public Economies*, Washington: ACIR.

ACIR (1988), Advisory Commission on Intergovernmental Relations, *Metropolitan Reorganization: The St. Louis Case*, Washington: ACIR.

ACIR (1989a), Advisory Commission on Intergovernmental Relations, *Significant Features of Fiscal Federalism*, 1989 edn, vol. 1, Washington: ACIR.

ACIR (1989b), Advisory Commission on Intergovernmental Relations, *Significant Features of Fiscal Federalism*, 1989 edn, vol. 11, Washington: ACIR.

ADC (1987), Association of District Councils, *Economic Development Initiatives and Innovations*, London: ADC.

Agnew, J. (1987), *Place and Politics. The Geographical Mediation of State and Society*, London and Boston: Allen and Unwin.

Altenberger, C., Kearns, K. and Peters, B.G. (1988), 'Strengthening Pennsylvania Local Governments: Implications for the Mon Valley', conference on Mill Towns, University of Pittsburgh.

Arocena, J. (1986), *Le développement par l'initiative locale*, Paris: L'Harmattan.

Ashford, D. (1982), *British Dogmatism and French Pragmatism. Central–Local Policymaking in the Welfare State*, London: Allen and Unwin.

Ashford, D. (1989), 'British Dogmatism and French Pragmatism Revisited', in Crouch, C. and Marquand, D. (eds), *The New Centralism*, Oxford: Blackwell.

Audit Commission for Local Authorities in England and Wales (1989), *Urban Regeneration and Economic Development. The Local Government Dimension*, London: HMSO.

Bachrach, P. and Baratz, M. (1962), 'The Two Faces of Power', *American Political Science Review*, 56(4), pp. 947–52.

Balligand, J.-P. and Maquart, D. (1990), 'Aménagement du territoire: la mosaïque disloquée', *Revue Politique et Parlementaire*, 946, pp. 54–67.

Barker, A. and Keating, M. (1977), 'Public Spirits. Amenity Societies and Others', in Crouch, C. (ed.), *British Political Sociology Yearbook*, London: Croom Helm.

Barnekov, T., Boyle, R. and Rich, D. (1989), *Privatism and Urban Policy in Britain and the United States*, Oxford: Oxford University Press.

Barnes, J. (1990), 'Urban development corporations – the lessons from London's docklands', in Montgomery, J. and Thornley, A. (eds), *Radical Planning Initiatives*, Aldershot: Gower.

Barnes, W. (1990), 'Urban Policies and Urban Impacts after Reagan', *Urban Affairs Quarterly*, 25(4).

Beauregard, R. (1989), 'Space, Time and Economic Restructuring', in Beauregard, R. (ed.), *Economic Restructuring and Political Response*, Urban Affairs Annual Reviews, vol. 34, Newbury Park and London: Sage.

Bélorgey, G. (1984), *La France décentralisée*, Paris: Berger–Levrault.

Bennett, R. (1989), 'Central and local government taxes and responsibilities: the arguments for assignment and the demands for restructuring', in France, G. (ed.), *Local Public Services and Crisis of the Welfare State*, Rimini: Maggioli.

Bernier, L. (1991), 'Decentralisation and Policy in France', *Journal of Urban Affairs*.

Bird, R. and Slack, N.E. (1983), *Urban Public Finance in Canada*, Toronto: Butterworth.

Birnbaum, N. (1988), *The Radical Renewal. The Politics of Ideas in Modern America*, New York: Pantheon.

Birnbaum, P. (1982), *La logique de l'état*, Paris: Fayard.

Boddy, M. and Fudge, C. (eds) (1984), *Local Socialism? Labour Councils and New Left Alternatives*, London: Macmillan.

Body-Gendrot, S. (1987), 'Grass-roots Mobilization in the Thirteenth Arrondissement of Paris: A Cross-National View', in Stone, C. and Sanders, H., (eds), *The Politics of Urban Development*, Lawrence: University of Kansas Press.

Brindley, T., Rydin, Y. and Stoker, G. (1989), *Remaking Planning. The Politics of Urban Change in the Thatcher Years*, London: Unwin Hyman.

Brownstone, M. and Plunkett, T. (1983), *Metropolitan Winnipeg: Politics and Reform of Local Government*, Berkeley: University of California Press.

Bulpitt, J. (1983), *Territory and Power in the United Kingdom. An Interpretation*, Manchester: Manchester University Press.

Carlson, D.B. (1981), 'How Cities Use Block Grants for Economic Development', *Urban Institute Working Paper 1448–01*, Washington: Urban Institute.

Castells, M. (1978), *City, Class and Power*, London: Macmillan.

Castells, M. (1983), *The City and the Grassroots,* Berkeley: University of California Press.

CED (1966), Committee for Economic Development, *Modernizing Local Government*, Washington: CED.

Clavel, P. (1986), *The Progressive City. Planning and Participation, 1969–84*, New Brunswick: Rutgers University Press.

Clément, R. (1988), 'Les élections municipales. Une démarche unitaire conforme aux intérêts des habitants', *Economie et Politique*, 140, pp. 46–9.

CLES (1989), Centre for Local Economic Strategies, *Interim Monitoring Report. Urban Development Corporations*, Manchester: CLES.

Cochrane, A. and Clarke, A. (1990), 'Local Enterprise Boards: The short history of a radical initiative', *Public Administration*, 68(3), pp. 315–36.

Cockburn, C. (1977), *The Local State; management of cities and people*, London: Pluto.

Coleman, M. (1983), *Interest Intermediation and Local Urban Development*, Ph.D. thesis, University of Pittsburgh.

Committee of Public Accounts (House of Commons) (1986), *Tenth Report. The Urban Programme*, HC 81. 1985–6, London: HMSO.

Committee of Public Accounts (House of Commons) (1989), *Urban Development Corporations*, HC 385. 1988–9, London: HMSO.

Conseil des Impôts (1987), 'Neuvième rapport au président de la république, relatif à la fiscalité des entreprises', *Journal Officiel de la République Française*, 89, 26 August 1987.

Conseil Economique et Social (1987), 'Avis et Rapports', *Journal Officiel de la République Française*, 12, 3 June 1987.

Cooke, P. (1983), *Theories of Planning and Spatial Development*, London: Hutchinson.

Cooke, P. (1990), *Back to the Future. Modernity, Postmodernity and Locality*, London: Unwin Hyman.

Coulson, A. (1989), *Strategy and Impact of the Teesside Development Corporation*, Birmingham: Institute of Local Government Studies.

Cour des Comptes (1987), 'Rapport au président de la république', *Journal Officiel de la République Française*, 66, 3 July 1987.

Cour des Comptes (1988), 'Rapport au président de la république', *Journal Officiel de la République Française*, 59, 22 June 1988.

Crawford, P., Fothergill, S. and Monk, S. (1985), *The Effect of Rates on the Location of Employment. Final Report*, Cambridge: Department of Land Economy, University of Cambridge.

Crenson, M. (1971), *The Unpolitics of Air Pollution: A Study of Non-Decision-Making in the Cities*, Baltimore: Johns Hopkins Press.

Criqui, E. (1990), 'Les carrières des élites politiques locales', *Revue Politique et Parlementaire*, 946, pp. 44–53.

Crozier, M. (1964), *The Bureaucratic Phenomenon*, London: Tavistock.

Crozier, M. and Friedberg, E. (1977), *L'acteur et le système*, Paris: Seuil.

CSO (1990), Central Statistical Office, *Monthly Digest of Statistics*, 533, London: HMSO.

Cullingworth, J.B. (1987), *Urban and Regional Planning in Canada*, New Brunswick, N.J.: Transaction.

Cummings, S. (1988), 'Private Enterprise and Public Policy: Business Hegemony in the Metropolis', in Cummings, S. (ed.), *Business Elites and Urban Development*, Albany: State University of New York Press.

Dearlove, J. (1979), *The Reorganisation of British Local Government*, Cambridge: Cambridge University Press.

Dente, B. (1985), *Governare le frammentazione. Stato, Regioni ed enti locali in Italia*, Bologna: Il Mulino.

Deves, C. and Gouttebel, J.-Y. (1988), 'Que reste-t-il du dispositif d'aides de janvier-septembre 1982?', *Revue d'Economie Régionale et Urbaine*, 2, pp. 207–30.

Dion, S. (1986), *La politisation des mairies*, Paris: Economica.

Dogan, M. and Pelassy, D. (1990), *How to Compare Nations. Strategies in Comparative Politics*, 2nd edn, Chatham, N.J.: Chatham House.

Doig, J. (1987), 'Coalition-Building by a Regional Agency: Austin Tobin and the Port of New York Authority', in Stone, C. and Sanders, H. (eds), *The Politics of Urban Development*, Lawrence: University of Kansas Press.

Dolan, D. (1990), 'Local Government Fragmentation: Does it Drive Up the Cost of Government?', *Urban Affairs Quarterly*, 26(1), pp. 28–45.

Douence, J.-C. (1988), *L'action économique locale. Décentralisation ou récentralisation?*, Paris: Economica.

Dunleavy, P. (1980), *Urban Political Analysis*, London: Macmillan.

Dupoirier, E., Grunberg, G. and Roy, B. (1985), 'L'évolution électorale de la France urbaine (1971–83)', *Revue française de science politique*, 35(1), pp. 46–70.

Dupuy, F. and Thoenig, J.-C. (1985), *L'administration en miettes*, Paris: Fayard.

Dyson, K. (1980), *The State Tradition in Western Europe*, Oxford: Martin Robertson.

Edwards, R., Garonna, P. and Tödtling, F. (eds) (1986), *Unions in Crisis and Beyond*, Dover, Mass.: Auburn House.

Elkin, S. (1987), *City and Regime in the American Republic*, Chicago: University of Chicago Press.

Employment Committee (House of Commons) (1988), *3rd Report. The Employment Effects of Urban Development Corporations*, HC 327–1, 1987–8.

Fayolle, G. (1989), *La vie quotidienne des élus locaux sous la Ve république*, Paris: Hachette.

Ferman, B. (1989), 'The Politics of Exclusion: Political Organisation and Economic Development', Urban Affairs Association Annual Meeting, Baltimore.

Frisken, F. (1986), 'Canadian cities and the American example: a prologue to urban policy analysis', *Canadian Public Administration*, 29(3), pp. 345–76.

GAO (1983), US General Accounting Office, *States Are Making Good Progress in Implementing the Small Cities Community Development Block Grant Program*, E00602–003, Washington, D.C.: author.

Garraud, P. (1988), 'La sélection du personnel politique local', *Revue Française de Science Politique*, 38(3), pp. 402–32.

Garraud, P. (1989), 'Political mobilisation in France: a study of local protest', in Mabileau, A., Moyser, G., Parry, G. and Quantin, P., *Political Participation in Britain and France*, Cambridge: Cambridge University Press.

Gaudin, J.-P. (1988), 'La notion de politique urbaine. Evolutions et évaluations', *Espaces et Sociétés*, 48–49, pp. 259–75.

Gaudin, J.-P. (1989), *Technopolis. Crises urbaines et innovations municipales*, Paris: Presses Universitaires de France.

Giard, J. and Scheibling, J. (1981), *L'enjeu régional*, Paris: Messidor.

Giloth, R. and Mier, R. (1989), 'Spatial Change and Social Justice: Alternative Economic Development in Chicago', in Beauregard, R. (ed.), *Economic Restructuring and Political Response*, Urban Affairs Annual Reviews, vol. 34, Newbury Park and London: Sage.

Goldberg, M. and Mercer, J. (1986), *The Myth of the North American City*, Vancouver: University of British Columbia Press.

Goldsmith, M. and Page, E. (1987), 'Britain', in Goldsmith, M. and Page, E. (eds), *Central and Local Government Relations. A Comparative Analysis of West European States*, London: Sage.

Goldsmith, M. (1989), 'The Status of Local Government: A Consideration of the Political Position of Local Government in Britain, Canada and the United States', in Pratt, H., Elder, C. and Wolman, H. (eds), *Constitutional Regimes and the City. The US, Canada and Britain*, Detroit: Department of Political Science, Wayne State University.

Graziano, L. (1984), *Clientelismo e Sistema Politico. Il caso italiano*, Milan: Franco Angeli.

Greffe, X. (1989), *Décentraliser pour l'emploi*, 2nd edn, Paris: Economica.

Grémion, P. (1976), *Le pouvoir périphique. Bureaucrates et notables dans le système politique français*, Paris: Seuil.

Griffiths, R. (1990), 'Planning Retreat? Town Planning and the Market in the 1980s', in Montgomery, J. and Thornley, A. (eds), *Radical Planning Initiatives*, Aldershot: Gower.

Guengant, A. and Uhaldeborde, J-M. (1989), *Crise et réforme des finances locales*, Paris: Presses Universitaires de France.

Guglielmo, R. and Moulin, B. (1986), 'Les grands ensembles et la politique', *Hérodote*, 43, pp. 39–74.

Guichard, O. (1976), *Vivre Ensemble*, Paris: Documentation Française.

Gurr, T.R. and King, D.S. (1987), *The State and the City*, London: Macmillan.

Gyford, J. (1985), *The Politics of Local Socialism*, London: Allen and Unwin.

Gyford, J. and James, M. (1983), *National Parties and Local Politics*, London: Allen and Unwin.

Gyford, J., Leach, S. and Game, C. (1989), *The Changing Politics of Local Government*, London: Allen and Unwin.

Harrigan, J. (1989), *Political Change in the Metropolis*, 4th edn, Glenview, Ill.: Scott Foresman.

Harvey, D. (1989), *The Urban Experience*, Baltimore: Johns Hopkins University Press.

Hayward, J. (1982), 'Mobilising Private Interests in the Service of Public Ambitions: The Salient Element in the Dual French Policy Style?', in Richardson, J.J. (ed.), *Policy Styles in Western Europe*, London: Allen and Unwin.

Heald, D. (1983), *Public Expenditure*, Oxford: Martin Robertson.

Heidenheimer, A., Heclo, H. and Adams, C. (1983), *Comparative Public Policy. The Politics of Social Choice in Europe and America*, 2nd edn, New York: St. Martin's Press.

Hindess, B. (1971), *The Decline of Working Class Politics*, London: Paladin.

Hobsbawm, E. and Ranger, T. (eds.) (1983), *The Invention of Tradition*, Cambridge: Cambridge University Press.

Hoffmann-Martinot, V. and Nevers, J.-Y. (1989), 'French Local Policy Change in a Period of Austerity: A Silent Revolution', in Clarke, S. (ed.), *Urban Innovation and Autonomy*, Newbury Park and London: Sage.

Hogwood, B. and Keating, M. (eds) (1982), *Regional Government in England*, Oxford: Clarendon.

Iion, J. (1987), 'Cohabitations résidentielles en France: la règle et le conflit', *Politique Aujourd'hui*, 2, pp. 12–22.

Jacobs, J. (1984), *Cities and the Wealth of Nations*, New York: Random House.

Jones, B. and Bachelor, L. (1986), *The Sustaining Hand. Community Leadership and Corporate Power*, Lawrence: University of Kansas Press.

Jones, B. and Keating, M. (1985), *Labour and the British State*, Oxford: Clarendon.

Jones, G. (1969), *Borough Politics: A Study of the Wolverhampton Town Council, 1888–1964*, London: Macmillan.

Joyeux, P., Logié, G., Carles, J. and Dupuis, J. (1989), 'La réforme de la fiscalité directe locale', *Cahiers Français*, 239, pp. 68–78.

Judd, D. (1988), *The Politics of American Cities. Private Power and Public Policy*, 3rd edn, Glenview, Ill.: Scott Foresman.

Judd, D. and Parkinson, M. (eds) (1990), *Leadership and Urban Regeneration*, London and Newbury Park: Sage.

Kantor, P. (1987), 'The Dependent City. The Changing Political Economy of Urban Development in the United States', *Urban Affairs Quarterly*, 22(4), pp. 493–520.

Kantor, P. with David, S. (1988), *The Dependent City. The Changing Political Economy of Urban America*, Glenview, Ill.: Scott Foresman.

Katznelson, I. (1981), *City Trenches. Urban Politics and the Patterning of Class in the United States*, New York: Pantheon.

Keating, M. (1975), 'The Scottish Local Government Bill', *Local Government Studies*, 4, pp. 49–61.

Keating, M. (1988a), *The City that Refused to Die. Glasgow: The Politics of Urban Regeneration*, Aberdeen: Aberdeen University Press.

Keating, M. (1988b), *State and Regional Nationalism. Territorial Politics and the European State*, Hemel Hempstead: Harvester-Wheatsheaf.

Keating, M. (1988c), 'Does Regional Government Work? The Experience of Italy, France and Spain', *Governance*, 1(2), pp. 184–204.

Keating, M. (1988d), 'Local Government Reform and Finance in France', in Paddison, R. and Bailey, E. (eds), *Local Government Finance. International Perspectives*, London: Routledge.

Keating, M. (1989a), 'Local government and economic development in Western Europe', *Entrepreneurship and Regional Development*, 1.

Keating, M. (1989b), 'The Disintegration of Urban Policy. Glasgow and the New Britain', *Urban Affairs Quarterly*, 24(4).

Keating, M. (1991a), 'Local Growth Politics in France', *Journal of Urban Affairs*.

Keating, M. (1991b), 'Do the workers really have no country? Socialism and peripheral nationalism in France, Italy, Spain and Britain', in Coakley, J. (ed.), *The Social Origins of Nationalist Movements*, London and Newbury Park: Sage.

Keating, M. and Boyle, R. (1986), *Remaking Urban Scotland. Strategies for Local Economic Development*, Edinburgh: Edinburgh University Press.

Keating, M. and Hainsworth, P. (1986), *Decentralisation and Change in Contemporary France*, Aldershot: Gower.

Keating, M., Levy, R., Geekie, J. and Brand, J. (1989), 'Labour Elites in Glasgow', *Strathclyde Papers on Government and Politics*, Glasgow: University of Strathclyde.

Keating, M. and Rhodes, M. (1981), 'The Regional Water Authorities. Politics or Technocracy?', *Political Quarterly*, 52(4), pp. 487–90.

Kemmis, D. (1990), *Community and the Politics of Place*, Norman and London: University of Oklahoma Press.

Kiernan, M. and Walker, D. (1983), 'Winnipeg', in Magnusson, W. and Sancton, A. (eds), *City Politics in Canada*, Toronto: University of Toronto Press.

King, D. (1984), *Fiscal Tiers: The Economics of Multi-Level Government*, London: Allen and Unwin.

King, D.S. (1990), 'Economic Activity and the Challenge to Local Government', in King, D.S. and Pierre, J., *Challenges to Local Government*, London and Newbury Park: Sage.

Ladd, H. and Yinger, J. (1989), *America's Ailing Cities. Fiscal Health and the Design of Urban Policy*, Baltimore: Johns Hopkins University Press.

Laffin, M. (1986), *Professionalism and Policy: The Role of the Professions in the Central–Local Government Relationship*, Aldershot: Gower.

Lansley, S., Goss, S. and Wolmar, C. (1989), *Councils in Conflict. The Rise and Fall of the Municipal Left*, London: Macmillan.

Le Galès, P. (1990), 'Rennes: Social dynamics and the support of the state', in Judd, D. and Parkinson, M. (eds), *Leadership and Urban Regeneration*, London and Beverly Hills: Sage.

Leo, C. and Fenton, R. (1990), '"Mediated enforcement" and the evolution of the state: development corporations in Canadian city centres', *International Journal of Urban and Regional Research*, 14(2), pp. 185–206.

Levine, M. (1987), 'Downtown redevelopment as an urban growth strategy: a critical appraisal of the Baltimore renaissance', *Journal of Urban Affairs*, 9(2), pp. 103–23.

Levitan, S. and Taggart, R. (1976), *The Promise of Greatness. The social programs of the last decade and their achievements*, Cambridge, Mass.: Harvard University Press.

Lindblom, C. (1959), 'The Science of Muddling Through', *Public Administration Review*, 19, pp. 79–88.

Lindblom, C. (1977), *Politics and Markets. The World's Political–Economic Systems*, New York: Basic Books.

Lipset, S.M. (1990), *Continental Divide. The Values and Institutions of the United States and Canada*, London and New York: Routledge.

Lloyd, G. and Newlands, D. (1990), 'Business interests and planning initiatives: a case study of Aberdeen', in Montgomery, J. and Thornley, A. (eds), *Radical Planning Initiatives*, Aldershot: Gower.

Logan, J.R. and Molotch, H. (1987), *Urban Fortunes: The Political Economy of Place*, Berkeley: University of California Press.

Lowe, S. (1986), *Urban Social Movements. The City after Castells*, London: Macmillan.

Lubove, R. (1969), *Twentieth Century Pittsburgh. Government, Business and Environmental Change*, New York: Wiley.

Lyon, L. (1987), *The Community in Urban Society*, Chicago: Dorsey.

Mabileau, A., Moyser, G., Parry, G. and Quantin, P. (1989), *Political Participation in Britain and France*, Cambridge: Cambridge University Press.

Machin, H. (1977), *The Prefect in French Public Administration*, London: Croom Helm.

Mackay, D. (1989), 'Central Power, Urban Government and Civic Community', in Pratt, H., Elder, C. and Wolman, H. (eds), *Constitutional Regimes and the City. The US, Canada and Britain*, Detroit: Department of Political Science, Wayne State University.

Mackintosh, J. (1968), *The Devolution of Power*, Harmondsworth: Penguin.

Magnusson, W. (1981), 'Metropolitan Reform in the Capitalist City', *Canadian Journal of Political Science*, X1V(3), pp. 557–87.

Magnusson, W. (1989), 'Statism and the Closure of Urban Politics: Canada, Britain and the USA', in Pratt, H., Elder, C. and Wolman, H. (eds), *Constitutional Regimes and the City. The US, Canada and Britain*, Detroit: Department of Political Science, Wayne State University.

Magnusson, W. (1990), 'Progressive Politics and Canadian Cities', in King, D. and Pierre, J. (eds), *Challenges to Local Government*, London and Newbury Park: Sage.

Marquand, D. (1988), *The Unprincipled Society. New Demands and Old Politics*, London: Jonathan Cape.

Mawson, J. and Miller, D. (1985), 'Employment', in Ranson, S., Jones, G. and Walsh, K., *Between Centre and Locality*, London: Allen and Unwin.

McLean, I. (1983), *The Legend of Red Clydeside*, Edinburgh: John Donald.

McNaught, K. (1988), *The Penguin History of Canada*, Harmondsworth: Penguin.

Mellors, C. and Pijnenburg, B. (eds) (1989), *Political Parties and Coalitions in European Local Government*, London and New York: Routledge.

Mény, Y. (1974), *Centralisation et décentralisation dans le débat politique français (1945–1969)*, Paris: Pichon et Durand-Auzias.

Mény, Y. (1987), 'France' in Goldsmith, M. and Page, E. (eds), *Central and Local Government Relations. A Comparative Analysis of West European States*, London: Sage.

Mény, Y. (1989), 'La décentralisation sans la démocratie locale', *Le Journal des Elections*, 6, pp. 6–9.

Mény, Y. and Wright, V. (eds) (1985), *Centre-Periphery Relations in Western Europe*, London: Allen and Unwin.

Midwinter, A., Keating, M. and Mitchell, J. (1991), *Politics and Public Policy in Scotland*, London: Macmillan.

Mill, J.S. (1912), *Considerations on Representative Government*, Oxford: Oxford University Press.

Miller, W. (1988), *Irrelevant Elections?*, London: Macmillan.

Ministère de l'Economie, des Finances et du Budget (1989), *Les Notes Bleus*, 456.

Ministère de l'Economie, des Finances et du Budget (1990), *Les Notes Bleus*, 482.

Ministère de l'intérieur (1988), *Guide Statistique de la fiscalité directe locale*, Paris: Documentation Française.

Mollenkopf, J.H. (1983), *The Contested City*, Princeton: Princeton University Press.

Molotch, H. (1976), 'The City as a Growth Machine', *American Journal of Sociology*, 82(2), pp. 309–30.

Molotch, H. (1988), 'Strategies and Constraints of Growth Elites', in Cummings, S. (ed.), *Business Elites and Urban Development*, Albany: State University of New York Press.

Nanetti, R. (1988), *Growth and Territorial Politics. The Italian Model of Social Capitalism*, London: Pinter.

Nairn, T. (1981), *The Break Up of Britain*, London: New Left Books.

Nairn, T. (1988), *The Enchanted Glass. Britain and its Monarchy*, London: Hutchinson Radius.

National Audit Office (1988a), *Scottish Development Agency. Involvement with the Private Sector*, 478, London: HMSO.

National Audit Office (1988b), *Urban Development Corporations*, 492, London: HMSO.

National Audit Office (1990), *Regenerating the Inner Cities*, 169, London: HMSO.

Némery, J.-C. (1989), 'Les collectivités locales, l'économie et l'emploi', *Cahiers Français*, no. 239.

Neubeck, K. and Ratcliff, R. (1988), 'Urban Democracy and the Power of Corporate Capital: Struggles over Downtown Growth and Neighbourhood Stagnation in Hartford, Connecticut', in Cummings, S. (ed.), *Business Elites and Urban Development*, Albany: State University of New York Press.

Newton, K. (1984), 'American Urban Politics: Social Class, Political Structure, and Public Goods', in Hahn, C. and Levine, H., *Readings in Urban Politics. Past, Present and Future*, 2nd edn, New York and London: Longman.

Niskanen, W.A. (1973), *Bureaucracy: Servant or Master?*, London: Institute of Economic Affairs.

OECD (1987), Organisation for Economic Cooperation and Development, *New Roles for Towns and Cities, Local Initiatives for Employment Creation*, Paris: OECD.

O'Connor, J. (1973), *The Fiscal Crisis of the State*, New York: St. Martins Press.

O'Leary, B. (1987), 'British Farce, French Drama and tales of two cities; explaining the reorganization of Paris and London governments, 1957–1986', *Public Administration*, 65(4), pp. 369–89.

Onslow (1927), Royal Commission on Local Government, Chairman, Lord Onslow, *First Report, Constitution and Extension of County Boroughs*, Cmd. 2506, London: HMSO.

Ostrom, V., Bish, R. and Ostrom, E. (1988), *Local Government in the United States*, San Francisco: Institute for Contemporary Studies.

Paddison, R. (1983), *The Fragmented State. The Political Geography of Power*, Oxford: Blackwell.

Page, E. and Goldsmith, M. (1987), 'Centre and locality: functions, access and discretion', in Goldsmith, M. and Page, E. (eds), *Central and Local Government Relations. A Comparative Analysis of West European States*, London: Sage.

Page, E., Wolman, H. and McCarty, K. (1987), *America's Big City Mayors. A 1987 Profile*, Washington: National League of Cities.

Pahl, R. (1964), *Whose City?*, London: Longman.

Paris, C. (1984), 'Mais que font les Chambres de Commerce et d'Industrie?', *CFDT Aujourd'hui*, 33, pp. 31–42.

Parkinson, M., Foley, B. and Judd, D. (eds) (1987), *Regenerating the Cities: The UK Crisis and the US Experience*, Glenview, Ill.: Scott Foresman.

Parkinson, M., Foley, P. and Judd, D. (eds) (1989), *Regenerating the City*, Glenview, Ill.: Scott Foresman.

Parks, R. and Oakerson, R. (1989), 'Metropolitan Organization and Governance. A Local Public Economy Approach', *Urban Affairs Quarterly*, 25(1), pp. 18–29.

Parks, R. and Ostrom, E. (1981), 'Complex Models of Urban Service Systems', in Clark, T.N. (ed.), *Urban Policy Analysis. Directions for Future Research*, Urban Affairs Annual Reviews, vol. 21, Newbury Park and London: Sage.

Peterson, P. (1981), *City Limits*, Chicago: University of Chicago Press.

Phares, D. (1989), 'Big is Better, or is Smaller? Restructuring Local Government in the St. Louis Area', *Urban Affairs Quarterly*, 25(1), pp. 5–17.

Plan Urbain (1986), Commissariat Général du Plan, Délégation à l'Aménagement du territoire et à l'Action Régionale, *Mutations Economiques et Urbanisation*, Paris: Documentation Française.

Portz, J. (1990), *The Politics of Plant Closings*, Lawrence: University of Kansas Press.

Pratt, H., Elder, C. and Wolman, H. (eds) (1989), *Constitutional Regimes and the City, The US, Canada and Britain*, Detroit: Department of Political Science, Wayne State University.

Preteceille, E. (1987), 'La décentralisation: pour qui; pour quoi?', *Politique Aujourd'hui*, 2, pp. 38–53.

Prim, M. (1988), 'Pas de richesses locales nouvelles sans création d'emplois', *Economie et Politique*, 140, pp. 58–9.

Ratcliffe, J. (1981), *An Introduction to Town and Country Planning*, 2nd edn, London: Hutchinson.

Redlich, J. and Hirst, F. (1903), *Local Government in England*, London: Macmillan.

Rex, J. and Moore, R. (1967), *Race, community and conflict*, Oxford: Oxford University Press.

Rhodes, R.A.W. (1981), *Control and Power in Central–Local Government Relations*, Aldershot: Gower.

Rhodes, R.A.W. (1988), *Beyond Westminster and Whitehall. The subcentral governments of Britain*, London: Allen and Unwin.

Ritaine, E. (1989), 'La modernité localisée? Leçons italiennes sur le développement régional', *Revue Française de Science Politique*, 39(2), pp. 154–77.

Ronai, S. (1986), 'La crise des grands ensembles et les nouvelles politiques municipales', *Hérodote*, 43, pp. 75–89.

Ross, J. (1980), 'Local Government in Scotland. Some Subversive Reflections', mimeo, University of Strathclyde.

Sancton, A. (1983), 'Montreal', in Magnusson, W. and Sancton, A. (eds), *City Politics in Canada*, Toronto: University of Toronto Press.

Sancton, A. (1989), 'The Tri-Level Politics of Social Services in Canada and the United States', in Pratt, H., Elder, C. and Wolman, H. (eds), *Constitutional Regimes and the City. The US, Canada, and Britain*, Detroit: Department of Political Science, Wayne State University.

Sancton, A. (1990), 'Local Government Reorganization in Canada since 1975', paper for Intergovernmental Committee on Urban and Regional Research, London, Ontario: University of Western Ontario.

Sancton, A. and Woolner, J. (1991), 'Full-time councillors in Canadian local government', *Canadian Public Administration*, 34(1).

Saunders, P. (1984), 'Rethinking Local Politics', in Boddy, M. and Fudge, C. (eds), *Local Socialism? Labour Councils and New Left Alternatives*, London: Macmillan.

Saunders, P. (1986), 'Reflections on the dual politics thesis: the argument, its origins and its critics', in Goldsmith, M. and Villadsen, S. (eds), *Urban Political Theory and the Management of Fiscal Stress*, Aldershot: Gower.

Savitch, H.V. (1988), *Post-Industrial Cities. Politics and Planning in New York, Paris and London*, Princeton: Princeton University Press.

Sbragia, A. (1983), 'Politics, Local Government, and the Municipal Bond Market', in Sbragia, A. (ed.), *The Municipal Money Chase*, Boulder: Westview.

Schain, M. (1985), *French Communism and Local Power*, London: Frances Pinter.

Schneider, M. (1989), *The Competitive City. The Political Economy of Suburbia*, Pittsburgh: University of Pittsburgh Press.

Self, P. (1982), *Planning the Urban Region. A Comparative Study of Policies and Organizations*, London: Allen and Unwin.

Seyd, P. (1990), 'Radical Sheffield: From Socialism to Entrepreneurialism', *Political Studies*, XXXVIII(2).

Shaw, K. (1990), 'The Politics of Public–Private Partnership', Newcastle upon Tyne Polytechnic, Local Authority Management Unit, *Discussion Paper*, 90.2.

Shlay, A.B. and Rossi, P.H. (1981), 'Putting Politics into Urban Ecology: Estimating Net Effects of Zoning', in Clark, T.N. (ed.), *Urban Policy Analysis. Directions for Future Research*, Urban Affairs Annual Reviews, vol. 21, Newbury Park and London: Sage.

Smith, R. and Wannop, U. (eds) (1985), *Strategic Planning in Action. The Impact of the Clyde Valley Plan, 1946–82*, Aldershot: Gower.

Steib, J. (1987), Rapport présenté au nom du Conseil Economique et Social, Avis et Rapports du Conseil Economique et Social, *Journal Officiel de la Republique Française*, 12, 3 June 1987.

Stewart, J. (1971), *Management in Local Government*, London: Charles Knight.

Stewart, J. (1983), *Local Government. The Conditions of Local Choice*, London: Allen and Unwin.

Stewart, J. (1986), *The New Management of Local Government*, London: Allen and Unwin.

Stewart, M. (1984), 'Talking to Local Business: The involvement of Chambers of Commerce in local affairs', *Working Paper 38*, School of Advanced Urban Studies, University of Bristol.

Stewman, S. and Tarr, J. (1982), 'Four Decades of Public–Private Partnerships in Pittsburgh', in Fosler, R. and Berger, R., *Public–*

Private Partnership in American Cities, Lexington, Mass.: Lexington Books.

Stone, C. (1984), 'Systemic Power in Community Decision Making: A Restatement of Stratification Theory', in Hahn, H. and Levine, A. (eds), *Readings in Urban Politics. Past, Present and Future*, New York: Longman.

Stone, C. (1987), 'The Study of the Politics of Urban Development', in Stone, C. and Sanders, H.T. (eds), *The Politics of Urban Development*, Lawrence: University of Kansas Press.

Stone, C. (1989), *Regime Politics. Governing Atlanta, 1946–1986*, Lawrence: University of Kansas Press.

Stone, C.N. and Sanders, H.T. (eds) (1987), *The Politics of Urban Development*, Lawrence: University of Kansas Press.

Swanstrom, T. (1985), *The Crisis of Growth Politics: Cleveland, Kucinich and the Challenge of Urban Populism*, Philadelphia: Temple University Press.

Swanstrom, T. (1988), 'Urban Populism, Uneven Development, and the Space for Reform', in Cummings, S. (ed.), *Business Elites and Urban Development*, Albany: State University of New York Press.

Thornley, A. (1990), 'Thatcherism and the erosion of the planning system', in Montgomery, J. and Thornley, A. (eds), *Radical Planning Initiatives*, Aldershot: Gower.

Tiebout, C. (1956), 'A Pure Theory of Local Expenditures', *Journal of Political Economy*, 64, pp. 416–24.

Tocqueville, A. de (1986), *De la Démocratie en Amérique*, Paris: Laffont.

Travers, T. (1989), 'The Threat to the Autonomy of Elected Local Government', in Crouch, C. and Marquand, D. (eds), *The New Centralism*, Oxford: Blackwell.

Treasury (UK) (1990), *Civil Service Statistics*, London: HMSO.

Tym, Roger and Partners (1984), *Monitoring Enterprise Zones. Three Year Report*, London: Roger Tym and Partners.

Tyman, J. and Nogues, H. (1988), *Action Sociale et Décentralisation. Tendances et prospectives*, Paris: L'Hartmann.

Wachter, S. (1987), *Etat, décentralisation et territoires*, Paris: Harmattan.

Walker, D. (1983), *Municipal Empire*, London: Temple Smith.

Wannop, U. (1989), 'The Planning Case for Regions and the Evolution of Strathclyde', in Garside, P. and Hebbert, M. (eds), *British Regionalism, 1900–2000*, London: Mansell.

Warren, R. (1990), 'National Urban Policy and the Local State. Paradoxes of Meaning, Action and Consequences', *Urban Affairs Quarterly*, 25(4), pp. 541–62.

Warwick, P. (1990), *Culture, Structure or Choice. Essays in the Interpretation of the British Experience*, New York: Agathon.

Wassmer, R. (1990), 'Local fiscal variables and intrametropolitan firm location: regression evidence from the United States and research suggestions', *Environment and Planning C: Government and Policy*, 8, pp. 283–96.

Weber, E. (1977), *Peasants into Frenchmen. The modernisation of rural France*, London: Chatto and Windus.

Weber, M. (1988), *Don't call me boss. David Lawrence, Pittsburgh's Renaissance Mayor*, Pittsburgh: University of Pittsburgh Press.

Welch, S. and Bledsoe, T. (1988), *Urban Reform and its Consequences*, Chicago: University of Chicago Press.

Wheatley (1969), Royal Commission on Local Government in Scotland, 1966–69, *Report*, Cmnd. 4150, Edinburgh: HMSO.

Widdicombe, D. (1986), *Report of Committee of Inquiry into the Conduct of Local Authority Business*, London: HMSO.

Williams, (1971), *Metropolitan Political Analysis: A Social Access Approach*, New York: Free Press.

Wolman, H. (1986), 'The Reagan Urban Policy and its Impacts', *Urban Affairs Quarterly*, 21(3).

Wolman, H. (1988), 'Local economic development policy: what explains the divergence between policy analysis and political behaviour', *Journal of Urban Affairs*, 10(1), pp. 19–28.

Wolman, H. and Goldsmith, M. (1990), 'Local Autonomy as a Meaningful Analytic Concept', *Urban Affairs Quarterly*, 26(1), pp. 3–27.

Worms, J.-P. (1966), 'Le prefet et ses notables', *Sociologie du travail*, 3.

Wright, D.S. (1988), *Understanding Intergovernmental Relations*, 3rd edn, Pacific Grove: Brooks Cole.

Zeldin, T. (1973), *France, 1848–1945*, vol. 1, Oxford: Clarendon.

Index